DISCOVER MEANINGFUL WORK

A Career Transition Workbook
for Professionals in the Tech Industry

JULIA STEGMAN

For more information, email Julia@DiscoverMeaningfulWork.com

ISBN: 979-8-89694-070-8 (Paperback)
ISBN: 979-8-89694-071-5 (Hardcover)

BONUS CONTENT

This workbook is designed to be interactive, with numerous forms and exercises to guide you through your career transition. To get the maximum value from this process, I encourage you to write directly in the workbook as you complete each exercise. Engaging actively with the content will help you clarify your thoughts and make tangible progress toward your goals.

Access Templates and Tools

Throughout the book, I reference additional tools to support your journey, such as the Marketing Plan spreadsheet template. These resources are available for download via the URL below.

Take advantage of these bonus tools to stay organized and confident as you navigate your career transition.

https://DiscoverMeaningfulWork.com/

To my husband, Terry: *Thank you for supporting me through all the ups and downs of my career. I couldn't have done it without you.*

To my sons and grandchildren: *May you enjoy meaningful careers that leverage your special talents, bring joy to your life, and enable you to explore this amazing world that God has created.*

TABLE OF CONTENTS

INTRODUCTION

"How we spend our days is, of course, how we spend our lives."

– Annie Dillard

The tech industry attracts many professionals, often because of the promising income potential. However, working in tech comes with both pros and cons.

On the positive side, salaries in tech are significantly higher than the national average, ranging from 32 percent to 85 percent higher[1], depending on the state. However, this can result in the golden handcuffs—staying for the money at the expense of your other priorities, dreams, or your well-being.

Beyond compensation, managing a career in the tech industry is not for the faint of heart. It is notoriously volatile, whether you're at a fast-moving startup or a large enterprise. This volatility can bring instability, both financially and emotionally, for you and your loved ones.

Consider this: the typical American employee will spend 90,000[2] hours at work in their lifetime—a full third of their life. The sad truth is job satisfaction in the tech industry is at an all-time low. Massive layoffs, return-to-office mandates, and restructurings have left many professionals dissatisfied, uncertain, and uninspired.

Having spent twenty years as a tech executive at Hewlett-Packard, I saw firsthand how tech companies managed profitability with their two favorite levers: *layoffs and reorganizations*. Year after year, I witnessed restructurings that frequently failed to address deeper challenges such as lack of innovation, unmet customer outcomes, or internal politics that prioritized individual agendas over company success.

The reality is, whether you're at a small startup or a global enterprise, no one is immune from this volatility.

---

[1] https://www.zippia.com/advice/tech-industry-statistics/

[2] https://www.zippia.com/advice/career-change-statistics/

Let me share an example. As an executive recruiter, I once worked with an amazing co-founder and CEO of a thriving SaaS company. After securing private equity investment to accelerate growth, the PE firm ultimately decided he should step down, replacing him with a new CEO. If a company can remove its co-founder, it can remove anyone.

Unfortunately, these stories are not rare. In 2023 alone, tech companies laid off 429,608 employees globally,[3]. The financial strain and emotional toll on these tech employees and their families were profound. It was heartbreaking.

Why I Wrote this Book

As a certified career coach and former executive recruiter, I've had the privilege of speaking with thousands of tech professionals about their careers. I've listened to their aspirations, frustrations, and disappointments. Many felt unfulfilled, stuck in roles they no longer loved. Others faced the shock of unexpected layoffs and found themselves unsure of their next steps.

I wrote this book for two main groups of people:

- Tech professionals who feel stuck or unfulfilled in their current roles.

- Those who have been laid off and need guidance navigating their next career move.

Wherever you are in your career journey, this workbook will help you make a meaningful and effective career transition—whether that means staying within the tech industry, exploring new roles, or pursuing entirely different opportunities. This book will empower you to:

- Find meaning and fulfillment in your current role.

- Plan a clear career progression with your current employer.

- Explore opportunities with other tech companies or in tech-adjacent industries.

- Consider starting your own business if you're ready to take the leap.

Drawing on my experience as a career coach, I've developed a proven five-phase process to help professionals like you navigate career transitions with clarity and confidence. Through reflective exercises, practical strategies, and structured planning, you'll uncover your unique strengths, values, and priorities. You will create actionable short-term, two-year, and five-year career roadmaps.

A Hands-On Workbook

This workbook is designed to guide you through a process of discovery. I encourage you to carve out time on your calendar to work through each section thoughtfully and deliberately. Writing directly in the workbook will help you fully engage with the exercises and maximize the value you gain.

---

[3] https://www.trueup.io/layoffs

By the end, you'll have the tools and strategies to take charge of your career and drive your own success—on your terms. Together, let's celebrate what makes you unique and uncover the path to a more fulfilling, meaningful career.

A Legacy of Meaningful Work

A dear friend of mine, Pete, ran a highly successful construction company. He taught many subcontractors how to build strong small businesses. At his celebration of life service, it was standing-room-only; hundreds of people honored him for his mentorship and friendship. It impressed me so much I asked myself that day, "What will my legacy be?"

Well, my hope and my prayer is to help thousands of tech professionals discover greater meaning in their careers and, as a result, live more fulfilling lives. Devoting time to a career you enjoy and that plays to your strengths will have an immeasurable impact on your quality of life.

Time to Take Action

So I ask you:

- How satisfied are you with your career?

- How meaningful is the work you do?

- Is your career contributing to your life goals?

- Do you have the flexibility to create balance in your life?

- Are you achieving your financial goals?

If not, it's time to roll up your sleeves. No one can do this work for you, but I'll be your guide every step of the way.

I often remind my sons, Corey and Josh, that every day is a gift and we need to make the most of it. I remind myself of this too.

Will you join me on this journey to discover what will create a more meaningful career for you?

Let's get you looking forward to Mondays!

CHAPTER 1

THE FIVE PHASES OF A CAREER TRANSITION

*"A career is not just about earning a paycheck.
It's about pursuing the essence of who you want to become
and what you want to contribute to the world."*

– Candace Bushnell

The title of this book is intentional, especially the word *discover*.

What I have learned as a career coach is that the client already has the answers to their own questions, even if they don't realize it. But most people do need a process to help them *get* to the answers. So, a career coach's role is to act as a facilitator to take the client on a process of discovery.

This is also my objective with this workbook—to emulate the coaching I've done with clients and take you on a *process of discovery*.

Another design principle in this workbook is that the process is interactive and requires your participation. Please have a pen or pencil with you when reading this book. I encourage you to write in the workbook and make lots of notes; let your thoughts, instincts, and feelings flow.

Invest Positive, Proactive Energy in Your Career

Studies indicate that most of us will change jobs twelve times, on average, over the course of our careers.[4]

Some people don't enjoy looking for their next position. In fact, based on conversations with some clients I have coached, if given a choice between the two activities, some would rather visit the dentist than take time to write their resumes or engage in networking activities.

We must change our mindsets about how we manage our careers.

---

[4] https://www.zippia.com/advice/career-change-statistics/

Let's start by thinking of your career as a good friend that you lovingly spend time with. To *have* good friends, you need to *be* a good friend. The way to cultivate a good friend is to spend regular time with that friend.

Think of two friends you have. One friend reaches out when they need something from you. The other friend enjoys your company, seeks out opportunities to be with you, and supports your growth.

If you invest energy in your career only when it is time to change positions (when you need something from your career), your career will fall short of its potential. However, if you regularly spend time planning your career goals, building new skills, and expanding your network, your career could soar to new heights (when you spend time lovingly with your career).

A Meaningful Career

This book will provide a methodology for you to take the reins and manage your career proactively to create a more meaningful career. If you lean into what needs to be done to evolve your career, your efforts will produce fruit. Defining what is meaningful in your career is very personal. And our priorities often vary depending on whether we are in the early, middle, or late stage of our careers.

Maybe your next career move will include a promotion, a larger scope, and higher compensation. Maybe your next career move will be centered on making changes to improve meaning and fulfillment or to get your life and career priorities in sync. So, your next role could include a lateral move or a position with a reduced scope.

The process you are embarking upon with this book can help you achieve your career goals regardless of what creates meaning for you.

Here's a story about one of my career coaching clients. Mike was a senior executive for a well-known software company, where he led a team of fifteen hundred employees in a post-sales function. Mike was concerned about his company's direction and impending layoffs. So, he was on the hunt for his next career move.

He worked diligently to fill his pipeline with career opportunities with small, medium, and large companies that were interesting to him. This increased his chances of getting an offer from a company he was excited about.

Microsoft was high on his list of companies to work for, so Mike and I started contacting people we each knew at Microsoft. He got into some interviews, and conversations were going well. The challenge was timing. Microsoft had just started creating its budgets and hiring plans for the year—no small task for a company the size of Microsoft. It was taking months to work through the budgets, which lengthened the hiring process for Mike.

Then we had a breakthrough. One of the people I had introduced Mike to at Microsoft was promoted to corporate vice president, which put him in a position to hire Mike. And he did. Mike accepted an offer with a title and compensation that was a bit lower than his prior role. At that point, this was what it took to get in the door with a great company and a well-led organization with leaders who cared about their employees. He is now enjoying a challenging role and is spending more time with his wife and children. Mike is experiencing a more balanced, meaningful career and life. He is happier than he has ever been in his career.

Mike has since been promoted, and his compensation has increased to the level it was when he was a senior executive in the prior company. He is very well-respected by the leadership team and has a bright future in front of him at Microsoft.

This story leads me to highlight a couple of points:

- Navigating your next career move requires proactive effort on your part to build a pipeline of opportunities with companies that interest you.

- Persistence and patience are key. This was a four-month process with Microsoft.

- Not all career transitions are linear, resulting in a larger scope and more compensation. To find more balance or meaning in your career, you have to think outside the box and evaluate meandering routes. We will discuss this in Chapter 8, where you will create your career path.

Would you like to optimize your career, feel more in control of your career, and achieve career goals that are meaningful to you? If so, this process will empower you to create and execute your career action plans to achieve your goals.

Activities and Outcomes for Each of the Five Phases of a Career Transition

Let's discuss the process we will be taking a journey on. There are five distinct phases of a career transition to ensure an effective outcome in a job search.

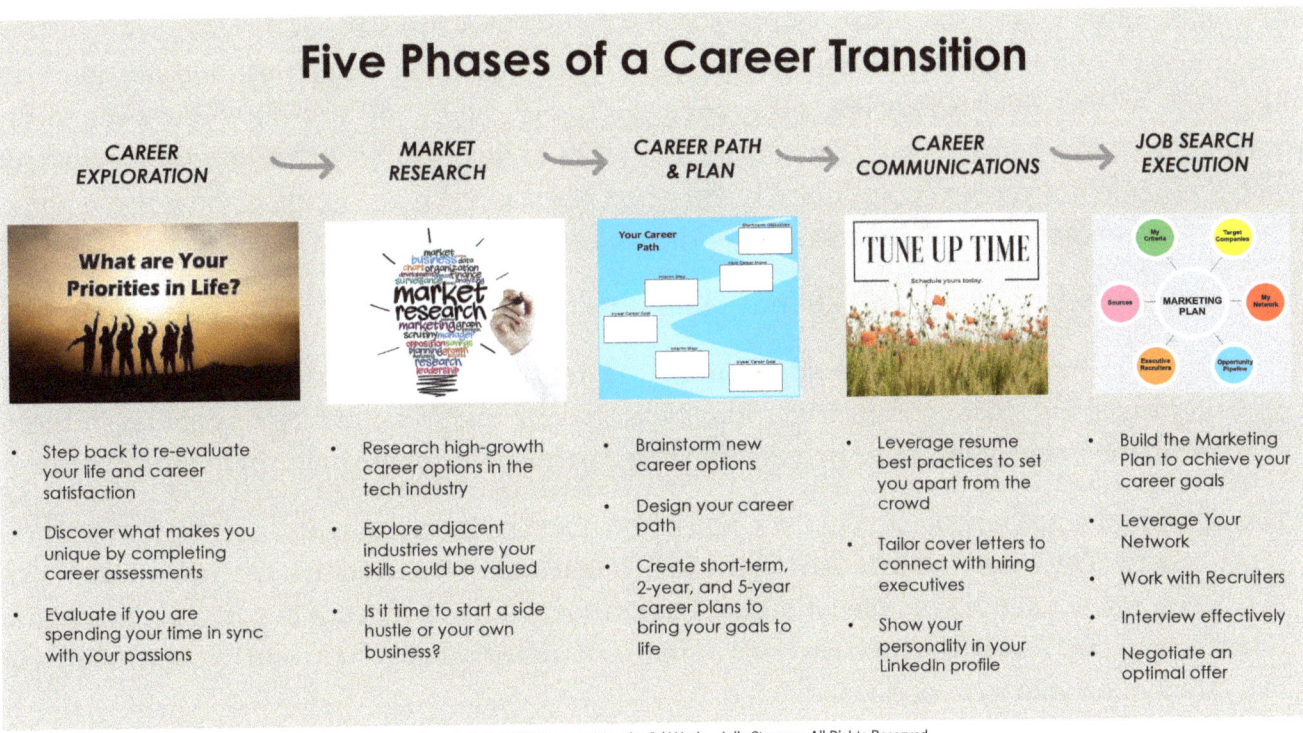

Five Phases of a Career Transition

CAREER EXPLORATION	MARKET RESEARCH	CAREER PATH & PLAN	CAREER COMMUNICATIONS	JOB SEARCH EXECUTION
What are Your Priorities in Life?	market research	Your Career Path	TUNE UP TIME	MARKETING PLAN
• Step back to re-evaluate your life and career satisfaction	• Research high-growth career options in the tech industry	• Brainstorm new career options	• Leverage resume best practices to set you apart from the crowd	• Build the Marketing Plan to achieve your career goals
• Discover what makes you unique by completing career assessments	• Explore adjacent industries where your skills could be valued	• Design your career path	• Tailor cover letters to connect with hiring executives	• Leverage Your Network
• Evaluate if you are spending your time in sync with your passions	• Is it time to start a side hustle or your own business?	• Create short-term, 2-year, and 5-year career plans to bring your goals to life	• Show your personality in your LinkedIn profile	• Work with Recruiters
				• Interview effectively
				• Negotiate an optimal offer

The key activities and outcomes in each phase are below.

Phase 1: Career Exploration

Most working adults are going eighty miles per hour with their hair on fire. Add family responsibilities to work, and you might be going a hundred miles per hour. It is important to step back from the hustle and bustle of daily life to evaluate your satisfaction with your life and career.

In Phase 1, you will participate in career assessments and exercises designed to help you:

- Rate your life and career satisfaction

- Evaluate how you are spending your time

- Get in touch with your God-given strengths, values, and unique capabilities

You will identify key satisfaction gaps in your life and career, along with solutions that will be included in your career action plans. You will decide if you need to make adjustments in how you spend your time. And you will receive insights from career assessment tools that will help you create a meaningful career path and define your personal brand.

Phase 2: Market Research

Steering yourself toward positions and industries with strong growth will create a tailwind instead of a headwind for your career.

In Phase 2, I will introduce a broad set of market factors for you to explore. These chapters are significantly longer than other chapters in the book. They are designed to expose you to a wide range of career options in the tech industry, in tech-adjacent industries, and outside tech altogether. As you think about not only your next career move but also how you want to set yourself up for the future, these chapters are resources to help you broaden your thinking about what a meaningful career could look like for you. You can skim or dig deep into these three chapters, depending on your interest level in the career opportunities. You will:

- Evaluate which of the top eight hot spots in tech to incorporate into your career path.

- Explore industries that are adjacent to the tech industry, such as the automotive or industrial automation industries. Your skills may be highly valued by companies in these industries, especially those that are building a software business unit inside their company.

- Consider whether you should own a business. Explore the possibilities of venturing out on your own by creating a side hustle or a full-time business. I added this chapter because I've seen many talented people who built their careers in tech venture out to start successful businesses. The skills you have built in the tech industry could help you successfully pivot to owning your own business.

You will identify career options to incorporate into your career path for the next five years. Guiding your career toward the top eight hot spots in the tech industry will help create career growth and career sustainability. Incorporating career options in tech-adjacent industries will expand the number of career possibilities to consider. And exploring self-employment options, whether a side hustle or a full-time business, might spark your entrepreneurial fire.

Phase 3: Career Path and Plan

"People are 76% more likely to achieve goals if they write action commitments and share weekly progress reports. Writing down goals helps you achieve them by providing clarity, commitment, and motivation."[5]

The shocking fact is only 3 percent of people write down their goals.[6]

Do you have written career goals and a clear path to achieve them?

In Phase 3, you will complete templates to:

- Summarize insights from prior chapters onto two pages to enable you to identify patterns of what could create more meaning in your career, specifically for you.

- Create your career path.

- Document your career action plans into short-term, two-year, and five-year plans.

Creating and documenting your career plans will set you up to be in an elite category of people, and this significantly increases your ability to bring your career goals to life.

Phase 4: Career Communication Documents

Career communication documents contain insights about your strengths, skills, values, experience, and competencies—what makes you unique.

In Phase 4, you will build your portfolio of career communication documents.

- You will design your resume to communicate your personal brand to prospective employers.

- Your LinkedIn profile will reflect your career experience as well as your personality.

- You will create tailored cover letters that help you connect with hiring executives.

You will incorporate insights from the career assessments into your resume, LinkedIn profile, and cover letters to articulate what makes you original and sets you apart from the crowd.

---

[5] https://www.zippia.com/advice/goal-setting-statistics/

[6] https://www.zippia.com/advice/goal-setting-statistics/

Phase 5: Job Search Execution

With the prior phases complete, you are now ready to execute your job search effectively and efficiently.

In Phase 5, you will put together everything from the prior chapters to launch an effective job search. You will:

- Utilize the marketing plan template to create and manage a pipeline of career opportunities.

- Learn new networking skills.

- Understand how to work effectively with recruiters.

- Prepare to interview effectively and avoid the most common interview pitfalls.

- Understand current labor laws to help you optimize your compensation during negotiations.

Staying organized during your job search with your marketing plan, along with a plan to increase your professional network, will create momentum and provide motivation to continue working toward your goals. Your confidence will increase with networking, building relationships with recruiters, interviewing effectively, and negotiating an optimal offer upon reviewing and implementing recommendations in these chapters.

Focus on What You Can Control

In the introduction, we talked about layoffs and restructurings in the tech industry, and they are unsettling. We typically don't have control over them. What do we have control over?

If you desire to continue your career in the tech industry, it is critical to:

1. Commit to continuously evolving and growing your skill set, staying relevant and marketable.

2. Engage regularly with people across your organization and outside your company to create a vibrant network you can lean on when it's time for a career transition.

3. Create cash reserves (or other investments) to carry you through a period of unemployment.

Recently, I was discussing the three bullet points above with my financial advisor, Chad Johnson, of Bulwark Capital Management. Chad relayed to me that his grandfather, Frosty Westering, was one of the top ten winning coaches in the history of college football. In fact, he was inducted into the National Football Foundation and College Hall of Fame.

While Frosty experienced much on-field success, his coaching philosophy and style were unique compared to many other coaches. Throughout his forty-year coaching career, he was a sought-after motivational speaker for business executives and leadership teams, and he wrote *The Strange Secret of the Big Time.*

The key to Frosty's philosophy was to challenge this popular mindset: "Winning isn't everything. It is the only thing." He taught that if winning is determined only by your success on the scoreboard, your focus becomes more about comparing yourself to others and getting distracted by many things you cannot control. This mindset leads to a fear of failure. Negative thought patterns and emotions begin to emerge, such as anxiety, tension, stress, and frustration.

Instead of defining winning as being the best, he focused more on *being your best* and *giving it your best shot.* With this mindset, the focus became more on the areas you can control, building up your specific individual skills, and collaborating as a team to give it your best shot. This creates meaning and purpose in each step of the journey. When the effort goes into making you the best you can be, winning becomes the by-product.

The essence of Frosty's book and his coaching approach is to focus on what you can control—to be at your best. The results will follow.

The same could be said for your career. You can't control mergers and acquisitions, internal politics, or management changes—all of which can slow your career progression or put your career at risk.

What you *can* control is investing in yourself to continuously improve your skills and performance. And give your work your best shot. The results will follow.

A Special Message If You Just Left or Lost Your Job

Leaving or losing a position can be challenging. While you are in transition with your career, I offer the following advice:

- Take a break to catch your breath. Many people find it helpful to take a week and be with the people who love and support them. For example, a former employee of mine, Mark, was laid off from a senior executive position, and he didn't see it coming. It was a shock to his system. So he and his wife put together a last-minute camping trip to the beach with their children, and it reset him. He gained an important perspective on what is most important in his life—his family. Our careers are very important, but life is bigger than our careers alone.

- After you catch your breath, your current job is to find your next job. Set up regular routines for yourself. Schedule five to six hours a day in your calendar to invest in your job search.

- Chapters 2 to 4 take less than a half day to complete, so I encourage you to complete them. These assessments and exercises will help you get reacquainted with your priorities, gifts, and talents, which will build confidence in your job search.

- It can be uplifting to do something *every day* that brings you joy. Joy comes from God, and no one can take this from you.

- Don't hesitate to ask others for help. If someone was in your shoes and asked you for help, you would likely offer assistance. Giving others an opportunity to help you can be positive for both of you.

This career transition won't last forever; it too shall pass, and you will be on your way to the next phase of your career journey. You will get through this.

Closing

Before you advance to the next chapter, please do yourself a favor and book appointments on your calendar with yourself to complete this workbook. I suggest you schedule blocks of time and make it a priority to go through every section of the workbook from beginning to end.

Find a quiet place where you aren't disrupted by day-to-day obligations and can do some self-reflection and critical thinking.

This is the journey we will embark upon together. I hope you embrace the process with an open mind, an open heart, and boatloads of curiosity.

PHASE 1
CAREER EXPLORATION

"The only way to do great work is to love what you do.
If you haven't found it yet, keep looking. Don't settle."

– Steve Jobs

I commend you for making the commitment to discover what will create more meaning in your career. Let's get started!

In Phase 1, you will participate in career assessments and exercises designed to help you:

- Rate your life and career satisfaction

- Evaluate how you are spending your time

- Get in touch with your God-given strengths, values, and unique capabilities

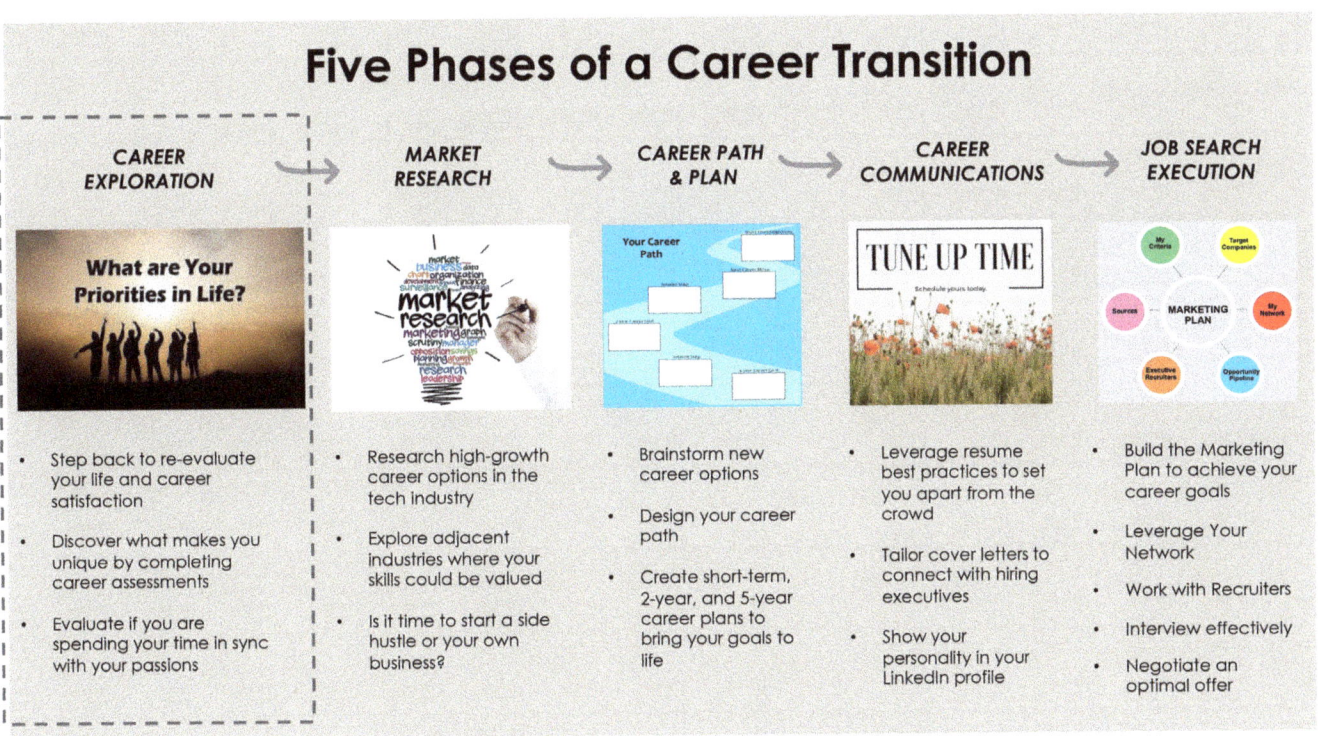

Five Phases of a Career Transition

CAREER EXPLORATION

- Step back to re-evaluate your life and career satisfaction
- Discover what makes you unique by completing career assessments
- Evaluate if you are spending your time in sync with your passions

MARKET RESEARCH

- Research high-growth career options in the tech industry
- Explore adjacent industries where your skills could be valued
- Is it time to start a side hustle or your own business?

CAREER PATH & PLAN

- Brainstorm new career options
- Design your career path
- Create short-term, 2-year, and 5-year career plans to bring your goals to life

CAREER COMMUNICATIONS

- Leverage resume best practices to set you apart from the crowd
- Tailor cover letters to connect with hiring executives
- Show your personality in your LinkedIn profile

JOB SEARCH EXECUTION

- Build the Marketing Plan to achieve your career goals
- Leverage Your Network
- Work with Recruiters
- Interview effectively
- Negotiate an optimal offer

In each chapter, there are spaces in the workbook for you to document your insights or decisions from the assessments and exercises. It's important to not skip any sections since we will use these insights and decisions in subsequent chapters; the content in the workbook builds on itself.

The outcomes from Phase 1 will include:

- Identification of key satisfaction gaps with your life and career, along with possible solutions

- Course corrections you wish to make with how you are spending your time in the short term, as well as self-reflection on envisioning your future

- Confirmation of what makes you unique in terms of your strengths, values, and capabilities

First, we will start with the ten-thousand-foot view of your broader life satisfaction. And then, we will explore your satisfaction with your career.

CHAPTER 2

LIFE AND CAREER SATISFACTION

"In the end, it's not the years in your life that count.
It's the life in your years."

– Abraham Lincoln, sixteenth president of the United States

Tech companies are notorious for operating at breakneck speed. During my career in tech, I found it challenging, on occasion, to maintain a healthy and holistic view of the big picture of my life. Let's face it: Working in tech can be all-consuming. So, let's start by pulling back the lens, reviewing the big picture, and evaluating where you are in your life and career right now.

- What is your level of satisfaction with your life and career?

- Is your career so consuming that you have lost sight of your life goals?

- What will be your life's legacy? We will all leave a legacy. How intentional are you about yours?

You will start by assessing your satisfaction with your life and the many facets that touch your life. Second, you will assess your career and the many elements that can contribute to or take away from your satisfaction with your career.

Life Satisfaction Assessment

Rate your satisfaction with each category[7] by circling the number that reflects your current level of satisfaction, with 1 being "completely dissatisfied" and 10 being "highly satisfied." Connect the circled numbers with lines to see where any imbalances lie.

---

[7] Based on Paul J. Meyer's Wheel of Life®. Wheel of Life® is a registered trademark of Success Motivation® International, Inc. Used with permission.

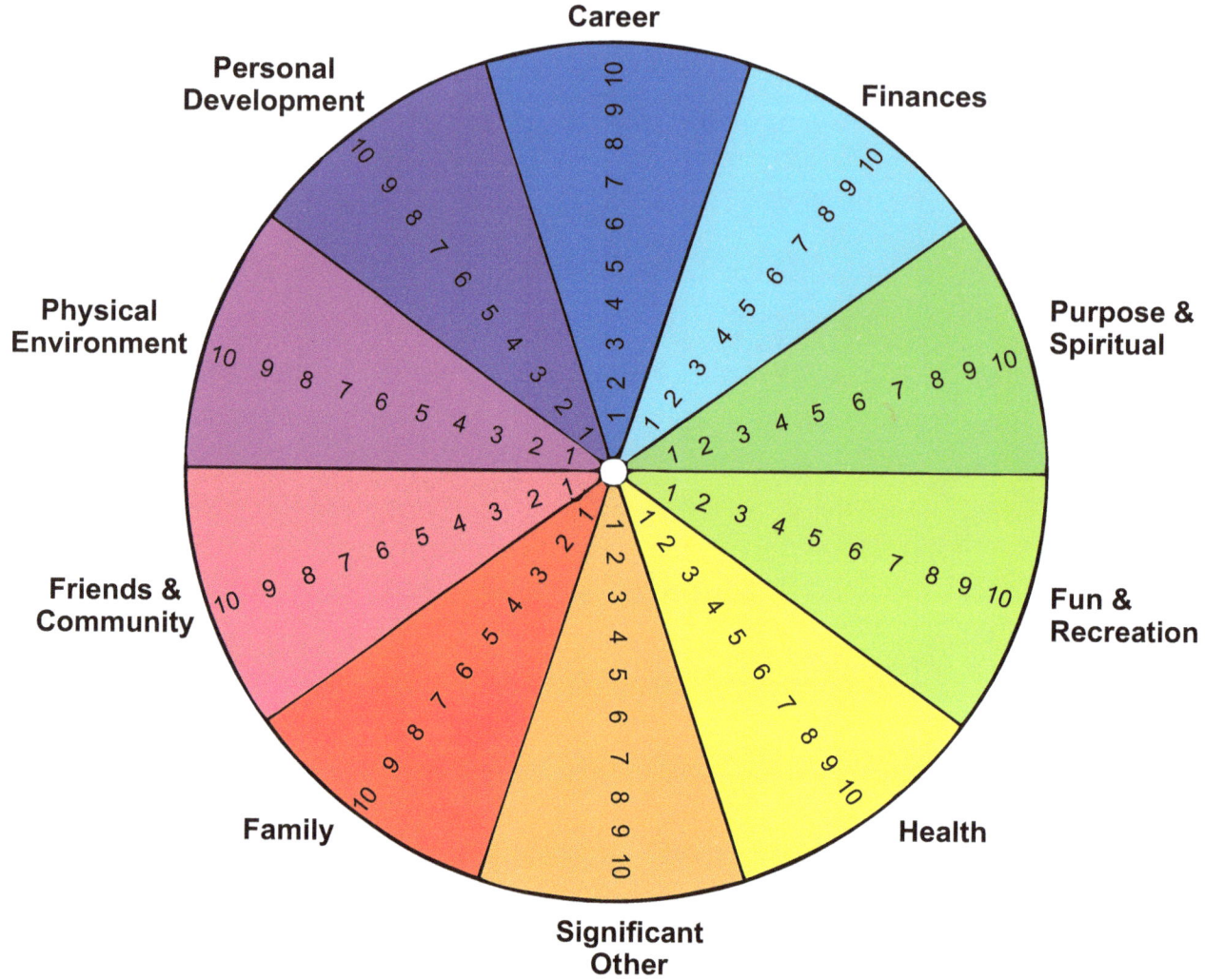

Career: You look forward to Monday mornings. You spend most of your time doing what you enjoy and are good at. Your career contributes to your other life goals.

Finances: You are satisfied with your income, investments, debt, and savings.

Purpose & Spiritual: You are living your life in alignment with your spiritual beliefs or values. You understand your personal mission and are using your gifts and talents to contribute to society.

Fun & Recreation: You are having fun in life. You have hobbies or recreational activities that bring you joy. You have sufficient 'me' time.

Health: You are thriving in terms of your physical health, mental health, and emotional well-being. You exercise regularly and have good eating habits. You are resilient during challenging situations.

Significant Other: You have a strong emotional connection with your spouse, partner, or significant other. You feel supported and loved.

Family: Your family relationships are positive. You feel supported by your family.

Friends & Community: You have healthy friendships with people who support you and your goals.

Physical Environment: You are comfortable and satisfied with your living environment—the city and state you live in, your specific neighborhood, and your home or apartment.

Personal Development: You are pleased with your level of personal growth, maturity, coping skills, and overall mindset. Your actions are aligned with your values and goals.

Sample:

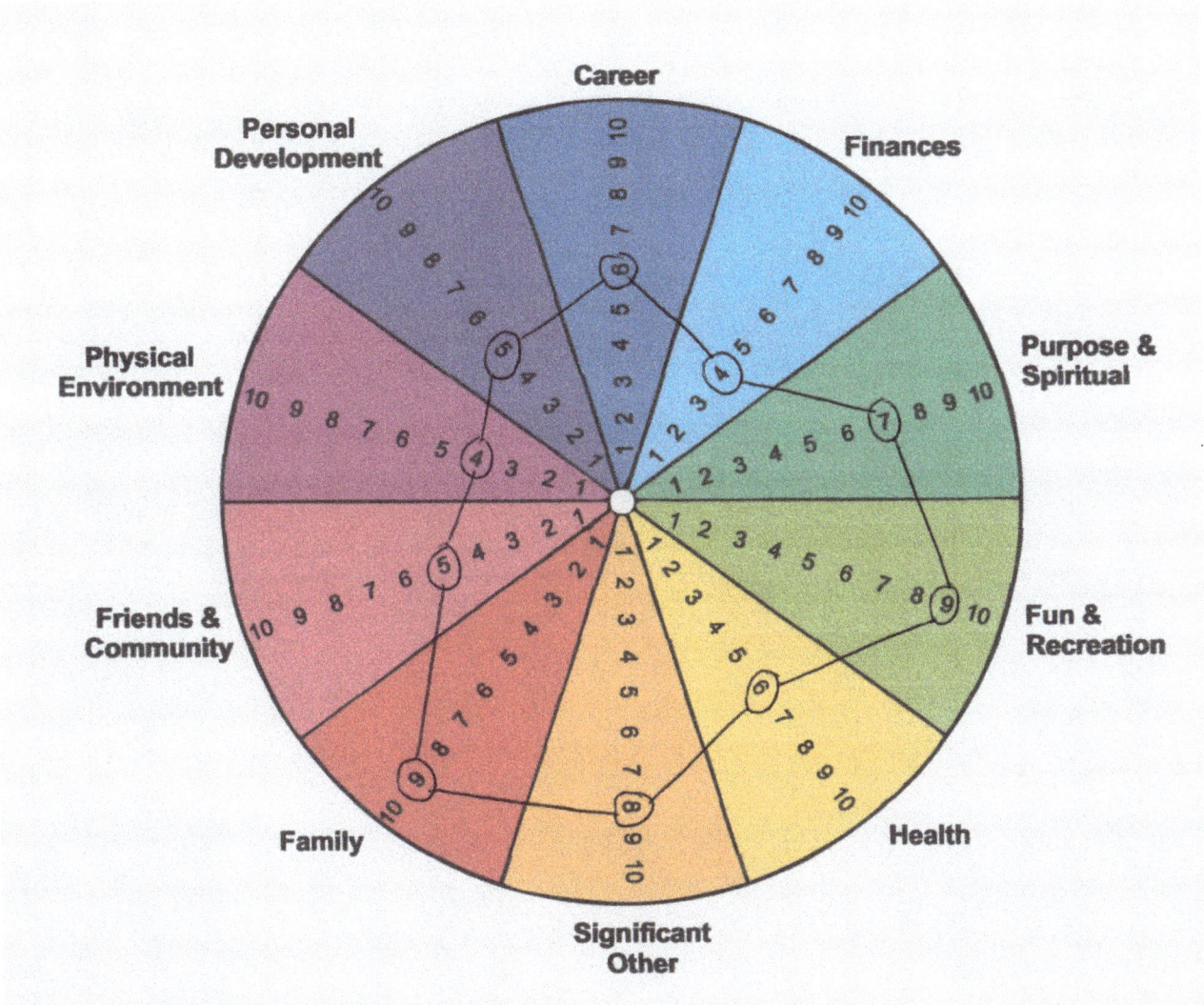

Life Satisfaction – Identify Gaps and Solutions

Some categories might be more important to you than others. Not every category needs to be rated a 10 for you to be satisfied with that particular category of your life.

With this in mind, choose the top three gaps you are most concerned about. For each of the three top gaps, enter your current rating from the Life Satisfaction assessment as well as what you would like this rating to be in the future. Document what makes you dissatisfied with each category and note some initial possible solutions.

Life Category	Current Ranking	Desired Ranking	Dissatisfiers and Possible Solutions
Concern #1:			
Concern #2:			
Concern #3:			

Some questions to consider:

- What do you want in these areas of your life?

- What would that look like? How would it feel?

- What's in the way?

- What are you thinking or doing that's keeping you from more satisfaction?

- What are the consequences if you do nothing?

- What is the upside if you do something?

Next, let's drill deeper into satisfaction with your career.

Career Satisfaction Assessment

Please rate each category[8] based on your current role. If you are in a career transition, please answer based on your most recent role.

---

[8] Career categories inspired by The Academies for Coaching, Inc. Used with permission.

Rate your satisfaction with each category by circling the number that reflects your level of satisfaction, with 1 being "completely dissatisfied" and 10 being "highly satisfied." Connect the circled numbers with lines to see where any imbalances lie.

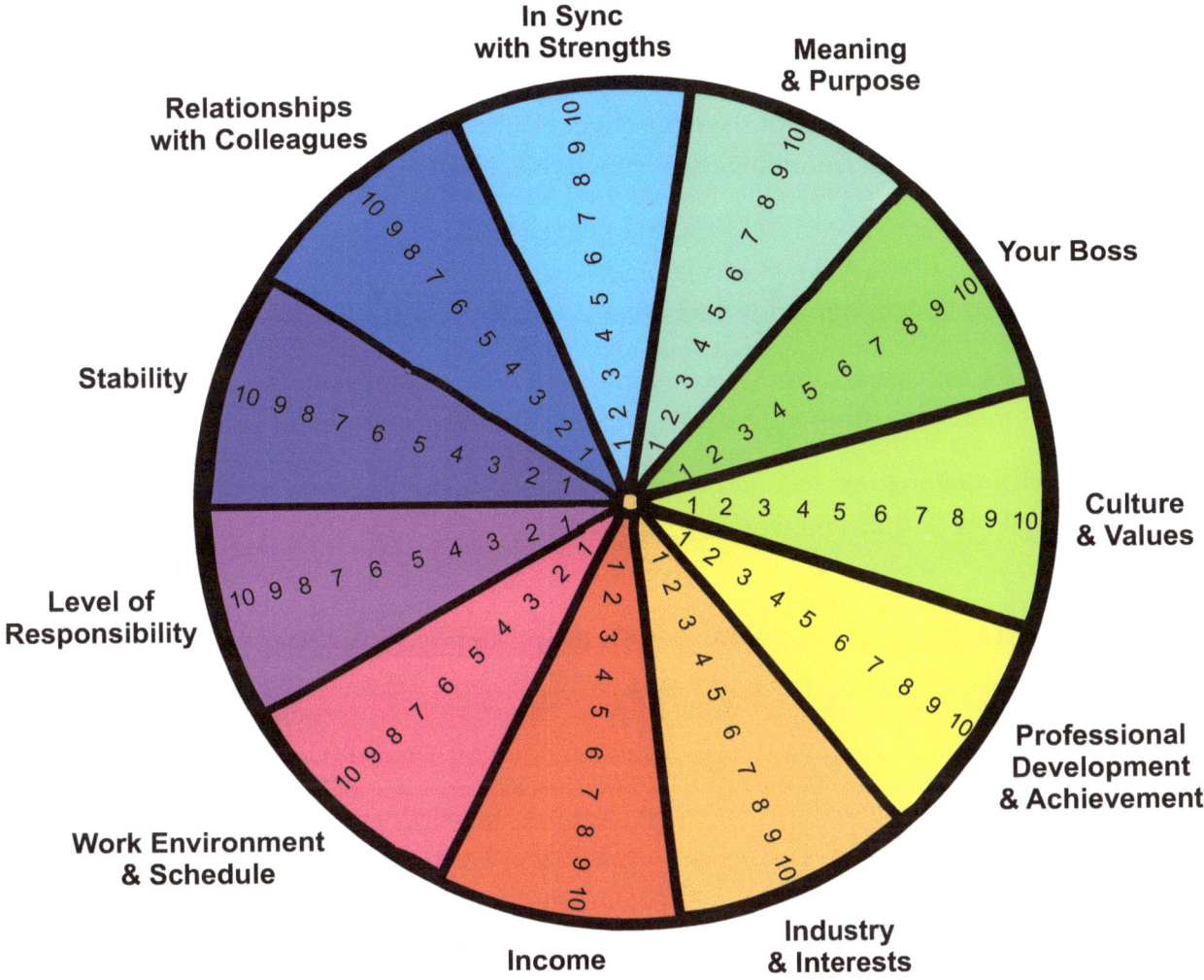

In Sync with Strengths: Your role allows you to use your strengths, natural talents, and favorite skills most of the time.

Meaning & Purpose: You receive internal fulfillment from meaningful work. Your career contributes to your life goals.

Your Boss: You and your boss have a productive relationship, which includes mutual respect. Your boss is fair, supports your development, and recognizes your contributions.

Culture & Values: Your values and your employer's values are aligned. Your employer has integrity and is transparent with key business decisions. Your employer treats employees and customers with respect.

Professional Development & Achievement: You have acquired new skills over the past year. You have opportunities to grow and increase your ability to contribute to the company. You are satisfied with the results you achieve.

Industry & Interests: You have a genuine interest in your professional field. You like the products or services your organization brings to market.

Income: Your financial needs are met, and your income supports your desired lifestyle. Your compensation is appropriate for the work you do. You are comfortable with the mix of compensation across base salary, incentive compensation, and equity.

Work Environment & Schedule: Your work schedule allows you time for a balanced life. Your work location and physical surroundings are acceptable. The balance of working remotely versus in the office suits you.

Level of Responsibility: You have the responsibility, authority, and flexibility you want. There aren't excessive pressures or demands placed on you.

Stability: You aren't concerned about your employer's financial viability. You don't feel that your position is threatened. The company benefits provide stability for you and your loved ones.

Relationships with Colleagues: You and your colleagues work collaboratively to achieve results. You enjoy many of the people you work with.

Career Satisfaction – Identify Gaps and Solutions

Some categories might be more important to you than others. Not every category needs to be rated a 10 for you to be satisfied with that particular category of your career.

With this in mind, choose the top three gaps you are most concerned about. For each of the three top gaps, enter your current rating from the Career Satisfaction assessment as well as what you would like this rating to be in the future. Document what makes you dissatisfied with each category and note some initial possible solutions.

Career Category	Current Ranking	Desired Ranking	Dissatisfiers and Possible Solutions?
Concern #1:			
Concern #2:			
Concern #3:			

Some questions to consider:

- What do you want in these areas of your career?

- What would that look like? How would it feel?

- What's in the way?

- What are you thinking or doing that's keeping you from more satisfaction?

- What are the consequences if you do nothing?

- What is the upside if you do something?

Taking time for self-reflection can help you make sense of what's going on around you. You can be grateful for the good things in your life and career; appreciate and hold on to the positive. I also hope these exercises bring to the forefront of your mind the things that aren't working so well, along with the courage to build a plan to make these elements of your life or career better.

What would a more fulfilled life feel like? Is it worth the effort to create a new career path and career action plan that is more meaningful for you and aligns with your life priorities?

If so, there are plenty of exercises and tools in this book to help you achieve this, so let's keep going.

While the two exercises above are fresh in your mind, please flip to Chapter 8 and log the concerns and possible solutions for your Life Satisfaction and Career Satisfaction on the Putting It All Together forms. Although I am the author of this workbook, you will be authoring your new story through your participation in the assessments, exercises, and templates. I look forward to going on this journey with you!

CHAPTER 3

HOW YOU SPEND YOUR TIME IS HOW YOU SPEND YOUR LIFE

"Time is more valuable than money.
You can get more money, but you cannot get more time."

– Jim Rohn

When we're in our twenties and thirties, the tendency is to focus on the here and now and not so much on the distant future. One can feel a bit immortal at this age. And then the forties come.

Many of our family's friends threw fortieth-birthday parties for their spouses. When I turned forty, I told my husband I didn't want a party since turning forty hit me like a ton of bricks. I moped around for a week. It dawned on me that I had now been living with my husband longer than I had lived with my parents as a child. Suddenly, I didn't feel so immortal.

As someone who is now entering the third season of life, I assure you that this can be a wonderful time. My husband and I are traveling while also focusing on writing and launching this book. We are doing things we didn't have time to do during the prime earning years of our lives, given the demands of working for a tech company and raising a family. We have more flexibility to travel to see our grandchildren, my time lingering in the garden gives me great peace, and we are picking up golf again.

In this chapter, we will continue with self-reflection. It's an opportunity to celebrate the milestones, achievements, and experiences you have had thus far—and ponder and envision what your future could hold.

If we think about the typical lifespan of a working adult, we can divide it into three seasons:

Seasons of Life

1. **The spring**: Childhood & Formal Education

2. **The summer**: Prime Earning Years

3. **The fall**: Self-Actualization & Paying It Forward

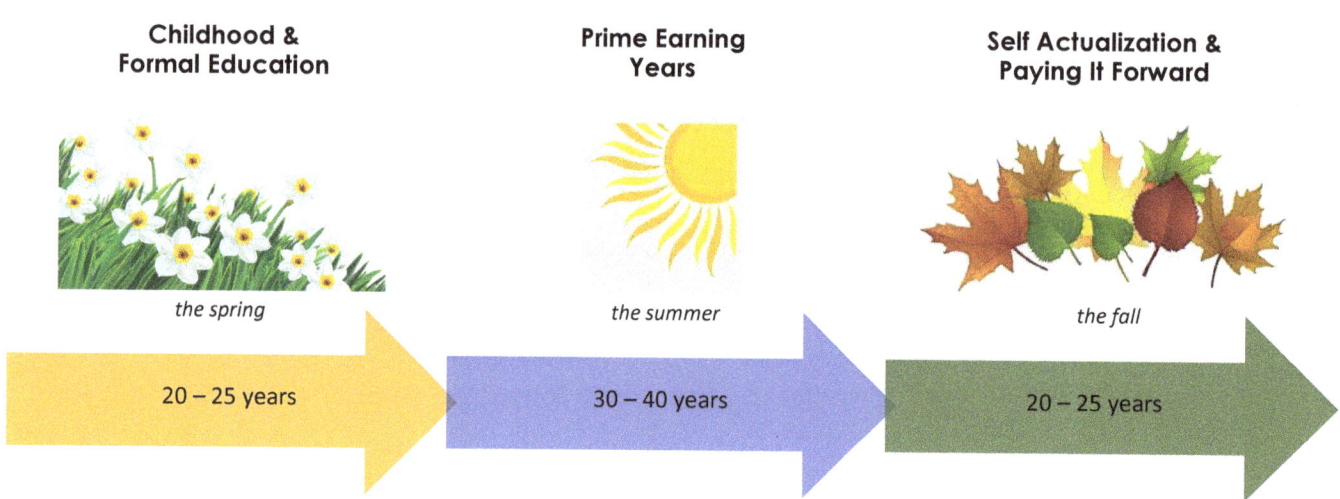

Everyone has their own journey and their own time in each season, and they manage the transitions differently. Some people work while going to college or vocational school; others go back to school during their prime earning years. So, one size does not fit all.

There are two seasons I'd like to focus on:

1. The summer

2. The fall

In your prime earning years (the summer), you may be concerned about maximizing your income to achieve your goals, for example, to have the lifestyle you desire, live in a nice home, send your children to college, or make other investments that require a significant amount of money. If you are in your prime earning years, now is a good time to conduct a checkpoint review with yourself to evaluate the progress toward your goals. Whether you are early, midway, or late in your prime earning years, I also encourage you to think about what you'd like to experience in your later years (the fall). You may know people who didn't plan activities or have goals for their later years, and they just seem lost or bored. This is such a shame because the fall years are such a gift to enjoy.

As we think about the future, the tough reality is we each have a finite number of years on this planet. The average life expectancy for a person in the United States is 76.4 years.[9] Of course, many people live into their eighties or early nineties. How much thought have you given to the fall season of your life? What do you envision for the fall season, and when do you want it to begin?

---

[9] https://www.npr.org/sections/health-shots/2022/12/22/1144864971/american-life-expectancy-is-now-at-its-lowest-in-nearly-two-decades

Gallup states the average retirement age is sixty-one, but many will work until sixty-five or longer. For many working adults, most of their lives have been full of obligations related to work, raising families, raising pets, pursuing education, etc. And hopefully, there has been a lot of joy along the way. In the fall season, there is more freedom to define how you spend your time. It could be:

- **Doing something you are passionate about**: Hobbies, recreation, travel, etc.

- **Serving others**: Giving back, helping family or friends, helping someone with their small business, volunteering, etc.

- **Working part-time**: Doing work that is fun, earning some additional money during retirement, running a nonprofit, serving on a board, etc.

Whatever stage of life you are in, I encourage you to reflect on each of the seasons of your life. What are you grateful for, and what do you look forward to?

Below are questions to help you conduct a checkpoint review of the summer and fall seasons of your life and envision what your future could hold:

Exercise: Some Questions to Ponder for the Summer Season of Life

What are you grateful for at this stage of your life?	
What significant life and career goals have you achieved thus far? (For example, you share your life with someone you enjoy, live in a nice home, sent children to college, built retirement investments, achieved certain level of position in career, etc.)	
What significant life and career goals do you still want to achieve?	
How long will you prolong your prime earning years? What are the trade-offs between earning money in your prime earning years and enjoying a longer period of self-actualization and pursuing your personal interests?	

Exercise: Some Questions to Ponder About Planning for the Fall Season of Life

When is it time to start the transition to the fall?	
What is your plan for the fall season of your life? What activities do you want to engage in?	
Do you want to semi-retire? (Work part-time, enjoy longer weekends.)	
What do you want your legacy to be?	

In the exercise above, we explored the broader seasons of life, celebrating what you're grateful for and envisioning what your future could entail. In the next exercise, let's get more granular about how you are currently spending your time.

What Is Work-Life Balance?

As I was conducting research to write this book, I came across the rule of 888.[10] I think it is simple and profound.

The Rule of 888

8 + 8 + 8 = 24 hours

---

[10] https://www.actiu.com/en/articles/inspiration/the-three-eights/

With this exercise, you will evaluate how you are spending your days in terms of sleep, work time, and personal time. And then you will assess whether you want to make changes to how you are spending your time.

Time is finite. There are twenty-four hours in a day. Many of us find ourselves wishing there were more than twenty-four hours in a day, but such is not the case. This can be especially true for professionals working in the tech industry, where long work hours can be the expectation.

What we *do* have influence over is *how* we spend our time.

Many people struggle with managing their time effectively, which can lead to burnout, stress, and poor health. Let's explore each of the three areas of work, sleep, and my time.

Work: For the hours that you decide to work, give it your all and be as effective and efficient as possible. Delegate, prioritize, and guard against perfectionism.

Sleep: Sleep is critical to overall good health and well-being.

My Time: Personal time is precious.

- Spending time doing activities you enjoy and being with people you care about can create happiness and improve your mental health.

- Nurturing your spiritual life can create a sense of calm and peace, and this requires stepping away from the day-to-day obligations of life to pray or meditate.

- Proper exercise and nutrition contribute to good physical health, but how often are other parts of your life hijacking this time?

- Hobbies you enjoy can contribute to a better quality of life. When was the last time you engaged in your favorite hobby?

- Giving back to others can make our problems seem not so big.

You must carve time out of your day for these activities, or the busy-ness of life will consume all your time.

Thirty-five percent of survey respondents to a CultureAmp survey reported that work-life balance and burnout would be a primary reason for leaving their employer. Ninety-four percent of respondents also indicated that work-life balance and salary are of equal weighting in terms of their criteria for their next career move. How important is work-life balance to you?

Please look at your calendar and activities for the past week. How did you spend your twenty-four hours per day? If you have an Apple Watch or a similar device that collects the number of hours you sleep, the device's app can provide concrete data on your sleep hours. In fact, you might be sleeping more or less than you think.

Exercise: Evaluate How You Are Spending Your Time

Please log how you spent your time last week. If last week wasn't typical, please look at a prior week that is more typical.

Last Week or a Typical Week	Sleep	Work	My Time
Monday			
Tuesday			
Wednesday			
Thursday			
Friday			
Saturday			
Sunday			

If work is eating into your personal time, is this conscious? Some people are okay with working long hours during the week, and some are okay with working on the weekends. But is it chronic? And is it desired?

During the pandemic, I talked with an executive who was starting to think about making a career change. Sharon had a global role with an enterprise software company, and she was working twelve to fourteen hours a day. She talked with people in Europe in the early mornings, North America during regular work hours, and then with people in Asia late at night. Young families had so many challenges during the pandemic. Sharon's two young sons (who had lots of energy) were also now at home with her as she tried to manage this all-consuming tech work schedule.

Sharon confided in me, "I want to run away from home. I'm serious."

It broke my heart.

I know Sharon loves her family. The issue was that she wasn't setting boundaries at work. There was a strong fear factor running through the tech industry during the pandemic, and some employers took advantage of employee fear to get them to work very long hours. Sharon was overwhelmed with work and family responsibilities. So we talked about having specific days of the week for talking with people in Europe and *different* days for talking with people in Asia so she could get more personal time back into her calendar.

The key point is that Sharon didn't *want* to be working those hours, so she needed to make adjustments.

Exercise: Identify Concerns About How You Are Spending Your Time

Let's identify any concerns you have about how you are spending your twenty-four hours a day.

Concerns	Sleep	Work	My Time
Monday through Friday			
Saturday and Sunday			

What steps can you take to create more balance in your life? The 80/20 rule, or Pareto Principle, is such a powerful concept. The reality is there is never enough time to do all the things in your job that could be done. Such is life in tech. No empty inboxes here! If 80 percent of the results come from 20 percent of the activities, focus on what you can *stop* doing. Learn to say *no*. Become an expert at planning, setting, and resetting priorities. Delegate every chance you get.

You are the only one who can create time in your calendar for the things that bring you joy outside of work.

Exercise: Identify Possible Solutions to Create More Balance

Let's list possible solutions below to create more balance across work, sleep, and my time.

Possible Solutions	Sleep	Work	My Time
Monday through Friday			
Saturday and Sunday			

As discussed in the introduction, money can cloud the issue and become overly dominant in terms of career choices. This is especially true for tech professionals. So, let's put money to the side for this next exercise, open up the possibilities, and get reacquainted with your passions and dreams.

If Money Wasn't an Issue

Let's tap the imaginative and envisioning part of your brain.

Imagine you have no bills to pay for a year and get to explore activities that interest you.

I encourage you to ponder the three scenarios below. Don't just fill in the worksheet. Rather, let your mind be free and curious. Don't let the realities of *how* to make this happen come into your mind right now. Freeing yourself from the practicalities of life can remind you of some of your passions.

Search your soul.

For this exercise, you have twelve months to pursue new activities that interest you. Envision yourself in each of the three scenarios below and jot down the descriptions.

First Scenario: How would you spend four months in some type of paid employment that interests you? This is a job that interests you and pays *some* amount of money (but you have no bills).

Second Scenario: How would you spend the next four months learning something new that interests you? It could be related to your career or not. It could be taking classes, reading, learning a new hobby, traveling, getting a certification, or interning to learn a new role. This is unpaid time.

Third Scenario: How would you spend the last four months helping others? This service would be unpaid. You could be a volunteer helping people you don't know, or you could help family or friends.

Insights from the Exercise – If Money Wasn't an Issue

How did it feel when you thought about these scenarios and envisioned yourself in them?

Did a passion of yours rise to the surface?

Did one scenario jump out above the other two scenarios? If so, why?

How did your life change when you envisioned yourself in these scenarios?

Were there any surprises?

I hope this exercise opened up some thoughts about your passions.

And great job spending time in self-reflection with the three exercises above! While the insights from the three exercises are fresh in your mind, please flip to Chapter 8 and log your top observations and decisions from the Seasons of Life and Work-Life Balance exercises on the Putting It All Together forms, as well as the passions you wish to explore from the exercise If Money Wasn't an Issue.

Next, you will participate in three career assessments, which will help with brainstorming your career path and defining your personal brand.

CHAPTER 4

DISCOVER WHAT MAKES YOU ORIGINAL AND UNIQUE

"Be yourself; everyone else is already taken."

– Oscar Wilde

Over the course of my career, I've observed a number of challenging situations for tech professionals that make it difficult for them to stay connected to who they are. For example:

1. Companies going through hypergrowth create an exciting opportunity, but it can also contribute to burnout with long work hours.

2. Toxic or political environments, and those with a continuous threat of layoffs, require professionals to be vigilant about their values and what lines they will or will not cross.

3. Leadership changes—including CEO changes, PE firm buyouts, or executives exiting the company who were your advocates—can be very disruptive to managing and advancing your career.

In challenging business scenarios like those mentioned above, we can lose a bit of ourselves and possibly lose some confidence in our capabilities.

So, the objective of this chapter is to get clarity on your God-given strengths, revisit your values, and get reacquainted with your unique capabilities. The insights from these three assessments reflect the core of who you uniquely are. Now more than ever, it's critical to have this clarity.

From my perspective, one of the shortcomings of other career development books is they ask us to document what our strengths are. Well, we are often too close to ourselves to make objective assessments of our strengths. Or maybe we take our gifts for granted.

So, I have opted to include three career assessments that are highly regarded in the coaching community and have significant research behind them. These career assessments focus on your strengths, values, and personality type. Careers that land in the intersection of these three areas can significantly increase your satisfaction with your career.

My career coaching clients have enjoyed insights from taking these career assessments, and I hope you do too. The findings from these assessments provide insights that are helpful to draw from when creating your career path in Chapter 8. Sharing your strengths, values, and unique capabilities with people you trust can result in productive brainstorming for a meaningful career path. It could be a mentor, a loved one, a colleague, a former boss, a leader who has knowledge of the industry you are interested in, or a career coach. More on this later.

Overview and Instructions for Taking the Career Assessments

While completing the assessments, it's important to self-assess and be honest with your answers. There are no right or wrong answers! This process is about learning more about your gifts and perspectives on life; celebrate them and leverage them more in your career so you can put yourself on a path for a more meaningful and successful career.

Values Career Assessment

The Values in Action survey is an assessment tool created by the VIA Institute on Character, and it provides insights into your character strengths.

The VIA Institute defines character strengths as "the positive parts of your personality that make you feel authentic and engaged." Their findings show that "workers who use four or more of their top five character strengths at work have more positive work experiences and report their work is a calling in their life. The insights reflect the *real* you, who you are at your core."[11]

My career coaching clients have enjoyed the accuracy of the insights that come from this assessment and have said things like "This assessment nailed who I am."

To take the Value in Actions Survey, go to:

https://www.viacharacter.org/account/register

Register your name, email address, and password. Accept their terms and conditions. Then click "Register Now," and the survey will begin.

This is a free survey. You can also purchase additional reports to get more in-depth insights and recommendations, but the free survey works well for our purposes.

---

[11] https://www.viacharacter.org/character-strengths-via

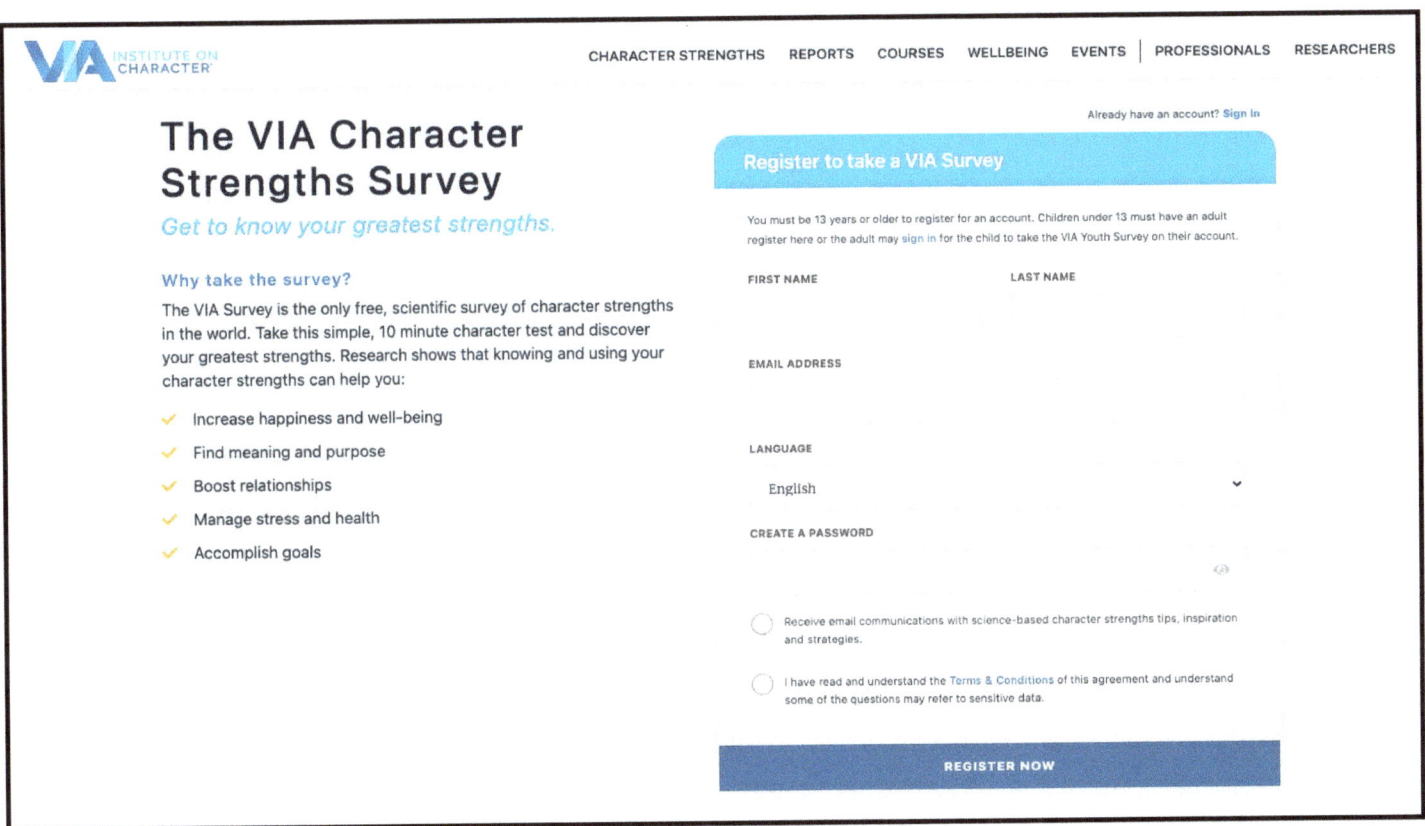

The survey takes about ten minutes to complete.

Upon completion of the survey, your results will be reflected on the screen. Scroll down and click on "Download your VIA Character Strengths Profile."

You will be provided with a ranking of twenty-four character strengths, with your strongest five on the top, then your middle strengths, and last, your lesser strengths. The top of the report will look like the figure below with your personalized insights.

1. Spirituality
TRANSCENDENCE

Having coherent beliefs about the higher purpose and meaning of the universe; knowing where one fits within the larger scheme; having beliefs about the meaning of life that shape conduct and provide comfort.

2. Creativity
WISDOM

Thinking of novel and productive ways to conceptualize and do things; includes artistic achievement but is not limited to it.

3. Bravery
COURAGE

Not shrinking from threat, challenge, difficulty, or pain; speaking up for what's right even if there's opposition; acting on convictions even if unpopular; includes physical bravery but is not limited to it.

4. Leadership
JUSTICE

Encouraging a group of which one is a member to get things done and at the same time maintain good relations within the group; organizing group activities and seeing that they happen.

5. Hope
TRANSCENDENCE

Expecting the best in the future and working to achieve it; believing that a good future is something that can be brought about.

You can go back any time to view your insights by clicking the "My Dashboard" button on top, then "View Results" in the "My Survey Results" box.

With this assessment, it is important to focus on your top and middle strengths. Know and celebrate these strengths. Build a career that plays to these strengths.

None of us are great at everything. So be aware of your lesser strengths and just don't build a career where you need to lean on your lesser strengths a significant amount of the time.

The chart below will help you understand which categories your top strengths fall into.

The VIA Classification of 24 Character Strengths

Wisdom

CREATIVITY
- Clever
- Original & Adaptive
- Problem Solver

CURIOSITY
- Interested
- Explores new things
- Open to new ideas

JUDGMENT
- Critical thinker
- Thinks things through
- Open-minded

LOVE OF LEARNING
- Masters new skills & topics
- Systematically adds to knowledge

PERSPECTIVE
- Wise
- Provides wise counsel
- Takes the big picture view

Courage

BRAVERY
- Shows valor
- Doesn't shrink from fear
- Speaks up for what's right

PERSEVERANCE
- Persistent
- Industrious
- Finishes what one starts

HONESTY
- Authentic
- Trustworthy
- Sincere

ZEST
- Enthusiastic
- Energetic
- Doesn't do things half-heartedly.

Humanity

LOVE
- Warm and genuine
- Values close relationships

KINDNESS
- Generous
- Nurturing
- Caring
- Compassionate
- Altruistic

SOCIAL INTELLIGENCE
- Aware of the motives and feelings of self/others
- Knows what makes others tick

Justice

TEAMWORK
- Team player
- Socially responsible
- Loyal

FAIRNESS
- Just
- Doesn't let feelings bias decisions about others

LEADERSHIP
- Organizes group activites
- Encourages a group to get things done

Temperance

FORGIVENESS
- Merciful
- Accepts others' shortcomings
- Gives people a second chance

HUMILITY
- Modest
- Lets one's accomplishments speak for themselves

PRUDENCE
- Careful
- Cautious
- Doesn't take undue risks

SELF-REGULATION
- Self-controled
- Disciplined
- Manages impulses and emotions

Transcendence

APPRECIATION OF BEAUTY & EXCELLENCE
- Feels awe and wonder in beauty
- Inspired by goodness of others

GRATITUDE
- Thankful for the good
- Expresses thanks
- Feels blessed

HOPE
- Optimistic
- Future-minded
- Future Orientated

HUMOR
- Playful
- Brings smiles to others
- Lighthearted

SPIRITUALITY
- Searches for meaning
- Feels a sense of purpose
- Senses a relationship with the sacred

Strengths Career Assessment

The CliftonStrengths survey is an assessment tool created by Don Clifton, who had a mission to empower human development. You may also know the survey by its original name, Clifton StrengthsFinder. *This survey measures your natural patterns of thinking, feeling, and behaving.* These strengths are core to your DNA. Another way to think of these strengths is they are God-given.

Most of the books Clifton read on human development were focused on what is wrong with people. So Clifton's work went out to solve the question "What would happen if we studied what was *right* with people versus what's wrong with people?" Over 31 million people have taken this survey. I think Clifton accomplished his mission.

Gallup later acquired CliftonStrengths, which allows Don Clifton's work to carry on. What a legacy he left!

The findings from this survey are particularly useful for identifying *skills* that can inform your career choices; this will help you build a career path that plays to your strengths. Clifton's premise is to focus your energies on strengthening your top and middle themes and just navigate or manage the other themes that are ranked lower.

Per Gallup, focusing on your top strengths will help you become the best version of yourself. "Do more of what you do best, and you'll feel more engaged, empowered, and energized."[12]

There is a fee for this survey, but I think it's worth it. The outcomes of this assessment translate very well to skills needed in business.

There are a number of tailored reports. For our purposes, I recommend you buy the Clifton Strengths Top 5 report for $24.99.

You will receive a sixteen-page report that identifies your top five strengths with descriptions for each strength area; your combination of strengths will help you understand what makes you unique. The report goes deep for each of the five strength areas.

---

[12] https://www.gallup.com/cliftonstrengths/en/253676/how-cliftonstrengths-works.aspx

GALLUP

 # CliftonStrengths® Top 5

1. Strategic®

You create alternative ways to proceed. Faced with any given scenario, you can quickly spot the relevant patterns and issues.

2. Individualization®

You are intrigued with the unique qualities of each person. You have a gift for figuring out how different people can work together productively.

3. Self-Assurance®

You feel confident in your ability to take risks and manage your own life. You have an inner compass that gives you certainty in your decisions.

4. Significance®

You want to make a big impact. You are independent and prioritize projects based on how much influence they will have on your organization or people around you.

5. Focus®

You can take a direction, follow through and make the corrections necessary to stay on track. You prioritize, then act.

EXECUTING themes help you make things happen.

RELATIONSHIP BUILDING themes help you build strong relationships that hold a team together.

INFLUENCING themes help you take charge, speak up and make sure others are heard.

STRATEGIC THINKING themes help you absorb and analyze information that informs better decisions.

STRATEGIC THINKING

1. Strategic®

What Is Strategic?

People with strong Strategic talents can sort through the clutter to find the best route. You can't teach this skill. It is a distinct way of thinking — a unique perspective on the world at large. This outlook allows them to see patterns where others see complexity. Mindful of these patterns, they envision alternative scenarios, always asking, "What if this happened?" This recurring question helps them see, plan and prepare for future situations. They see a way when others assume there is no way. Armed with this strategy, they move forward.

Why Your Strategic Is Unique

These Strengths Insights are personalized based on your CliftonStrengths results.

Strategic	Individualization	Self-Assurance	Significance	Focus

It's very likely that you usually identify problems others fail to notice. You repeatedly create solutions and find the right answers. You yearn to improve things about yourself, other people, or situations. You are drawn to classes, books, or activities that promise to give you the skills and knowledge you seek.

By nature, you commonly opt to work by yourself. You trust your talents, knowledge, and skills to identify problems. You consider numerous solutions before you pinpoint the most appropriate course of action. Questions and answers materialize without a lot of effort on your part.

Chances are good that you generate ideas quickly. You draw clever linkages between facts, events, people, problems, or solutions. You present others with numerous options at a pace some find dizzying. Your innovative thinking tends to foster ongoing dialogue between and among the group's participants.

Because of your strengths, you notice that multiple solutions to nagging problems automatically pop into your mind. You usually study each option from many different angles. After carefully evaluating the entire situation, you likely choose the alternative that makes the most sense. Why? You habitually aim to outscore or outperform most of your rivals most of the time.

To take the CliftonStrengths assessment, go to:

https://store.gallup.com/c/en-us/1/cliftonstrengths

Select the CliftonStrengths Top 5 assessment by clicking the "Shop Now" button.

Personality Type Assessment

The Myers-Briggs Type Indicator assessment is the most popular personality tool worldwide, with about 2 million people completing it every year. It was created by a mother-and-daughter team, Katharine Cook Briggs and Isabel Myers, and was made available in 1962. "Briggs was inspired to research personality type theory when she met her daughter's future husband, Clarence Myers. She noticed he had a different way of seeing the world. This intrigued her enough to start a literature review to understand different temperaments. World War II was a huge influence on the project's development. Myers believed that if people understood each other better, they'd work together better and there'd be less conflict."[13]

Even if you have taken the Myers-Briggs personality type in the past, please take this personality assessment again. Your preferences, and therefore your findings, can change over time.

- Go to https://www.truity.com/test/type-finder-personality-test-new and please take the survey.

- Assessment takes about ten minutes to complete.

- Upon completion of the survey, your results will be reflected on the screen.

- Your results will be a four-letter personality type. For example, ENFJ. And the graph will indicate how strong your preferences are.

The graph will look something like this:

---

[13] https://eu.themyersbriggs.com/en/tools/MBTI/Myers-Briggs-history

Write down your four-letter personality type:

There is a short summary about your personality type on the website. You can read it below your four-letter designation.

Then, go to the MTBI website (https://www.mbtionline.com/en-US/) to read more about your type. Click on the menu at the upper right of the website (four bars) and choose "MBTI Types." Click on your four-letter designation.

You will see another summary about your personality type, along with how common it is. See sample below:

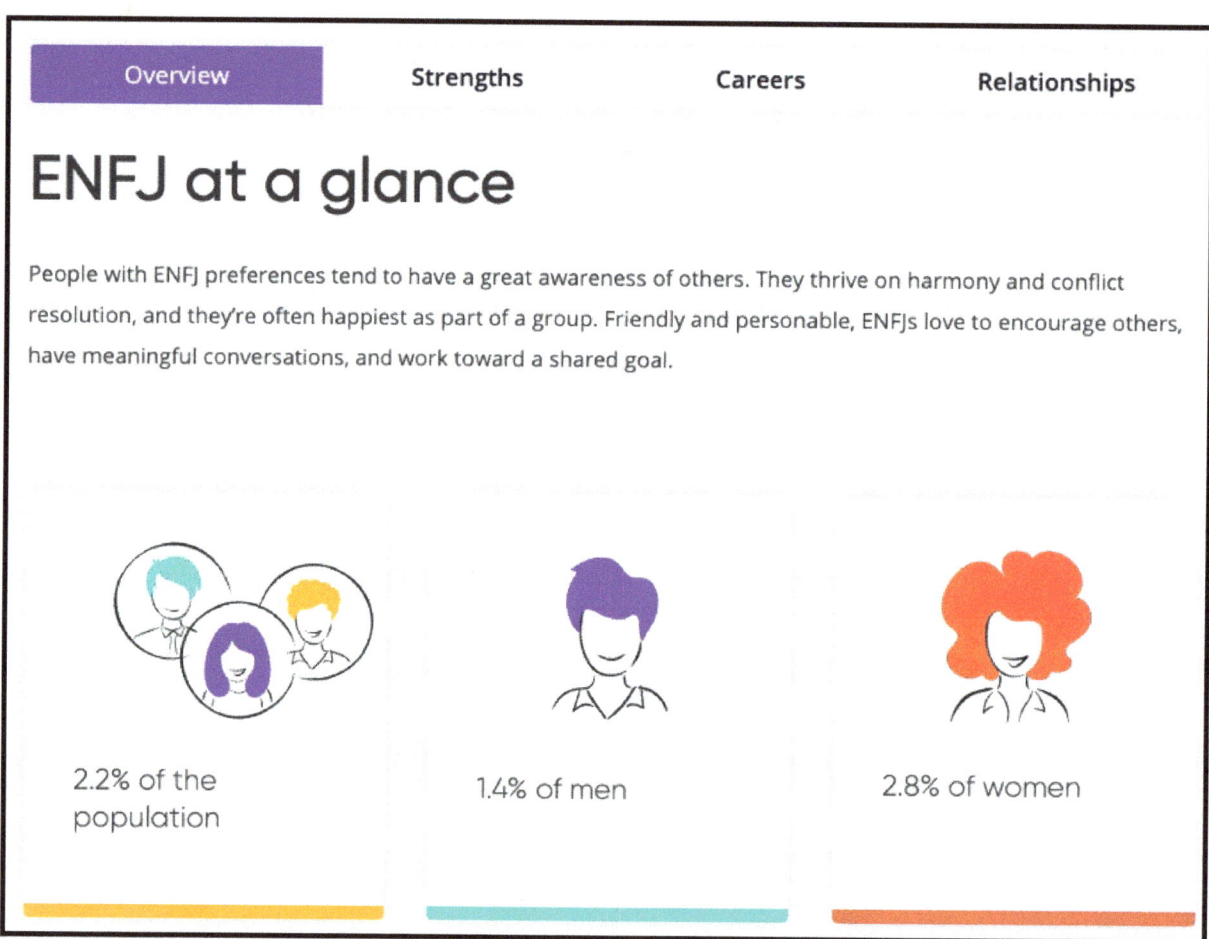

And finally, there is a list of words or phrases that describe people with your personality type. See sample below:

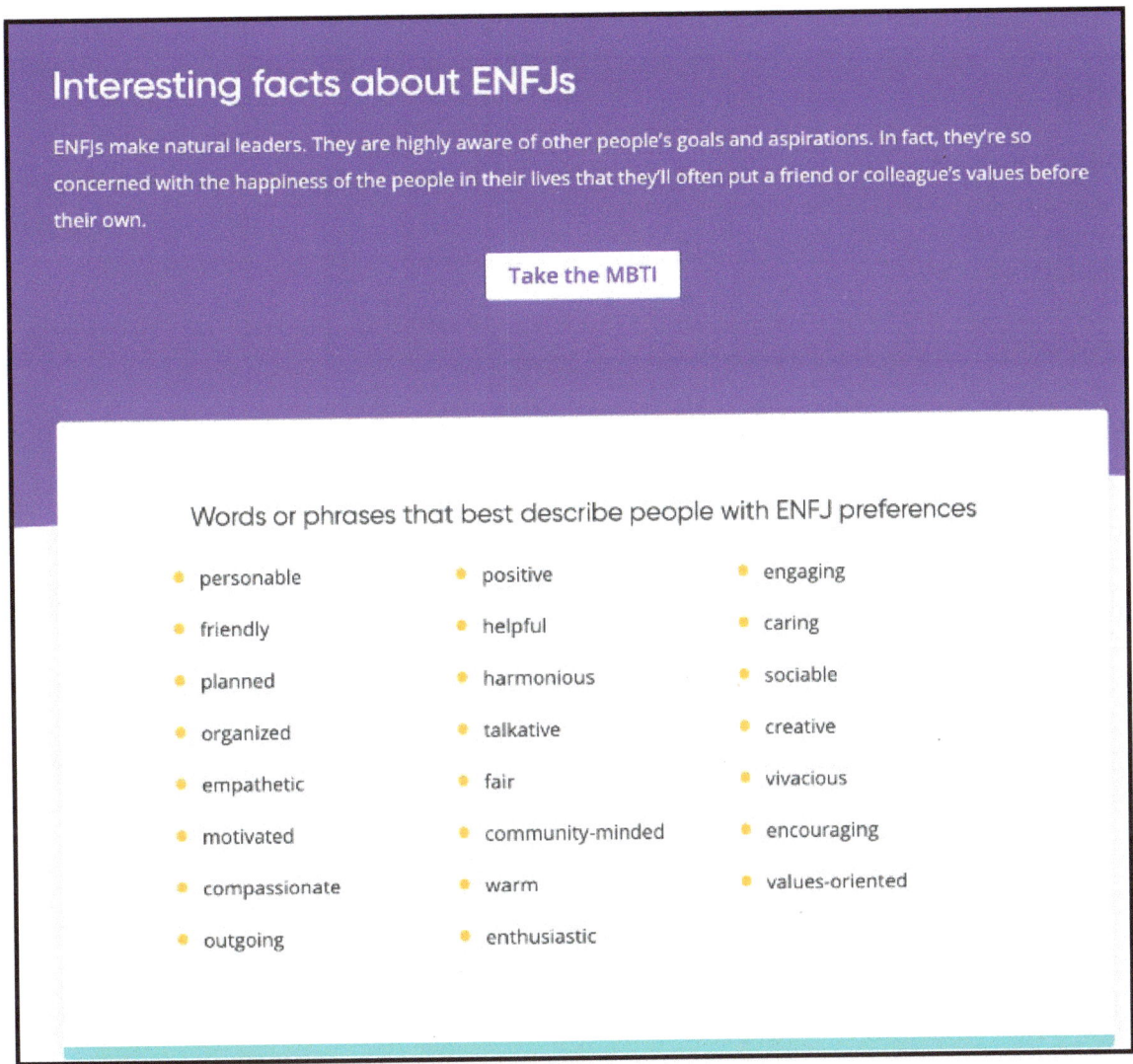

After you read the two summaries and review the words and phrases list, choose five characteristics about your personality type that resonate with you—each characteristic can be one word or a short phrase.

Write Five Characteristics That Resonate with You About Your Personality Type:

1.

2.

3.

4.

5.

Your personality is core to who you are. I have had positive and negative experiences in tech companies when people have differing personalities. I'll start first with the negative experience.

I was part of a leadership team at Hewlett-Packard, where two of my peers, William and Katie, were very close with our boss. William and Katie seemed to have his ear, and they won every battle. It became clear to me why this was.

A member of the leadership team, Tom, was in a master's program for organizational development, and he put all of us through the Myers-Briggs personality type assessment. Tom's objective was to try to reduce some of the tension and division that existed in this leadership team.

Tom acted as a facilitator after we all completed the assessment. Tom had the *Introverts* stand on one side of the room and the *Extroverts* on the other side.

Then Tom had the people who used their *Intuition* skills stand on one side of the room and the people who used their *Sensing* skills on the other side.

Then he had those who had strong *Thinking* tendencies stand on one side of the room while people who used their *Feeling* tendencies on the other side.

The last of the four letters was *Judgment* versus *Perception*. Tom had those people take their places.

Well, our boss, as well as William and Katie, who had our boss's ear, were *always* standing on the same side of the room. I was on the other side of the room for three of the four scenarios, and most of my peers usually joined me.

Unfortunately, the insight that most of us took away was, "Oh, that's why I find it difficult to work with you. We are opposites." The group missed the opportunity to leverage the differences in the leadership team. Tensions didn't reduce on that team. I eventually left and joined a team where my strengths were welcomed and appreciated.

On the flip side, I had an extremely positive experience with varying personality types with a team of eighteen sales representatives who worked for me at Hewlett-Packard. I am not exaggerating. We had one of each of the sixteen personality types. It was mind-blowing how diverse our personalities were! We all couldn't have been more different from each other.

I had two peers who led teams of sales representatives similar to my team, and they could never figure out our secret sauce for always being the top-performing team.

Here is the secret sauce: We *respected* and leveraged each person's strengths. This was the difference between this sales team and the leadership team I described above. For example, when I held forecasting calls every month with the sales reps, I put them in groups of three. They listened to each other's sales scenarios and shared best practices with each other. It was such a joy to work with this team. And we enjoyed tremendous success together.

The moral of this story is that assessment tools are not meant to judge anyone. There are no right or wrong insights from career assessments. These tools should be used to celebrate your unique gifts and talents and help you put them into play more often. And they help you appreciate others' gifts and talents too and leverage them for the good of the company.

While the insights from these three career assessments are fresh in your mind, please flip to Chapter 8 and log your top five values from the Values in Action assessment, your top five strengths from the Clifton Strengths assessment in the God-given Strengths field, and the top five characteristics that resonate with you from the Personality Type assessment. Please log these on the Putting It All Together forms.

This concludes Phase 1, Career Exploration.

I hope you enjoyed learning new insights or were reacquainted with your special gifts and perspectives. You should be celebrated for your unique combination of strengths, values, and capabilities! We will use these insights in Chapter 8 as input for crafting your career path, then again in Chapter 10 when we build your personal brand for your resume.

We will now turn our attention to market research in Phase 2.

PHASE 2
MARKET RESEARCH

In Phase 2, we will explore three main topics:

- High-growth career options in the technology industry, including the top eight hot spots

- Adjacent industries where your tech experience could be valued

- Whether it's time for you to explore owning a business or starting a side hustle

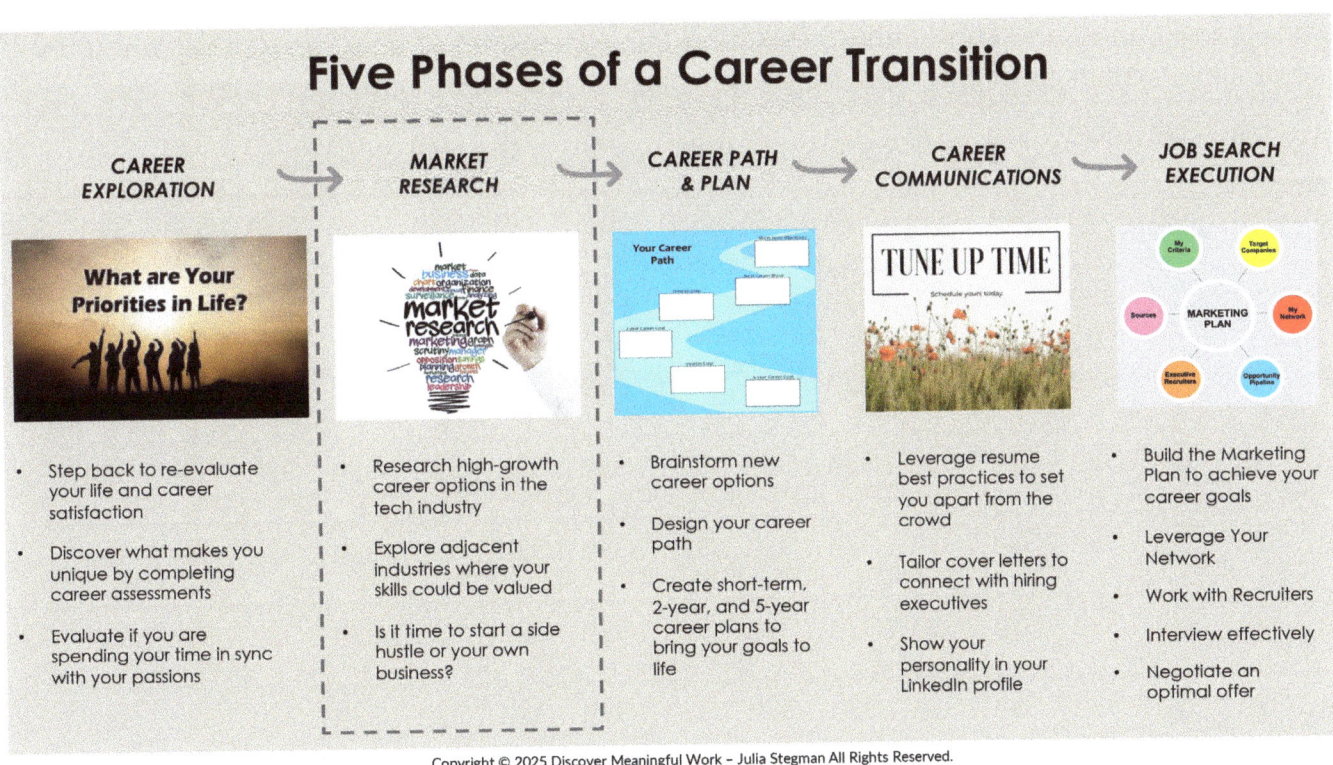

Before we dive into the content, I'd like to point out what is different about Phase 2. First of all, these chapters are significantly longer than the other chapters in the book. This is by design.

You are welcome to read through all the content. Or you can dive into the sections that interest you the most and just skim the sections that are less interesting to you.

Here is some help on navigating the three chapters in this phase:

If you are committed to staying in the tech industry, Chapter 5 will be your primary focus area.

If you are open to also exploring industries that are adjacent to tech, where your tech experience could be valued, Chapter 6 will be useful. In Chapter 6, we explore industries that are adjacent to tech, such as the industrial automation and automotive industries. Tech-adjacent companies are heavily utilizing technology in their business models to create value for customers, so you will find many of the same roles in these industries that you will find in a traditional tech company. By considering tech-adjacent companies, you will open yourself up to more career opportunities and more high-growth companies versus just focusing on the traditional tech industry. There are a lot of exciting companies in these tech-adjacent industries.

If you would like to explore side hustles or full-time business ownership, Chapter 7 will be your guide to evaluating a broad list of self-employment options, as well as an assessment to gauge your affinity for entrepreneurship. As you pondered the three seasons of your life along with the other exercises in Phase 1, is there a business ownership opportunity in your future, either now or down the road?

At a minimum, I recommend you read the first several pages of all three chapters to get a flavor for the exciting set of career options this book will put in front of you. I encourage you to take some time to think outside the box before deciding on your career path in Chapter 8.

We will start with evaluating fast-growing career options in the tech industry.

CHAPTER 5

EIGHT HIGH-GROWTH CAREER OPTIONS IN THE TECHNOLOGY INDUSTRY

"Opportunities come infrequently.
When it rains gold, put out the bucket, not the thimble."

– Warren Buffett

The tech industry continuously innovates. This is due to the nature of technology, which is ever evolving. Innovation is also *required* to keep tech company valuations high. The market expects it.

We are on the horizon of exciting technologies that will dramatically change how we work and play. Now more than ever, it's critical to get in front of these technologies and take the offensive to apply them to your employer's business. If you aren't on the offensive, by default, you are on the defensive.

Tech companies went through a significant shift in business strategies in 2023 and 2024, resulting in massive layoffs. On a human level, this was very painful for the tech employees whose jobs were impacted. On a business level, many large tech companies were freeing up investment and directing it toward new, innovative technologies.

So, it is critical to:

- Keep your eyes on where the investments are being made so you can ride the wave of growth

- Learn new skills to improve and evolve your marketability

In this chapter, we will review:

- Hot spots in the technology industry

- Jobs projected to grow

I'll first offer a description of the research methodology for this chapter.

As a vice president of research and advisory services for eight years at TSIA, I led a research practice and worked with hundreds of tech companies to help them optimize their recurring revenue streams. I had eight peers who led their own distinct areas of research. We were all exposed on a regular basis to each other's research, and it was a unique time in my career to get a broad view of the tech industry. So, I had a strong foundation regarding the tech industry coming into writing this chapter.

I then started conducting internet research to confirm my understanding of the areas in tech where high job growth was expected. Subsequently, I created my top-eight list.

The next step was to create a detailed list of technical roles and customer-facing roles where high job growth was expected in each of the eight categories. Boy, was this time-consuming. So, I engaged the help of ChatGPT to generate the high-growth jobs lists. I was blown away by the results. As a subject matter expert, I knew the results were correct. The advantage was I didn't have to spend months consolidating this analysis; ChatGPT did it for me in a matter of minutes. Later in this chapter, we will talk more about the critical role of artificial intelligence (AI) in the tech industry, how it can accelerate productivity, and how important human intervention is. Writing this chapter, I experienced firsthand that AI is a powerful productivity enhancer.

Below is my list of the top eight hot spots in the technology industry, where job growth is expected.

The hot spots fall into two broad categories:

1. Innovative technologies

2. Optimization of functional areas

You don't have to be excited about all these areas, but it's important to embrace two or three hot spots and build new skills to harness these high-growth areas. The skills landscape is evolving rapidly, and you don't want to be left behind.

Top Eight Hot Spots in the Tech Industry

Innovative technologies:

1. Artificial intelligence and machine learning

2. Advanced technology—big data and quantum computing

3. Cybersecurity

4. E-commerce and digital trade

5. 3D and 4D printing and modeling

6. Cleantech and sustainability

Optimization of functional areas:

7. Evolving role of sales and marketing leaders

8. Scaling customer success and customer support

There is a mix of leadership roles and individual contributor (IC) roles listed below for your review. If you are a people leader, the projected growth at the IC level also translates to growth in management roles to lead these teams or functions. You can also consider expanding your current leadership charter by adding some of these high-growth functions to your organization.

In each of the eight hot spots listed below, there are examples of software or tools that are commonly utilized in these roles, so you can evaluate where you might need to invest in training to expand your skill set.

This chapter has a lot of content, so feel free to dive into the sections that interest you the most and skim the sections that are less interesting to you.

INNOVATIVE TECHNOLOGIES

Artificial Intelligence and Machine Learning

Artificial intelligence (AI) continues to be a major focus for technology companies, with investments in machine learning (ML), natural language processing, computer vision, and other AI technologies to develop intelligent systems, automation solutions, and personalized experiences across industries. AI and ML are predicted to have the most transformative impact on the tech industry for the next five years.

According to the TSIA, tech companies are using AI to:

- Create efficiencies that result in cost reductions

- Improve decision-making with data

- Enhance the customer experience

CEOs of large tech companies, including Dell Technologies, Google Cloud, HP Inc., Hewlett Packard Enterprise, IBM, Cisco Systems, AMD, Intel, Hitachi Vantara, Lenovo, and Vertiv, have stated that artificial intelligence is one of their largest opportunities for revenue growth.[14]

Given the importance of this topic, I interviewed an AI expert to get his perspective on AI and its impact on careers in the tech industry.

---

[14] CRN.com, February 22, 2024, https://www.crn.com/news/computing/2024/why-10-top-tech-ceos-see-ai-as-one-of-2024-s-biggest-opportunities?page=1

Abhijeet Khadilkar and I worked together when I was at TSIA and he was at Cisco. Abhijeet is now the managing director of Spearhead. He and his team help clients with their transformational AI projects.

I asked him, "Abhijeet, how impactful is AI now, and what will it mean in the future?"

"AI is a fast-moving topic. AI is here to stay. It will have a massive impact on life, work, and play. The recent developments, especially with generative AI, make it very compelling and easy for everybody to interact with AI. One analogy I like to give in terms of how impactful and invasive AI will become is the cell phone. We all use smartphones today. When we are using our cell phones, texting, doing email, or watching a video, we don't say we are using the internet even though we *are* using the internet. So AI will be kind of like that. We will be using AI without saying we are using AI. It will be pervasive across everything. It will be in our devices that we use for work; it will be in our homes. It's an opportunity for people to interact easily with technology—this is always the goal, to get more from computing and technology."

"That's amazing to think how pervasive AI will become," I replied. "It will be an interesting journey for all of us. It seems like this is a wide-open frontier—a bit like the Wild, Wild West. How are you approaching the implementation of AI and making it practical with your clients?"

"Everyone is getting on the journey to AI. There will be winners and losers. We don't want to be on the losing side; we want to be on the winning side. At Spearhead, we think of AI in five different dimensions. To make it easier, we call it CARES. This is our hypothesis for helping clients with AI-fication, which is the strategic process of integrating AI into an organization's operations, workflows, and decision-making systems to enhance efficiency, drive innovation, and create sustainable value."

He went on to explain that CARES stands for:

- **Create value in the flow of work.** AI-fication starts with embedding AI seamlessly into the natural workflows of the business. This ensures that AI drives tangible value without disrupting existing operations, enabling smooth transitions and immediate productivity enhancements.

- **Always have a human in the loop**. In the journey of AI-fication, human oversight is critical to maintaining ethical governance, ensuring quality outcomes, and fostering trust. AI should enhance human capabilities, not replace them, positioning people as key drivers of success. Also, AI (and gen AI in particular) does hallucinate which can be a good thing or not a good thing depending on the use case. Human judgment is required to address hallucinations and maintain quality output.

- **Right AI for the right use case**. AI-fication involves carefully selecting and implementing the AI algorithms, tools, technology platforms, and solutions that align with specific business challenges. By deploying the most suitable technologies, organizations can unlock maximum value while avoiding misaligned efforts and inefficiencies.

- **Experience enables AI adoption**. User experience is central to AI-fication. Intuitive, user-friendly AI solutions reduce resistance and accelerate adoption, making AI a natural and welcomed part of daily operations. This includes customer experience and also employee experience because employees are customers for internal AI solutions.

- **System, not tools**. AI-fication goes beyond deploying isolated tools and towards building cohesive AI ecosystems. These systems provide scalable and integrated solutions that align with strategic goals and deliver long-term value across the business. So rather than looking for piece-meal outputs from different AI tools, leaders should look at the system as a whole that could have multiple AI components.

I responded, "A lot of people are concerned about what AI means for their career. You talked about wanting to be on the winning side of AI. It sounds like subject matter experts are going to be really important with the appropriate implementation of AI."

Abhijeet then said, "You might have seen the meme going around that says you will not lose your job to AI, but you will lose your job to a person using AI. People who are using AI correctly are definitely getting the productivity benefits. Microsoft came up with a survey that showed productivity increases that ranged from 15 percent to 40 percent. For any individual who wants to increase their productivity, AI can be an accelerator. AI can also be an accelerator in learning new topics. You can ask AI to explain very complex topics to a seventh grader so it can be absorbed easily and quickly."

If you aren't using AI today, you will fall behind quickly from a career perspective. Abhijeet and I both challenge you: Wherever you are on your AI journey, take it to the next level today.

Abhijeet has an informative newsletter on generative AI and digital transformation that you can subscribe to: https://spearhead.so/subscribe/

EMERGING LEADERSHIP ROLES

As artificial intelligence (AI) and machine learning (ML) continue to transform the technology industry, new leadership roles are emerging to oversee the development, implementation, and ethical use of these technologies. These roles are critical for driving AI and ML innovation, ensuring data security, managing AI-driven operations, and guiding strategic decisions based on AI-powered insights. Here are the key emerging leadership roles in the technology industry due to the rise of AI and ML:

1. Chief AI Officer (CAIO)

- Description: The chief AI officer is responsible for overseeing the strategic direction and implementation of AI initiatives in an organization. They guide AI research, development, and deployment across products and services, ensuring alignment with business goals.

- **Why It's Emerging**: As AI becomes a core element of digital transformation, companies need a dedicated leader to drive AI strategies, ensuring that the technology delivers business value while managing associated risks.

2. Head of Machine Learning

- **Description**: The head of machine learning leads the development and implementation of machine learning models and systems that enhance business operations, products, or services. They manage ML teams and work on developing scalable algorithms and AI systems.

- **Why It's Emerging**: With the growing use of ML to power automation, personalization, and predictive analytics, leadership in this space is needed to develop, optimize, and manage ML capabilities across organizations.

3. Vice President of AI Ethics and Responsible AI

- **Description**: The vice president of AI ethics ensures that AI and ML technologies are developed and deployed ethically, addressing issues like bias, transparency, and fairness. This role also focuses on the governance and compliance of AI systems with legal and regulatory standards.

- **Why It's Emerging**: As AI adoption grows, companies face increasing scrutiny regarding the ethical implications of AI systems. This role is critical for ensuring that AI systems are responsible, fair, and aligned with societal values and regulatory frameworks.

Example: Microsoft has created a new executive position, chief responsible AI officer, to help build and guide the principles around the deployment of AI. The woman currently in this position is focused on defining Microsoft's approach to AI and writing the policies that govern AI deployments. She also works with other tech companies and governments to create the guardrails to ensure that AI is deployed beneficially.

4. Chief Data Scientist

- **Description**: The chief data scientist leads data-driven decision-making by overseeing AI and ML data models, analytics, and research. They ensure that AI technologies leverage the vast amounts of data that organizations collect for predictive insights and business optimization.

- **Why It's Emerging**: As companies continue to collect and analyze massive datasets, the role of the chief data scientist is pivotal in driving AI initiatives that harness data for AI-powered insights and innovation.

5. Director of AI Product Management

- **Description**: The director of AI product management focuses on guiding AI and ML products from conception to deployment. They work closely with AI engineers, data scientists, and cross-functional teams to create AI-driven products that solve business challenges.

- **Why It's Emerging**: As AI becomes integral to product innovation, this leadership role ensures that AI-driven products are developed with a strategic focus, aligning technical capabilities with market needs and customer expectations.

6. Chief Data and AI Officer (CDAO)

- **Description**: The chief data and AI officer combines the roles of data management and AI leadership, overseeing how data is collected, stored, and leveraged for AI and ML initiatives. They manage data infrastructure, analytics, and the development of AI models across the organization.

- **Why It's Emerging**: The increasing convergence of data and AI is driving the need for leaders who can integrate data management with AI initiatives, ensuring that data is leveraged effectively to create AI-driven business value.

7. Director of AI Operations

- **Description**: The director of AI operations manages the day-to-day operations of AI and ML systems. They focus on ensuring that AI models are deployed, maintained, and optimized for continuous performance, working closely with data engineers and AI engineers to resolve operational challenges.

- **Why It's Emerging**: With the growing complexity of AI systems, this role ensures that AI models are continuously optimized, maintained, and scaled to meet the demands of the business, supporting real-time decision-making and automation.

8. Head of AI-Driven Automation

- **Description**: The head of AI-driven automation leads initiatives focused on automating business processes using AI and ML technologies. They identify areas where automation can increase efficiency and oversee the implementation of AI-powered solutions, such as robotic process automation (RPA) and AI-driven workflows.

- **Why It's Emerging**: As AI becomes central to automating workflows, leadership in AI-driven automation is critical for scaling business processes, reducing costs, and improving operational efficiency.

9. Vice President of Natural Language Processing (NLP)

- **Description**: The vice president of NLP leads initiatives related to language technologies, such as chatbots, voice recognition, sentiment analysis, and language translation systems. They focus on developing AI systems that can process, understand, and generate human language.

- **Why It's Emerging**: NLP applications are expanding across industries, especially in customer support, healthcare, and e-commerce, driving demand for leadership that can guide the development of NLP systems.

10. Head of AI Partnerships and Ecosystem

- Description: The head of AI partnerships and ecosystem leads the development of strategic partnerships with AI technology providers, academic institutions, and other key stakeholders. They build an ecosystem that supports the organization's AI innovation and deployment efforts.

- Why It's Emerging: AI ecosystems are crucial for driving innovation, and leadership in partnership development is key to ensuring access to cutting-edge AI technologies, research, and talent.

These emerging leadership roles reflect the growing importance of AI and ML in shaping the future of business, operations, and technology. Leaders in these positions are responsible for driving AI innovation, ensuring ethical practices, managing AI operations at scale, and leveraging AI to create competitive advantages. As AI continues to expand, these leadership roles will become increasingly vital to organizations looking to harness the full potential of artificial intelligence.

ROLES THAT REQUIRE TECHNICAL SKILLS

Below are high-growth jobs in artificial intelligence (AI) and machine learning (ML) that require strong technical skills in the technology industry:

1. Machine Learning Engineer

- Description: ML engineers develop and deploy machine learning models to automate tasks, process large datasets, and solve complex problems. They work closely with data scientists to turn models into production-ready systems.

- Required Skills: Python, TensorFlow, PyTorch, deep learning frameworks, algorithm development, data preprocessing, cloud platforms (AWS, GCP, Azure).

2. Data Scientist

- Description: Data scientists analyze and interpret complex data using statistical methods and machine learning algorithms to extract actionable insights. They play a key role in building predictive models and optimizing business processes.

- Required Skills: Python, R, SQL, machine learning algorithms, data analysis, statistical modeling, data visualization, big data technologies (Hadoop, Spark).

3. AI Research Scientist

- Description: AI research scientists focus on developing new AI techniques, algorithms, and models, contributing to the advancement of AI technologies. They work on cutting-edge research in areas like natural language processing, computer vision, and reinforcement learning.

- **Required Skills**: Deep learning, neural networks, computer vision, NLP, reinforcement learning, Python, PyTorch, TensorFlow, research methodologies, mathematics.

4. Computer Vision Engineer

- **Description**: Computer vision engineers develop algorithms and systems that allow computers to interpret and process visual data from images and videos. This is widely used in areas such as autonomous vehicles, medical imaging, and augmented reality.

- **Required Skills**: OpenCV, TensorFlow, PyTorch, image processing, object detection, computer vision algorithms, C++, Python.

5. Natural Language Processing (NLP) Engineer

- **Description**: NLP engineers design and implement algorithms that allow computers to understand, interpret, and generate human language. They work on applications like chatbots, voice assistants, translation systems, and text analytics.

- **Required Skills**: NLP libraries (spaCy, NLTK, Hugging Face), deep learning, Python, text preprocessing, sentiment analysis, language modeling, transformer architectures (BERT, GPT).

6. Deep Learning Engineer

- **Description**: Deep learning engineers specialize in neural networks with multiple layers and architectures (convolutional neural networks, recurrent neural networks, GANs). They build AI systems that can learn complex patterns from large amounts of data.

- **Required Skills**: TensorFlow, PyTorch, Keras, deep learning architectures, neural networks, Python, model optimization, GPU programming, CUDA.

7. AI Ethics Specialist

- **Description**: AI ethics specialists focus on ensuring that AI systems are developed and deployed in a fair, transparent, and accountable manner. They work to address biases in machine learning models, data privacy concerns, and ethical implications of AI technologies.

- **Required Skills**: Understanding of AI and ML technologies, data privacy laws, ethics frameworks, algorithmic fairness, technical writing, policy understanding.

8. AI Infrastructure Engineer

- **Description**: AI infrastructure engineers design and manage the platforms and tools needed for AI and ML development, including distributed computing, cloud architecture, and model deployment infrastructure. They ensure scalability and efficiency.

- **Required Skills**: Kubernetes, Docker, cloud platforms (AWS, GCP, Azure), distributed computing, model deployment pipelines, DevOps, MLOps, Python, Terraform.

9. Robotics Engineer

- <u>Description</u>: Robotics engineers with a focus on AI work on integrating machine learning and AI algorithms into robotics systems. They develop systems capable of autonomous decision-making, object recognition, and environmental interaction.

- <u>Required Skills</u>: Python, C++, ROS (Robot Operating System), machine learning, computer vision, sensor fusion, path planning, deep learning, reinforcement learning.

10. Reinforcement Learning Engineer

- <u>Description</u>: Reinforcement learning engineers specialize in developing algorithms with which agents learn to make decisions by interacting with their environment. This approach is used in robotics, gaming, finance, and autonomous systems.

- <u>Required Skills</u>: Python, TensorFlow, PyTorch, reinforcement learning algorithms (Q-learning, DQN, PPO), deep learning, neural networks, simulation environments (OpenAI Gym).

11. AI Hardware Engineer

- <u>Description</u>: AI hardware engineers design specialized hardware (AI chips, GPUs, TPUs) optimized for the demands of machine learning and AI workloads. They work on improving the computational efficiency of AI applications.

- <u>Required Skills</u>: Hardware architecture, FPGA, GPU/TPU optimization, low-level programming (CUDA, OpenCL), Verilog, VHDL, ASIC design, machine learning model optimization.

These roles span a wide range of AI and ML applications and require strong technical skills in programming, algorithm development, data analysis, and deployment. As AI and ML technologies continue to advance, the demand for professionals in these roles is expected to grow rapidly across industries, making them some of the most promising career paths in tech.

Example: Artificial intelligence engineer is number ten on LinkedIn's fastest-growing jobs list;[15] there are eight AI engineer positions listed above in various AI specialty areas.

ROLES THAT REQUIRE CUSTOMER-FACING SKILLS

In the field of artificial intelligence (AI) and machine learning (ML), there are high-growth jobs that blend technical expertise with strong customer-facing skills. These roles often require professionals to communicate complex technical concepts to clients or stakeholders, manage projects, and ensure successful adoption and integration of AI and ML technologies. Here are some key roles:

---

[15] https://www.linkedin.com/pulse/linkedin-jobs-rise-2024-25-fastest-growing-roles-us-linkedin-news-dxmie/

1. AI/ML Solutions Consultant

- <u>Description</u>: AI/ML solutions consultants work directly with clients to understand their business needs and provide tailored AI or ML solutions. They bridge the gap between technical teams and customers, ensuring that solutions meet business objectives.

- <u>Customer-Facing Skills</u>: Strong communication, relationship building, requirements gathering, presentation skills.

- <u>Technical Skills</u>: Understanding of AI/ML technologies, cloud platforms (AWS, GCP, Azure), Python, data analysis.

Example: *Artificial intelligence consultant* is number eight on LinkedIn's fastest-growing jobs list.[16]

2. AI Product Manager

- <u>Description</u>: AI product managers oversee the development and deployment of AI-powered products, working closely with customers, development teams, and stakeholders to ensure that the product meets user needs. They often translate customer feedback into technical requirements.

- <u>Customer-Facing Skills</u>: Product road map management, customer feedback analysis, stakeholder communication, user experience (UX) understanding.

- <u>Technical Skills</u>: Basic understanding of AI/ML, data-driven decision-making, agile methodologies, product life cycle management.

3. AI Customer Success Manager

- <u>Description</u>: AI customer success managers ensure that clients successfully implement and maximize the value of AI/ML solutions. They focus on client onboarding, training, and continuous support to ensure customer satisfaction and retention.

- <u>Customer-Facing Skills</u>: Client relationship management, onboarding support, issue resolution, training and education, proactive customer engagement.

- <u>Technical Skills</u>: Understanding of AI tools, familiarity with data analytics platforms, cloud services knowledge, basic ML concepts.

4. AI Sales Engineer (Pre-Sales)

- <u>Description</u>: AI sales engineers support the sales process by demonstrating how AI/ML solutions can solve customer problems. They work closely with sales teams to present technical solutions to potential clients and customize proposals based on specific needs.

- <u>Customer-Facing Skills</u>: Sales presentations, product demonstrations, understanding client needs, negotiation.

---

[16] https://www.linkedin.com/pulse/linkedin-jobs-rise-2024-25-fastest-growing-roles-us-linkedin-news-dxmie/

- **Technical Skills:** Deep knowledge of AI/ML products, API integration, programming (Python or Java), cloud computing knowledge (AWS, GCP, Azure).

5. AI Technical Account Manager

- **Description:** Technical account managers act as liaisons between customers and AI/ML engineering teams. They ensure the successful deployment and ongoing maintenance of AI solutions, often managing post-sales technical relationships.

- **Customer-Facing Skills:** Account management, customer relationship building, issue troubleshooting, communication of technical solutions.

- **Technical Skills:** Familiarity with AI/ML platforms, cloud architecture, APIs; programming languages (Python, Java).

6. AI/ML Business Analyst

- **Description:** AI/ML business analysts identify opportunities to apply AI/ML technologies to solve business challenges. They work with customers to gather requirements, analyze data, and help build models that address client needs.

- **Customer-Facing Skills:** Requirements gathering, business analysis, customer workshops, stakeholder management.

- **Technical Skills:** Data analysis, SQL, basic knowledge of AI/ML algorithms, Excel, Python for data processing.

7. AI Implementation Specialist

- **Description:** Implementation specialists are responsible for guiding customers through the deployment of AI/ML systems. They ensure that the technology integrates smoothly into the customer's existing infrastructure and that end users are trained effectively.

- **Customer-Facing Skills:** Training and support, implementation management, problem-solving, customer consultation.

- **Technical Skills:** Familiarity with AI platforms, data integration, APIs, cloud platforms (AWS, Azure, GCP), scripting languages (Python).

8. AI/ML Trainer or Educator

- **Description:** Trainers or educators specialize in teaching customers how to use AI/ML tools and platforms. They provide training workshops, documentation, and ongoing educational support to ensure that customers fully understand the technology.

- **Customer-Facing Skills:** Teaching, communication, training material development, customer interaction.

- **Technical Skills:** Familiarity with AI/ML platforms, data analysis tools, coding (Python, R), AI/ML concepts.

9. AI Solutions Architect

- **Description**: AI solutions architects design end-to-end AI/ML solutions that meet customer requirements. They work closely with clients to understand their needs, design tailored architectures, and ensure that AI systems are scalable and sustainable.

- **Customer-Facing Skills**: Client consultation, presentation of architectural designs, solution alignment with business needs, stakeholder communication.

- **Technical Skills**: Knowledge of AI/ML frameworks, cloud platforms (AWS, Azure, GCP), system architecture, programming languages (Python, Java), API integration.

10. AI Evangelist/AI Advocate

- **Description**: AI evangelists promote the benefits of AI/ML technology to businesses, developers, and customers. They are often public speakers or content creators who explain how AI can be used to solve real-world problems and drive business outcomes.

- **Customer-Facing Skills**: Public speaking, networking, content creation (blogs, videos), community engagement.

- **Technical Skills**: Basic understanding of AI/ML, cloud platforms, coding; familiarity with the AI/ML ecosystem.

These high-growth roles in AI and ML require a mix of technical knowledge and strong customer-facing skills, such as communication, relationship building, and the ability to explain complex technologies in simple terms. They involve interacting with clients and stakeholders to ensure successful adoption, implementation, and use of AI/ML technologies, making them crucial to the commercial success of AI in various industries.

Advanced Technology– Big Data and Quantum Computing

A callout in this category is quantum computing, which enables computers to make massive calculations in seconds. "Quantum computing is the process of developing and applying computer technologies operating under the laws of quantum mechanics to solve complex real-world issues that exceed the capabilities of classical computers."[17] It could solve complex problems that have been elusive, like curing cancer.

Quantum computing promises to revolutionize computing power and enable breakthroughs in areas such as cryptography, optimization, and materials science. Technology companies are investing in quantum computing research, hardware development, and quantum algorithms to unlock the potential of quantum computing for practical applications.

According to the Bureau of Labor Statistics (BLS), quantum engineers, quantum software engineers, and quantum computing scientists have a job growth outlook of 22 percent between

---

[17] CareerKarma.com, July 23, 2022, https://careerkarma.com/blog/how-to-get-a-job-in-quantum-computing/

now and 2030, which is well above the national average for all professions. This is a very exciting tipping point for technology and could accelerate your career if you get in on the forefront of it.

ROLES THAT REQUIRE TECHNICAL SKILLS

Below are some high-growth jobs in advanced technology, big data, and quantum computing that require technical skills. These roles are critical in driving innovation in industries that rely on emerging technologies for solving complex problems, optimizing processes, and leveraging massive amounts of data.

1. Big Data Engineer

- Description: Big data engineers design, develop, and maintain large-scale data processing systems. They build robust data pipelines to ensure the collection, storage, and analysis of massive datasets in an efficient and scalable way.

- Required Skills: Hadoop, Spark, SQL/NoSQL databases (MongoDB, Cassandra), data pipeline frameworks, Python, Java, Scala, cloud platforms (AWS, GCP, Azure), distributed computing.

2. Quantum Software Developer

- Description: Quantum software developers work on writing software programs and algorithms that can run on quantum computers. They translate complex quantum theories into code and create quantum circuits for specific applications.

- Required Skills: Quantum programming languages (Qiskit, Cirq, Quipper), Python, linear algebra, quantum mechanics, quantum algorithms, classical computing fundamentals, quantum gates.

3. Big Data Architect

- Description: Big data architects design the overall architecture for large-scale data processing systems. They ensure that the infrastructure is scalable, secure, and optimized for processing massive amounts of data.

- Required Skills: Cloud platforms (AWS, GCP, Azure), Hadoop ecosystem, distributed systems, data architecture, ETL processes, data lakes, machine learning integration, data governance.

4. Quantum Research Scientist

- Description: Quantum research scientists focus on developing new theories, algorithms, and quantum computing techniques to push the boundaries of quantum technology. They work on applying quantum principles to solve real-world problems.

- Required Skills: Quantum mechanics, quantum algorithms, quantum computing platforms (IBM Q, Google's Quantum AI), linear algebra, cryptography, machine learning, physics.

5. Data Scientist

- Description: Data scientists working with big data develop models and perform statistical analysis to extract insights from large datasets. They leverage machine learning algorithms and statistical techniques to solve complex business problems.

- Required Skills: Python, R, SQL, machine learning frameworks (TensorFlow, PyTorch), big data tools (Hadoop, Spark), statistical modeling, data visualization, cloud computing, data preprocessing.

6. Quantum Hardware Engineer

- Description: Quantum hardware engineers design and develop the physical components of quantum computers, including qubits, control systems, and quantum gates. They work on overcoming the technical challenges of building reliable quantum computers.

- Required Skills: Quantum circuit design, superconducting qubits, cryogenic systems, FPGA programming, RF engineering, semiconductor physics, low-level programming, material science.

7. Quantum Cryptographer

- Description: Quantum cryptographers design encryption systems that leverage quantum principles to ensure secure communication. This includes developing quantum key distribution protocols and working on post-quantum cryptography solutions.

- Required Skills: Cryptography, quantum mechanics, quantum key distribution (QKD), quantum algorithms, information theory, linear algebra, computer security, programming languages (Python, C++).

8. Big Data Analytics Consultant

- Description: Big data analytics consultants help organizations leverage large datasets to make strategic decisions. They provide expertise in selecting tools, developing data models, and analyzing data to drive business outcomes.

- Required Skills: Data analytics tools (Power BI, Tableau, Excel), Python, SQL, Hadoop, machine learning algorithms, data visualization, business intelligence, cloud platforms.

9. Quantum Algorithm Developer

- Description: Quantum algorithm developers design and optimize algorithms that can be implemented on quantum computers to solve specific problems, such as optimization, cryptography, and material simulations.

- Required Skills: Quantum algorithms (Shor's, Grover's), linear algebra, quantum computing platforms, Python, C++, optimization techniques, computational complexity theory.

10. Big Data Security Engineer

- Description: Big data security engineers focus on protecting large datasets from cyber threats. They work on encryption, data masking, access controls, and security architecture to ensure data privacy and compliance.

- Required Skills: Cybersecurity protocols, encryption, Hadoop security, data access controls, cloud security (AWS, GCP, Azure), network security, data governance, security information and event management (SIEM) tools.

These high-growth jobs in advanced technology, big data, and quantum computing demand a strong technical background in areas such as distributed computing, quantum algorithms, data analytics, AI/ML integration, and cybersecurity. As these fields continue to advance, they offer exciting opportunities for professionals with expertise in both theory and practical applications, driving the future of technology across multiple industries.

ROLES THAT REQUIRE CUSTOMER-FACING SKILLS

Here are some high-growth jobs in advanced technology, big data, and quantum computing that require a combination of technical and customer-facing skills. These roles typically involve engaging with clients or stakeholders to explain complex technologies, manage projects, and help customers adopt and implement advanced solutions.

1. Big Data Solutions Architect

- Description: Big data solutions architects design and implement large-scale data solutions tailored to client needs. They collaborate with customers to understand their business challenges and design architectures using big data technologies.

- Customer-Facing Skills: Consulting, solution presentation, client relationship management, communication with technical and nontechnical stakeholders.

- Technical Skills: Hadoop, Spark, cloud platforms (AWS, GCP, Azure), data warehousing, ETL, data governance.

2. Quantum Computing Consultant

- Description: Quantum computing consultants work closely with businesses to understand how quantum technologies can solve specific problems, and they provide strategic advice on how to adopt quantum computing. This role often involves educating clients on quantum concepts and their applications.

- Customer-Facing Skills: Client consultation, strategic advising, solution scoping, translating complex technical concepts into business-friendly language.

- Technical Skills: Quantum computing frameworks (Qiskit, Cirq), quantum algorithms, Python, linear algebra, quantum cryptography.

3. Big Data Product Manager

- <u>Description</u>: Big data product managers are responsible for overseeing the development and marketing of big data solutions, ensuring that products align with customer needs. They serve as the liaison between customers, engineering teams, and marketing departments.

- <u>Customer-Facing Skills</u>: Product life cycle management, customer feedback analysis, market research, stakeholder communication, project management.

- <u>Technical Skills</u>: Understanding of big data technologies, data analysis, cloud platforms, AI/ML integration.

4. Quantum Computing Evangelist

- <u>Description</u>: Quantum computing evangelists promote the adoption and understanding of quantum technologies by engaging with developers, businesses, and the broader tech community. They act as public advocates for quantum technologies, often through speaking engagements, workshops, and technical demonstrations.

- <u>Customer-Facing Skills</u>: Public speaking, technical content creation, community engagement, relationship building with developers and businesses.

- <u>Technical Skills</u>: Quantum computing concepts, quantum programming languages (Qiskit, Cirq), cryptography, cloud computing.

5. Big Data Sales Engineer

- <u>Description</u>: Big data sales engineers support the sales process by demonstrating the capabilities of big data platforms and tools to potential clients. They work alongside sales teams to provide technical expertise and ensure that the proposed solutions align with customer needs.

- <u>Customer-Facing Skills</u>: Technical sales support, product demonstrations, client needs analysis, contract negotiation.

- <u>Technical Skills</u>: Big data platforms (Hadoop, Spark), cloud services (AWS, Azure, GCP), data analytics, database technologies.

6. Quantum Computing Business Development Manager

- <u>Description</u>: Quantum business development managers identify opportunities for quantum technologies in various industries and work to form partnerships or business relationships. They act as intermediaries between the technical quantum teams and business leaders.

- <u>Customer-Facing Skills</u>: Business development, strategic partnerships, sales, stakeholder engagement.

- **Technical Skills**: Understanding of quantum computing principles, market knowledge of quantum applications, ability to translate technical benefits into business opportunities.

7. Big Data Consultant

- **Description**: Big data consultants help organizations implement and optimize big data solutions. They provide strategic guidance on data architecture, analytics, and infrastructure while working closely with clients to ensure that the solutions meet business needs.

- **Customer-Facing Skills**: Consulting, customer requirements gathering, solution design, stakeholder communication.

- **Technical Skills**: Big data analytics tools (Hadoop, Spark, SQL, NoSQL databases), cloud platforms (AWS, GCP, Azure), machine learning, data governance.

8. Quantum Solutions Architect

- **Description**: Quantum solutions architects work with clients to design and implement quantum computing solutions that address specific business or research challenges. They help customers integrate quantum systems with classical computing infrastructure.

- **Customer-Facing Skills**: Client engagement, solution design, presenting complex quantum concepts, collaboration with technical and business teams.

- **Technical Skills**: Quantum algorithms, quantum programming (Qiskit, Cirq), cloud-based quantum computing, classical-quantum hybrid systems.

9. Big Data Customer Success Manager

- **Description**: Big data customer success managers ensure that clients successfully adopt and derive value from big data solutions. They provide ongoing support, handle issues, and work to maintain a strong relationship with the customer throughout their engagement.

- **Customer-Facing Skills**: Client relationship management, customer support, onboarding, issue resolution, training.

- **Technical Skills**: Understanding of big data platforms, data analytics, cloud infrastructure, SQL, data processing tools.

10. Quantum Computing Educator/Trainer

- **Description**: Quantum computing trainers work with customers, developers, and enterprises to train them in using quantum computing technologies. They create training programs, workshops, and courses that simplify complex quantum concepts.

- **Customer-Facing Skills**: Instruction, communication, curriculum development, public speaking.

- **Technical Skills**: Quantum computing principles, programming (Qiskit, Cirq), quantum algorithms, cryptography, machine learning integration with quantum systems.

These roles combine technical expertise with strong customer-facing skills, making them critical in driving the adoption of advanced technology, big data, and quantum computing. Professionals in these jobs work closely with clients to design solutions, manage deployments, and ensure that advanced technologies deliver business value. The ability to translate complex concepts into customer-friendly terms is essential for success in these positions.

Cybersecurity

Wide-spread cybercrime and cyber insecurity are a significant risk for companies globally.

As cyber threats continue to evolve, technology companies are investing in cybersecurity solutions, including threat detection, prevention, and response technologies, to protect data, networks, and critical infrastructure from cyberattacks and breaches.

According to Cyberseek.org, there are currently 572,000 open cybersecurity roles in the US. "Security experts have also predicted there will be 3.5 million unfilled positions in the industry by 2025, making it one of the best tech jobs."[18]

The US Infrastructure Investment and Jobs Act authorized $50 billion to protect infrastructure from cybersecurity attacks and weather disasters. This act will increase government spending over a ten-year period and is expected to increase the capacity of the US economy.

ROLES THAT REQUIRE TECHNICAL SKILLS

Below are high-growth jobs in cybersecurity in the technology industry that require strong technical skills. These roles are critical for defending organizations against cyber threats, securing digital assets, and ensuring the integrity of IT infrastructures:

1. Security Engineer

- **Description**: Security engineers are responsible for designing, implementing, and maintaining security systems to protect an organization's IT infrastructure. They work on firewalls, encryption, and vulnerability testing to safeguard against cyber threats.

- **Technical Skills**: Network security, firewalls, intrusion detection/prevention systems (IDS/IPS), encryption, penetration testing, Python, C++, vulnerability management tools.

2. Penetration Tester (Ethical Hacker)

- **Description**: Penetration testers simulate cyberattacks on an organization's systems to identify security weaknesses. They help organizations understand potential vulnerabilities and recommend solutions to prevent exploitation.

---

[18] 10 Highest Paying Tech Jobs for 2024, Techopedia, November 14, 2023, https://www.techopedia.com/highest-paying-tech-jobs

- **Technical Skills**: Penetration testing tools (Metasploit, Burp Suite, Kali Linux), scripting languages (Python, Bash), network protocols, vulnerability assessment, social engineering, exploit development.

3. Security Architect

- **Description**: Security architects design robust security frameworks to protect an organization's data and infrastructure. They develop strategies for preventing and mitigating security threats, ensuring that systems remain secure and compliant.

- **Technical Skills**: Network design, encryption protocols, firewalls, VPNs, security architecture frameworks, risk assessment, cloud security, security policies and standards.

4. Incident Response Analyst

- **Description**: Incident response analysts are responsible for responding to security breaches and cyberattacks. They investigate incidents, mitigate damage, and develop procedures for preventing future incidents.

- **Technical Skills**: Forensic analysis, malware analysis, intrusion detection, incident handling, SIEM tools (Splunk, ArcSight), Python, log analysis.

5. Cloud Security Engineer

- **Description**: Cloud security engineers focus on securing cloud-based environments, such as AWS, Azure, and Google Cloud. They are responsible for protecting cloud infrastructure, ensuring compliance with security standards, and implementing security controls.

- **Technical Skills**: Cloud platforms (AWS, Azure, GCP), identity and access management (IAM), encryption, firewalls, vulnerability management, DevSecOps, container security (Docker, Kubernetes).

6. Cybersecurity Analyst

- **Description**: Cybersecurity analysts focus on monitoring, analyzing, and responding to security threats across an organization's systems. They maintain security protocols, ensure compliance, and develop strategies for mitigating risks.

- **Technical Skills**: SIEM tools, firewall management, threat analysis, incident response, vulnerability scanning, endpoint security, risk assessment.

7. Application Security Engineer

- **Description**: Application security engineers focus on securing applications throughout the software development life cycle (SDLC). They conduct code reviews, perform security testing, and implement security measures to protect against application-level threats.

- **Technical Skills**: Secure coding practices, code review tools (Veracode, Checkmarx), OWASP Top 10, SAST/DAST tools, threat modeling, Java, Python, Ruby, C#.

Example: Product security engineer is number twelve on LinkedIn's fastest-growing jobs list.[19]

8. DevSecOps Engineer

- <u>Description</u>: DevSecOps engineers integrate security practices into the DevOps pipeline, ensuring that security is considered at every stage of software development and deployment. They automate security tests and maintain secure continuous integration and continuous deployment (CI/CD) workflows.

- <u>Technical Skills</u>: Automation tools (Jenkins, GitLab CI), security testing tools (SAST, DAST), cloud platforms, container security (Docker, Kubernetes), infrastructure as code (Terraform), scripting (Python, Shell).

9. Security Compliance Analyst

- <u>Description</u>: Security compliance analysts ensure that organizations adhere to cybersecurity laws, regulations, and standards. They perform audits, develop policies, and monitor systems to ensure compliance with security frameworks.

- <u>Technical Skills</u>: Compliance standards (ISO 27001, NIST, GDPR, HIPAA), risk assessment, security audits, SIEM tools, policy development, vulnerability management.

10. Network Security Engineer

- <u>Description</u>: Network security engineers focus on securing an organization's network infrastructure by implementing firewalls, VPNs, IDS/IPS systems, and monitoring network traffic to detect potential intrusions.

- <u>Technical Skills</u>: Firewalls, VPNs, IDS/IPS, network protocols (TCP/IP, DNS, HTTP), packet analysis, intrusion detection, encryption, networking equipment (Cisco, Juniper), Python, Bash.

These high-growth jobs in cybersecurity require a solid foundation in technical skills, such as network security, coding, reverse engineering, cloud infrastructure, and compliance management. As cyber threats continue to evolve, the demand for skilled cybersecurity professionals who can safeguard digital assets and respond to incidents will grow significantly.

ROLES THAT REQUIRE CUSTOMER-FACING SKILLS

Here are some high-growth jobs in cybersecurity in the technology industry that require a combination of customer-facing and technical skills. These roles are critical for interacting with clients, stakeholders, or internal teams to explain cybersecurity solutions, manage implementations, and ensure effective protection against cyber threats:

---

[19] https://www.linkedin.com/pulse/linkedin-jobs-rise-2024-25-fastest-growing-roles-us-linkedin-news-dxmie/

1. Cybersecurity Consultant

- **Description**: Cybersecurity consultants work closely with clients to assess security risks and vulnerabilities. They provide tailored advice on how to enhance cybersecurity practices, ensure compliance, and protect systems from cyber threats.

- **Customer-Facing Skills**: Client relationship management, consulting, security risk assessment, solution design, stakeholder communication.

- **Technical Skills**: Vulnerability assessments, penetration testing, risk management frameworks, cloud security, compliance (GDPR, HIPAA), encryption.

2. Cybersecurity Sales Engineer

- **Description**: Cybersecurity sales engineers collaborate with sales teams to present cybersecurity solutions to potential clients. They demonstrate how products and services can address specific client needs and provide technical guidance throughout the sales process.

- **Customer-Facing Skills**: Technical sales, product demonstrations, client needs analysis, solution customization, negotiation.

- **Technical Skills**: Firewalls, SIEM tools, endpoint security, cloud security, encryption, network security protocols.

3. Security Account Manager

- **Description**: Security account managers manage relationships with key clients, ensuring that they have the right cybersecurity solutions in place. They act as liaisons between the client and technical teams, resolving issues and providing ongoing support.

- **Customer-Facing Skills**: Client relationship management, communication, conflict resolution, project management, upselling.

- **Technical Skills**: Knowledge of cybersecurity products (firewalls, intrusion detection systems, VPNs), incident response, compliance, cloud security.

4. Cybersecurity Customer Success Manager

- **Description**: Customer success managers in cybersecurity ensure that clients are successfully implementing and maximizing the value of the security products or services they've purchased. They focus on client satisfaction, onboarding, and ensuring continued protection.

- **Customer-Facing Skills**: Onboarding support, relationship management, issue resolution, training, customer retention.

- **Technical Skills**: SIEM tools, endpoint security, firewall configuration, incident response, threat monitoring.

5. Cybersecurity Product Manager

- **Description**: Cybersecurity product managers oversee the development and life cycle of cybersecurity products and services. They work with customers, sales, and engineering teams to ensure that products meet client needs and solve relevant security problems.

- **Customer-Facing Skills**: Product road map management, client feedback analysis, market research, stakeholder communication.

- **Technical Skills**: Understanding of security protocols (SSL, TLS), data encryption, identity management, cloud security, compliance (ISO 27001, NIST).

6. Cybersecurity Training and Awareness Specialist

- **Description**: Training and awareness specialists create and deliver cybersecurity training programs for employees or clients. They educate teams on security best practices, phishing prevention, and recognizing potential cyber threats.

- **Customer-Facing Skills**: Teaching, presentation, training material development, communication.

- **Technical Skills:** Knowledge of cybersecurity threats, phishing attack prevention, secure password policies, social engineering tactics, compliance.

7. Cybersecurity Project Manager

- **Description**: Cybersecurity project managers oversee the implementation of security solutions, ensuring that they are delivered on time and meet client expectations. They coordinate between internal teams and clients to ensure smooth deployment and integration.

- **Customer-Facing Skills**: Project management, client communication, scope management, conflict resolution, stakeholder engagement.

- **Technical Skills**: Familiarity with security technologies (firewalls, IDS/IPS), compliance standards, incident response, cloud security, risk management.

8. Cybersecurity Evangelist

- **Description**: Cybersecurity evangelists promote cybersecurity products and services by engaging with the tech community, customers, and developers. They often speak at conferences, write technical blogs, and advocate for best practices.

- **Customer-Facing Skills**: Public speaking, content creation, community engagement, technical demonstrations, relationship building.

- **Technical Skills**: Knowledge of cybersecurity trends, threats, encryption, incident response, malware analysis, cloud security.

9. Cybersecurity Business Development Manager

- <u>Description</u>: Cybersecurity business development managers focus on expanding a company's cybersecurity business by identifying new markets, forming partnerships, and developing strategic relationships with clients.

- <u>Customer-Facing Skills</u>: Business development, strategic partnerships, sales, client relationship building, market analysis.

- <u>Technical Skills</u>: Understanding of cybersecurity solutions, compliance requirements, cloud security, network security, threat intelligence.

These high-growth jobs in cybersecurity demand a combination of technical knowledge and strong customer-facing skills, such as client relationship management, communication, and consulting. Professionals in these roles must be able to translate complex cybersecurity issues into business-friendly language while ensuring effective adoption and implementation of security solutions.

E-Commerce and Digital Trade

The pandemic permanently changed how we buy goods and services around the world, both as consumers (B2C) and as businesses (B2B). Online buying is projected to be a high-growth area in the coming years.

Technology companies are investing in e-commerce platforms, digital payment solutions, logistics, and supply chain technologies to support the growth of online retail, omnichannel experiences, and personalized customer engagement.

US online sales increased by $244 billion (43 percent year over year) during the first year of the pandemic, which resulted in total US online sales of $815 billion.[20]

2023 global e-commerce revenue was $3.15 trillion. By 2026, global e-commerce sales are expected to total over $8 trillion and represent almost 23 percent of all retail purchases.[21] This is a very significant growth opportunity.

ROLES THAT REQUIRE TECHNICAL SKILLS

Below are some high-growth jobs in e-commerce and digital trade in the technology industry that require strong technical skills. As the global demand for online shopping and digital transactions continues to rise, these roles are becoming essential for managing platforms, optimizing user experiences, and ensuring security.

---

[20] United States Census Bureau, https://www.census.gov/library/stories/2022/04/ecommerce-sales-surged-during-pandemic.html, April 27, 2022.

[21] Statista.com, February 8, 2024.

1. E-Commerce Developer

- **Description**: E-commerce developers are responsible for building and maintaining online stores, payment gateways, and digital marketplaces. They work on both front-end and back-end development to ensure seamless online shopping experiences.

- **Technical Skills**: HTML, CSS, JavaScript, React, Node.js, PHP, Python, e-commerce platforms (Shopify, Magento, WooCommerce), payment gateway integration, API development.

2. E-Commerce Solutions Architect

- **Description**: E-commerce solutions architects design the technical architecture for e-commerce platforms, ensuring scalability, security, and optimal performance. They work on integrating various systems, such as payment processors, CRMs, and inventory management tools.

- **Technical Skills**: Cloud platforms (AWS, Azure, GCP), microservices architecture, API integration, e-commerce platforms (Shopify, Magento, BigCommerce), security protocols (SSL, TLS), load balancing, DevOps tools.

3. DevOps Engineer

- **Description**: DevOps engineers in e-commerce automate infrastructure management and deployment processes for online stores and marketplaces. They ensure that the platforms are running smoothly with minimal downtime while optimizing the CI/CD pipeline.

- **Technical Skills**: Kubernetes, Docker, CI/CD tools (Jenkins, GitLab CI), cloud platforms (AWS, GCP, Azure), automation scripting (Python, Bash), monitoring tools (Prometheus, Grafana), security compliance.

4. Data Scientist

- **Description**: E-commerce data scientists analyze customer behavior, transaction data, and marketing performance to provide insights that help optimize sales strategies and customer retention. They develop models for recommendation engines and customer segmentation.

- **Technical Skills**: Python, R, SQL, machine learning algorithms, data analysis tools, big data platforms (Hadoop, Spark), cloud-based analytics (AWS Redshift, Google BigQuery), data visualization (Tableau, Power BI).

5. Digital Payment Integration Specialist

- **Description**: Digital payment integration specialists focus on integrating secure and reliable payment systems into e-commerce platforms. They ensure that the checkout process is seamless and supports multiple payment methods, including credit cards, digital wallets, and cryptocurrency.

- **Technical Skills**: Payment gateway APIs (Stripe, PayPal, Square), security standards (PCI DSS), encryption (SSL, TLS), blockchain technology, mobile payment integration, tokenization, JavaScript, Python.

6. E-Commerce Security Engineer

- **Description**: E-commerce security engineers safeguard online stores and digital trade platforms against cyber threats. They implement security protocols, conduct vulnerability assessments, and ensure that systems comply with relevant security regulations.

- **Technical Skills**: Firewalls, IDS/IPS, encryption (SSL/TLS), PCI DSS compliance, vulnerability scanning, penetration testing, incident response, cloud security, identity and access management (IAM).

7. E-Commerce Data Engineer

- **Description**: Data engineers in e-commerce are responsible for building and maintaining data pipelines that collect, process, and store large amounts of transactional and customer data. They ensure that data is easily accessible for analytics and decision-making.

- **Technical Skills**: Python, SQL, ETL pipelines, big data platforms (Hadoop, Spark), cloud data warehouses (AWS Redshift, Google BigQuery, Snowflake), NoSQL databases (MongoDB, Cassandra), data governance.

8. Mobile Commerce (M-Commerce) Developer

- **Description**: Mobile commerce developers specialize in building mobile-friendly e-commerce platforms and applications. They focus on creating responsive designs and ensuring seamless experiences on smartphones and tablets.

- **Technical Skills**: Swift (iOS), Kotlin (Android), JavaScript (React Native, Flutter), responsive design, mobile app frameworks, RESTful APIs, mobile payment integration, UX/UI design for mobile.

9. Supply Chain and Inventory Management Specialist

- **Description**: Specialists in this role manage the integration of e-commerce platforms with supply chain and inventory management systems. They ensure that stock levels are accurate and orders are fulfilled efficiently.

- **Technical Skills**: ERP systems (SAP, Oracle), inventory management software, API integration, automation, data analysis (SQL, Python), cloud platforms, supply chain optimization.

10. E-Commerce UX/UI Designer

- **Description**: E-commerce UX/UI designers focus on creating intuitive and engaging user experiences for online shoppers. They design interfaces that are user-friendly and optimized for conversions while ensuring a seamless shopping journey.

- Technical Skills: HTML, CSS, JavaScript, UX/UI design tools (Figma, Sketch, Adobe XD), user behavior analytics, A/B testing, responsive design, accessibility standards.

These high-growth jobs in e-commerce and digital trade demand a mix of technical skills, such as software development, data analysis, cloud platforms, and cybersecurity. As e-commerce continues to expand globally, there is a strong need for professionals who can design, build, and maintain scalable online shopping experiences while ensuring the security and performance of digital trade platforms.

ROLES THAT REQUIRE CUSTOMER-FACING SKILLS

Below are some high-growth jobs in e-commerce and digital trade that require a combination of customer-facing and technical skills. These roles focus on managing customer interactions, driving sales, optimizing the user experience, and ensuring smooth operations for digital businesses.

1. E-Commerce Product Manager

- Description: E-commerce product managers are responsible for overseeing the development, launch, and continuous improvement of digital commerce products. They gather customer feedback, work closely with technical teams, and ensure that the product meets customer needs.

- Customer-Facing Skills: Customer feedback analysis, stakeholder management, product road map development, market research.

- Technical Skills: Understanding of e-commerce platforms, product life cycle management, APIs, cloud platforms, basic analytics.

2. E-Commerce Customer Success Manager

- Description: Customer success managers in e-commerce ensure that clients and customers are successfully using the platform or service. They focus on onboarding, providing training, resolving issues, and maximizing customer satisfaction.

- Customer-Facing Skills: Client relationship management, onboarding support, customer training, issue resolution, account management.

- Technical Skills: Understanding of e-commerce platforms (Shopify, Magento), analytics tools (Google Analytics), CRM systems, basic technical troubleshooting.

3. E-Commerce Sales Engineer

- Description: Sales engineers work with e-commerce businesses to demonstrate and sell e-commerce solutions or platforms. They translate customer needs into technical requirements and help clients understand how the product can solve their business problems.

- **Customer-Facing Skills**: Technical sales, product demonstrations, customer consultation, needs assessment, negotiation.

- **Technical Skills**: E-commerce platforms, API integration, payment gateway solutions, basic coding knowledge (HTML, JavaScript).

4. E-Commerce Account Manager

- **Description**: Account managers in e-commerce are responsible for managing relationships with key clients and ensuring that the platform or service meets their needs. They work on upselling, client retention, and resolving any issues that arise.

- **Customer-Facing Skills**: Relationship management, customer support, upselling, conflict resolution.

- **Technical Skills**: Familiarity with e-commerce platforms (Shopify, Magento, WooCommerce), CRM tools, analytics (Google Analytics), order management systems (OMS).

5. E-Commerce Marketing Manager

- **Description**: E-commerce marketing managers develop and execute digital marketing strategies to increase online sales and improve customer engagement. They manage campaigns across multiple channels like SEO, PPC, email, and social media.

- **Customer-Facing Skills**: Campaign management, customer segmentation, client communication, content creation.

- **Technical Skills**: SEO/SEM tools (Google Ads, SEMrush), analytics (Google Analytics), CRM tools, email marketing platforms (Mailchimp, HubSpot).

6. E-Commerce UX/UI Designer

- **Description**: UX/UI designers for e-commerce platforms work on optimizing the customer experience by improving the look and feel of the website or app. They focus on user behavior, designing interfaces that are user-friendly and increase conversions.

- **Customer-Facing Skills**: User research, customer feedback analysis, wireframing, A/B testing.

- **Technical Skills**: Design tools (Figma, Sketch, Adobe XD), HTML/CSS, JavaScript, responsive design principles, user analytics.

7. Customer Support Specialist

- **Description**: Customer support specialists assist customers with issues related to the e-commerce platform, including order management, payment issues, and technical problems. They work directly with users to resolve concerns and ensure customer satisfaction.

- <u>Customer-Facing Skills</u>: Customer service, communication, problem-solving, issue resolution.

- <u>Technical Skills</u>: Knowledge of e-commerce platforms, payment gateways, basic troubleshooting, ticketing systems (Zendesk).

8. E-Commerce Operations Manager

- <u>Description</u>: E-commerce operations managers oversee an online store's day-to-day operations, including order fulfillment, logistics, customer service, and website performance. They ensure that the platform runs smoothly and customers have a seamless experience.

- <u>Customer-Facing Skills</u>: Operations management, client communication, customer service.

- <u>Technical Skills</u>: Order management systems (OMS), supply chain software, e-commerce platforms, basic analytics.

9. Digital Payment Specialist

- <u>Description</u>: Digital payment specialists ensure smooth payment processes for e-commerce platforms, helping customers with payment issues, integrating new payment gateways, and optimizing the checkout experience.

- <u>Customer-Facing Skills</u>: Payment issue resolution, customer communication, onboarding new payment methods.

- <u>Technical Skills</u>: Payment gateway APIs (Stripe, PayPal, Square), PCI compliance, encryption (SSL, TLS), tokenization.

10. E-Commerce SEO Specialist

- <u>Description</u>: E-commerce SEO specialists optimize online stores for search engines to drive organic traffic. They work closely with clients or internal teams to improve website visibility, conduct keyword research, and implement on-page and technical SEO strategies.

- <u>Customer-Facing Skills</u>: Client consultation, strategy development, content optimization.

- <u>Technical Skills</u>: SEO tools (Google Search Console, SEMrush), HTML, CSS, JavaScript, site speed optimization, keyword research.

These high-growth jobs in e-commerce and digital trade require a mix of customer-facing skills, such as relationship management, consulting, and customer support, alongside a strong understanding of e-commerce platforms, data analysis, UX/UI design, and marketing automation. As the digital commerce industry continues to expand, professionals who can bridge the gap between customers and technical teams are in high demand.

3D and 4D Printing and Modeling

3D and 4D modeling are expected to have a positive impact on job growth across various industries. These technologies offer powerful tools for visualizing, designing, prototyping, and simulating objects, products, and environments in three-dimensional space, leading to increased demand for skilled professionals in several fields. Here are some ways in which 3D and 4D modeling are expected to contribute to job growth.

ROLES REQUIRING TECHNICAL SKILLS

Below are some high-growth jobs in 3D and 4D printing and modeling in the technology industry that require strong technical skills. These roles are critical for designing, prototyping, and manufacturing complex products using advanced printing technologies.

1. 3D Printing Engineer

- Description: 3D printing engineers design, develop, and operate 3D printing systems to create physical models and prototypes. They are responsible for material selection, printer calibration, and the accuracy of printed components.

- Technical Skills: CAD software (AutoCAD, SolidWorks), 3D printing technologies (FDM, SLA, SLS), material science, printer setup and maintenance, G-code, CAM software.

2. 4D Printing Engineer

- Description: 4D printing engineers work with materials that change shape or properties over time or in response to environmental factors (e.g., temperature, humidity). They develop designs that incorporate smart materials and advanced printing techniques.

- Technical Skills: Smart materials, 4D printing techniques, CAD/CAM software, finite element analysis (FEA), material science, programming (Python, MATLAB), simulation tools.

3. 3D Modeler

- Description: 3D modelers create digital models of objects for use in 3D printing, animation, or virtual environments. They work closely with engineers and designers to produce accurate and detailed representations of products or components.

- Technical Skills: 3D modeling software (Blender, Maya, Rhino, ZBrush), rendering, animation tools, mesh generation, texturing, sculpting, and optimization for 3D printing.

4. Materials Scientist

- Description: Materials scientists develop and test new materials for use in 3D and 4D printing, focusing on improving material properties, such as strength, flexibility, or responsiveness to environmental stimuli. They work to expand the range of printable materials.

- **Technical Skills**: Material characterization, smart materials, polymer science, metal alloys, testing and analysis tools (SEM, X-ray diffraction), FEA, material behavior modeling.

5. Design Engineer

- **Description**: Design engineers specialize in creating products or components that are optimized for 3D and 4D printing technologies. They focus on designing structures that maximize material efficiency and leverage the unique capabilities of additive manufacturing.

- **Technical Skills**: CAD software (SolidWorks, CATIA), generative design, topology optimization, mechanical engineering principles, finite element analysis (FEA), 3D printing processes, material selection.

6. 3D Scanning and Reverse Engineering Specialist

- **Description**: Specialists in 3D scanning and reverse engineering use advanced scanning technologies to capture physical objects' geometry and recreate them in digital form. These models are used for 3D printing or modifying and enhancing existing products.

- **Technical Skills**: 3D scanning tools (Artec, FARO), reverse engineering software (Geomagic, Rapidform), point cloud processing, CAD modeling, mesh optimization, laser scanning, photogrammetry.

7. Additive Manufacturing Process Engineer

- **Description**: Additive manufacturing process engineers develop and optimize the manufacturing processes for 3D and 4D printing, focusing on improving production efficiency, reducing material waste, and ensuring high-quality outputs.

- **Technical Skills**: Process optimization, CAD/CAM software, G-code generation, lean manufacturing principles, machine calibration, data analysis, quality control systems.

8. Biomedical Engineer

- **Description**: Biomedical engineers in 3D printing work on designing and printing medical devices, prosthetics, implants, and even tissue scaffolds. They combine medical and engineering knowledge to create products customized to patients' needs.

- **Technical Skills**: 3D printing for medical applications (bioprinting, SLS, SLA), CAD modeling, material science (biocompatible materials), anatomy and medical device regulations, 3D scanning, simulation tools for biological systems.

9. Aerospace Engineer

- **Description**: Aerospace engineers working with 3D printing design and manufacture lightweight, high-strength components for aircraft and spacecraft. They use additive manufacturing to create complex geometries that are difficult to achieve with traditional methods.

- **Technical Skills**: CAD software, aerospace materials (composites, titanium, aluminum), topology optimization, FEA, additive manufacturing techniques (EBM, DMLS), simulation tools, regulatory standards for aerospace parts.

10. Industrial Designer

- **Description**: Industrial designers create products optimized for 3D and 4D printing technologies, focusing on aesthetics, functionality, and manufacturability. They work on consumer products, furniture, automotive components, and more.

- **Technical Skills**: CAD software (Rhino, Alias), 3D rendering and visualization, product design principles, 3D printing technologies, material selection, rapid prototyping.

These high-growth jobs in 3D and 4D printing and modeling require a strong understanding of CAD software, additive manufacturing processes, material science, and 3D scanning. As 3D and 4D printing continue to revolutionize industries such as healthcare, aerospace, automotive, and manufacturing, professionals with expertise in design, process optimization, and advanced materials will be in high demand.

ROLES THAT REQUIRE CUSTOMER-FACING SKILLS

Below are some high-growth jobs in 3D and 4D printing and modeling in the technology industry that require a combination of customer-facing and technical skills. These roles involve working directly with clients or customers, helping them adopt and implement 3D and 4D printing technologies while providing support and guidance throughout the process.

1. 3D Printing Solutions Consultant

- **Description**: 3D printing solutions consultants work with clients to identify their needs and recommend the most suitable 3D printing technologies and solutions. They guide customers through the selection and implementation process.

- **Customer-Facing Skills**: Client consultation, needs assessment, solution presentation, stakeholder management.

- **Technical Skills**: Understanding of 3D printing technologies (FDM, SLA, SLS), CAD software, material selection, printer setup and configuration.

2. Customer Success Manager

- **Description**: Customer success managers ensure that clients successfully implement and derive value from 3D or 4D printing solutions. They provide training, support, and ongoing guidance to help customers optimize their use of 3D printing technology.

- **Customer-Facing Skills**: Client onboarding, training, relationship management, issue resolution, post-sales support.

- Technical Skills: Familiarity with 3D printing platforms and processes, CAD software, material knowledge, troubleshooting printer issues.

3. 3D Printing Sales Engineer

- Description: Sales engineers work closely with customers to demonstrate and sell 3D printing products or services. They help clients understand how 3D printing can meet their needs, provide technical demonstrations, and support the sales process.

- Customer-Facing Skills: Technical sales, product demonstrations, solution presentations, client communication.

- Technical Skills: Knowledge of 3D printing technologies (FDM, SLA, DMLS), material properties, CAD modeling, printer software and hardware.

4. 3D Printing Account Manager

- Description: Account managers in 3D printing oversee relationships with key clients, ensuring that their needs are met and offer ongoing support. They manage customer inquiries, offer new product recommendations, and resolve any issues.

- Customer-Facing Skills: Account management, customer retention, upselling, relationship building, conflict resolution.

- Technical Skills: Knowledge of 3D printing platforms, materials (metals, plastics, resins), CAD software, technical troubleshooting.

5. 3D Printing Applications Engineer

- Description: Applications engineers work with customers to help them optimize their use of 3D printing technology for specific applications, such as prototyping, manufacturing, or product development. They provide technical advice and support to ensure successful implementation.

- Customer-Facing Skills: Client consultation, application support, technical training, project management.

- Technical Skills: 3D printing technologies (SLS, SLA, FDM), CAD software (SolidWorks, AutoCAD), material selection, generative design, rapid prototyping.

6. Technical Support Specialist (3D Printing)

- Description: Technical support specialists assist customers with troubleshooting and resolving technical issues related to 3D printers, software, or materials. They provide guidance on setting up equipment, performing maintenance, and optimizing prints.

- Customer-Facing Skills: Customer service, troubleshooting, issue resolution, communication, training.

- Technical Skills: 3D printing systems (SLA, FDM, SLS), slicing software, printer calibration, material handling, basic coding (G-code).

7. Field Service Engineer (3D Printing)

- Description: Field service engineers install, maintain, and repair 3D printers at customer sites. They ensure that machines are operating correctly and provide technical assistance for any hardware or software issues.

- Customer-Facing Skills: On-site customer support, technical troubleshooting, training, relationship management.

- Technical Skills: 3D printer operation and repair, hardware troubleshooting, CAD software, material properties, calibration techniques.

8. 3D Printing Training Specialist

- Description: Training specialists create and deliver training programs for customers who are adopting 3D or 4D printing technologies. They develop materials and conduct workshops or seminars to ensure that customers fully understand the technology and its applications.

- Customer-Facing Skills: Teaching, training development, public speaking, customer communication.

- Technical Skills: 3D printing processes (FDM, SLA, DMLS), CAD software, material science, post-processing techniques, printer maintenance.

9. 3D Printing Project Manager

- Description: Project managers oversee 3D printing projects from initiation to completion, ensuring that customer requirements are met. They manage timelines, coordinate with clients and internal teams, and ensure smooth project execution.

- Customer-Facing Skills: Project management, client communication, expectation setting, conflict resolution.

- Technical Skills: Knowledge of 3D printing technologies, CAD software, material properties, quality control, workflow optimization.

10. 4D Printing Product Manager

- Description: Product managers in 4D printing oversee the development and marketing of 4D printing solutions. They work with customers to understand their needs, guide product development, and ensure that the product meets market demands.

- Customer-Facing Skills: Product life cycle management, client feedback analysis, market research, stakeholder communication.

- Technical Skills: 4D printing technology, smart materials, product development, CAD software, prototyping.

These high-growth jobs in 3D and 4D printing require a blend of technical expertise and strong customer-facing skills. Professionals in these roles help customers understand and adopt new technologies, provide technical support, and ensure the successful implementation of 3D and 4D printing solutions in various industries. With the continued growth of additive manufacturing, these roles are critical for driving innovation and improving customer satisfaction.

Cleantech and Sustainability

With a focus on environmental sustainability, technology companies are investing in renewable energy solutions, energy-efficient technologies, and sustainability initiatives to reduce carbon emissions.

Cleantech is defined as "any process, product, or service that reduces negative environmental impacts through significant energy efficiency improvements, the sustainable use of resources, or environmental protection activities."[22]

Renewable energy, cleaner and greener transport, energy-efficient buildings, and sustainable water consumption are at the heart of cleantech trends. This is especially important for sustaining exponential technology growth (e.g., in high-power computing).

The US Inflation Reduction Act of 2022 is a federal law that included the largest investment in reducing carbon emissions in US history, including tax credits for households to offset energy costs and investments in clean energy production.

Moreover, Gartner predicts that "by 2027, 80% of CIOs will have performance metrics tied to the sustainability of the IT organization."[23]

ROLES THAT REQUIRE TECHNICAL SKILLS

Below are some high-growth jobs in cleantech and sustainability in the technology industry that require strong technical skills. These roles focus on developing and implementing sustainable technologies, renewable energy solutions, and environmentally friendly practices that help reduce carbon footprints and promote sustainable development.

1. Renewable Energy Engineer

- Description: Renewable energy engineers design and develop systems that generate power from renewable sources, such as solar, wind, and hydro. They focus on optimizing the efficiency and scalability of these systems to reduce dependence on fossil fuels.

---

[22] Wikipedia on Clean Technology.

[23] https://www.gartner.com/en/articles/gartner-top-10-strategic-technology-trends-for-2024

- **Technical Skills**: Solar photovoltaic (PV) systems, wind turbine design, energy storage systems, electrical engineering, grid integration, power electronics, CAD software, energy simulation tools.

2. Sustainability Engineer

- **Description**: Sustainability engineers design and implement systems that reduce the environmental impact of industrial processes, buildings, or products. They focus on energy efficiency, water conservation, and the use of sustainable materials in construction and manufacturing.

- **Technical Skills**: Life cycle assessment (LCA), energy modeling software (e.g., EnergyPlus, TRNSYS), water and waste management, green building standards (LEED, BREEAM), environmental impact assessments, sustainable materials science.

3. Energy Storage Engineer

- **Description**: Energy storage engineers work on developing and improving technologies like batteries, thermal storage, and other energy storage systems that store renewable energy for later use. They optimize energy storage solutions to enhance the reliability of renewable energy systems.

- **Technical Skills**: Battery technology (lithium-ion, solid-state), energy storage systems, grid integration, thermal energy storage, power electronics, system modeling, simulation tools (MATLAB, Simulink), control systems.

4. Environmental Engineer

- **Description**: Environmental engineers in cleantech work on reducing pollution, managing waste, and developing systems that improve environmental sustainability. They design solutions for air and water quality control, waste reduction, and energy efficiency.

- **Technical Skills**: Environmental impact assessments, waste management systems, pollution control technologies, renewable energy integration, environmental modeling software (GIS, MATLAB), air and water quality monitoring, sustainable materials.

5. Energy Efficiency Specialist

- **Description**: Energy efficiency specialists work to optimize the energy use of buildings, industrial processes, and systems. They design strategies to reduce energy consumption, enhance energy efficiency, and lower operating costs through innovative technologies.

- **Technical Skills**: Energy modeling software (eQUEST, RETScreen), HVAC systems, building automation, energy auditing, smart grid technology, IoT for energy management, building energy codes and standards (ASHRAE, IEC).

6. Green Building Architect

- Description: Green building architects design sustainable buildings that minimize environmental impact. They use eco-friendly materials, optimize energy efficiency, and integrate renewable energy sources into the design of residential, commercial, and industrial buildings.

- Technical Skills: Sustainable building design, energy-efficient materials, LEED or BREEAM certification, CAD and BIM software (AutoCAD, Revit), energy modeling software (EnergyPlus), passive solar design, thermal modeling.

7. Wind Energy Engineer

- Description: Wind energy engineers design, develop, and improve wind turbines and wind farms to generate renewable energy. They work on optimizing turbine performance, selecting sites, and integrating wind energy into the electrical grid.

- Technical Skills: Wind turbine design, aerodynamic modeling, mechanical and electrical engineering, wind farm layout optimization, energy storage integration, computational fluid dynamics (CFD), wind energy simulation tools (WAsP, WindPRO).

8. Smart Grid Engineer

- Description: Smart grid engineers work on modernizing the electrical grid to incorporate renewable energy, optimize energy distribution, and enable two-way communication between utilities and consumers. They focus on grid automation, energy storage, and demand response.

- Technical Skills: Smart grid technologies, SCADA systems, grid automation, energy storage, power electronics, grid integration of renewable energy, IoT systems, cybersecurity for smart grids.

9. Hydrogen Fuel Cell Engineer

- Description: Hydrogen fuel cell engineers design and develop hydrogen-based energy systems that convert hydrogen into electricity through chemical processes. They work on scaling up fuel cell technologies for transportation, industry, and energy storage.

- Technical Skills: Hydrogen fuel cell design, chemical engineering, electrochemical processes, energy storage systems, power electronics, thermodynamics, simulation tools (COMSOL, MATLAB).

10. Water Resources Engineer

- Description: Water resources engineers develop systems for sustainable water management, including water conservation, treatment, and recycling. They work on solutions to manage water resources efficiently and reduce waste in industrial and agricultural processes.

- Technical Skills: Hydrological modeling, water treatment systems, sustainable water management, environmental impact assessments, GIS for water resources, water quality monitoring, fluid dynamics.

These high-growth jobs in cleantech and sustainability require a combination of technical expertise in renewable energy systems, environmental engineering, energy efficiency technologies, and sustainability analysis. Professionals with strong technical skills in areas such as energy modeling, smart grids, carbon capture, and green building design will play a crucial role in shaping the future of sustainable technologies and addressing global environmental challenges.

ROLES THAT REQUIRE CUSTOMER-FACING SKILLS

Below are high-growth jobs in cleantech and sustainability that require a combination of customer-facing and technical skills. These roles focus on helping businesses and individuals adopt sustainable practices, renewable energy solutions, and environmentally friendly technologies while also ensuring client satisfaction and engagement.

1. Sustainability Consultant

- Description: Sustainability consultants work with organizations to assess their environmental impact and recommend strategies for improving sustainability. They guide businesses through implementing green technologies, reducing emissions, and improving resource efficiency.

- Customer-Facing Skills: Client consultation, sustainability strategy development, stakeholder communication, project management.

- Technical Skills: Carbon footprint analysis, life cycle assessment (LCA), regulatory compliance (ISO 14001, LEED), data analysis, renewable energy technologies.

2. Renewable Energy Sales Engineer

- Description: Renewable energy sales engineers work with customers to sell and implement renewable energy systems, such as solar, wind, and energy storage solutions. They translate customer needs into technical solutions and ensure a smooth installation process.

- Customer-Facing Skills: Sales, technical presentations, customer needs analysis, solution customization, relationship building.

- Technical Skills: Solar PV systems, wind energy, energy storage technologies, grid integration, power electronics, energy management software.

3. Customer Success Manager

- **Description**: Customer success managers ensure that clients are successfully implementing cleantech solutions and maximizing their value. They provide onboarding, training, and ongoing support to help customers achieve their sustainability goals.

- **Customer-Facing Skills**: Client onboarding, relationship management, issue resolution, customer engagement, training.

- **Technical Skills**: Understanding of clean energy systems (solar, wind, energy storage), energy monitoring tools, data analysis (usage data, energy savings), sustainability reporting.

4. Sustainability Account Manager

- **Description**: Sustainability account managers manage relationships with key clients and ensure that their sustainability goals are met. They collaborate with internal teams to provide the best sustainability solutions and drive continuous improvement for clients.

- **Customer-Facing Skills**: Account management, client communication, relationship building, cross-functional collaboration.

- **Technical Skills**: Sustainable product offerings, carbon emissions tracking, renewable energy solutions, regulatory compliance (LEED, BREEAM), life cycle assessment (LCA).

5. Green Building Consultant

- **Description**: Green building consultants work with architects, engineers, and building owners to design and implement sustainable building practices. They guide clients through certifications, such as LEED and BREEAM, ensuring that buildings meet sustainability standards.

- **Customer-Facing Skills**: Client consultation, project management, certification guidance, stakeholder communication.

- **Technical Skills**: LEED/BREEAM standards, sustainable materials, energy-efficient building design, energy modeling software (EnergyPlus, eQUEST), environmental impact assessments.

6. Sustainability Solutions Architect

- **Description**: Sustainability solutions architects design and implement custom sustainability solutions for organizations, including energy efficiency, waste reduction, and resource optimization. They work closely with clients to understand their specific needs and develop tailored solutions.

- **Customer-Facing Skills**: Solution design, client engagement, technical presentations, project scoping.

- **Technical Skills**: Energy efficiency technologies, renewable energy systems, carbon footprint reduction strategies, smart building solutions, resource optimization.

7. Clean Energy Project Manager

- **Description**: Clean energy project managers oversee the deployment of renewable energy projects, ensuring that they are completed on time and within budget. They act as the main point of contact between the client, contractors, and internal teams.

- **Customer-Facing Skills**: Project management, client communication, budgeting, stakeholder coordination.

- **Technical Skills**: Renewable energy systems (solar, wind, energy storage), project planning software (MS Project, Primavera), grid integration, permitting and regulatory compliance.

8. Carbon Reduction Specialist

- **Description**: Carbon reduction specialists help businesses lower their carbon emissions by assessing their carbon footprint and recommending strategies such as carbon offsets, renewable energy, and energy efficiency measures.

- **Customer-Facing Skills**: Carbon footprint assessments, client consultations, regulatory compliance guidance, reporting.

- **Technical Skills**: Carbon accounting, emissions tracking software, energy efficiency, renewable energy integration, carbon offset programs.

9. Smart Grid Sales Engineer

- **Description**: Smart grid sales engineers work with utilities and commercial clients to implement smart grid technologies, such as grid automation and energy management systems. They present technical solutions and help customers optimize energy distribution.

- **Customer-Facing Skills**: Technical sales, customer relationship management, solution customization, presentations.

- **Technical Skills**: Smart grid technologies, energy management systems, SCADA, grid automation, IoT for energy efficiency, power electronics.

10. Circular Economy Consultant

- **Description**: Circular economy consultants work with businesses to design processes and products that minimize waste by promoting recycling, reuse, and sustainable materials. They help clients transition to more sustainable, closed-loop systems.

- **Customer-Facing Skills**: Client consultations, sustainability strategy development, stakeholder engagement, reporting.

- **Technical Skills**: Circular economy modeling, waste reduction strategies, resource efficiency, life cycle assessment (LCA), sustainable materials.

These high-growth jobs in cleantech and sustainability combine customer-facing skills, such as consulting, relationship management, and technical presentations, with a solid understanding of renewable energy, energy efficiency, and sustainable practices. As businesses and individuals seek to reduce their environmental impact, these roles are crucial for guiding clients through the adoption and implementation of clean technologies and sustainable solutions.

Example: Sarah Swanson and I worked together at TSIA. At the time, she lived in San Diego. Recently, she posted on LinkedIn that she pivoted her career from the tech industry to the utility industry, specifically cleantech. So, I reached out to Sarah to talk with her about how she navigated to a new industry.

I asked, "How did you make your way into the utility industry?"

She replied, "I built my early career on a foundation of research, including positions such as senior research analyst at TSIA, user experience researcher at Best Buy, and senior CX researcher at 3M. I found my way into the utility industry when a recruiter at Xcel Energy reached out because she believed my skills were transferable for a user experience researcher role at Xcel Energy. While the utility industry itself was new for me, the position was a perfect combination of my field service and industrial knowledge gained at TSIA as well as my UX research expertise at 3M. I went through the interview process to check out the role and the company, and I accepted the job offer because I was excited by the prospect of combining these knowledge areas. I spent my first two years at Xcel working primarily on building a custom application to help Xcel's nuclear plant workers more efficiently plan and execute maintenance schedules without compromising the security of the plant."

"How different is the utility industry from the tech industry?"

"I feel like I had a soft landing into the utility industry since I was working in a tech role; most of my immediate peers and colleagues also came from the tech industry. There are quite a few challenges with embedding the fast-paced and agile working style of software development into an old-school bureaucratic structure. The biggest point of tension is how a utility makes money and how the internal structures are not easily adaptable to agile processes. It took me a year to understand how a utility makes money and why that was such a point of tension."

I asked her, "Were there people or resources that were helpful to you in learning a new industry?"

"I leveraged both internal company resources and external webinars and training to help me understand this new world I was living in."

"Are you able to navigate your career and achieve your career objectives in the utility industry?"

She explained, "After two years as a user experience researcher at Xcel Energy, I just started a new role with them as a product developer in Advanced Grid and Clean Energy. It is similar to a product manager role in a tech company. I will be developing service offerings to help facilitate the transition to clean energy. I have been environmentally conscious since I was a child. I remember when I was in grade school, I wrangled my parents to fix the leaky faucets so we could stop wasting water. So it feels good to be passionate about the work I'm doing."

"How do these changes fit into your career and life goals?"

"I don't see my career goals and life goals as separate things; my career has to fit into my life and not the other way around. When I moved back to Minnesota in 2020 to be closer to my family, my life satisfaction significantly improved. I love getting to spend time with my parents and extended family and have the joy of being an important part of my niece's life. Being her Aunt Sasa is the best thing in the world. In order to preserve this, I have made career moves and choices that align with the life I want to live. This new role serves me because it's a new challenge, and I value continued growth and learning. Plus, it has the perks of a strong career path with upward mobility without the need for me to make sacrifices to the life I have built."

I have several observations about Sarah's career pivot to a new industry:

1. She played to her strengths and articulated how her skills were transferable to the utility industry. That's what got her in the door with a new company in a new industry.

2. Once Sarah proved herself in the new company, she was able to navigate to a new role that would broaden her skill set, provide projects that are meaningful to her, and put her on a career path with increasing compensation over time.

3. She's living in a location of her choosing, which has increased her quality of life by allowing her to spend more time with her extended family.

OPTIMIZATION OF FUNCTIONAL AREAS

Evolving Roles of Sales and Marketing Leaders

Historically, sales and marketing have largely operated as separate functions, which has been problematic for decades in the tech industry.

With today's focus on leveraging AI for data-driven decision-making, the shift to digital sales and marketing channels, and account-based marketing, it is imperative that sales and marketing work seamlessly together.

EMERGING SALES AND MARKETING LEADERSHIP ROLES

In the fast-evolving technology industry, several emerging sales and marketing leadership positions are gaining prominence. These roles are being shaped by technological advancements, the shift to digital channels, and the need for more data-driven and customer-centric strategies. Here are the key emerging positions:

1. Chief Growth Officer (CGO)

- <u>Description</u>: The CGO is responsible for identifying and capitalizing on growth opportunities across multiple business areas. This role combines sales, marketing, product development, and customer success to drive overall business growth. It could also include partnerships, alliances, international expansion, innovation, and new ventures.

- <u>Key Responsibilities</u>: Growth strategy development, market expansion, customer acquisition, product-market fit, cross-functional leadership.

- <u>Why It's Emerging</u>: As businesses seek holistic growth across various functions, the CGO position aligns all departments toward a unified growth strategy.

Example: *Chief growth officer* is number one on LinkedIn's list of the twenty-five fastest-growing roles in the US.[24]

2. Head/Vice President of Revenue Operations (RevOps)

- <u>Description</u>: The head of revenue operations oversees the alignment of sales, marketing, and customer success operations. This role focuses on ensuring that all revenue-generating teams work together efficiently by providing data-driven insights and optimizing processes.

- <u>Key Responsibilities</u>: Revenue operations strategy, process optimization, CRM management, data analysis, sales and marketing alignment.

- <u>Why It's Emerging</u>: The need for seamless collaboration between sales, marketing, and customer success teams has given rise to the RevOps function, which eliminates silos and drives efficiency.

Example: *Director of revenue operations* is the fourth fastest-growing job on LinkedIn's list.[25]

3. Vice President of Product-Led Growth (PLG)

- <u>Description</u>: The vice president of product-led growth focuses on leveraging the product itself as a primary driver of customer acquisition, expansion, and retention. They develop strategies that enhance the user experience to turn product users into paying customers.

- <u>Key Responsibilities</u>: Product growth strategy, user onboarding and adoption, customer retention, data-driven product improvements.

- <u>Why It's Emerging</u>: The rise of SaaS and subscription models has made PLG critical, where the product itself is the key growth engine, minimizing the need for a large sales force.

---

[24] LinkedIn, Jobs on the Rise 2024: The 25 Fastest-growing Roles in the U.S. https://www.linkedin.com/pulse/linkedin-jobs-rise-2024-25-fastest-growing-roles-us-linkedin-news-dxmie/

[25] LinkedIn, Jobs on the Rise 2024: The 25 Fastest-growing Roles in the U.S. https://www.linkedin.com/pulse/linkedin-jobs-rise-2024-25-fastest-growing-roles-us-linkedin-news-dxmie/

4. Chief Digital Officer (CDO)

- <u>Description</u>: The CDO leads the company's digital transformation efforts and oversees all digital strategies. This role focuses on optimizing digital channels, improving customer experiences, and leveraging digital technologies to drive growth.

- <u>Key Responsibilities</u>: Digital transformation, customer experience optimization, data-driven decision-making, digital marketing strategy.

- <u>Why It's Emerging</u>: As companies increasingly shift to digital platforms, the CDO ensures that digital initiatives align with broader business goals, driving innovation and growth.

5. Vice President of Customer Experience (CX)

- <u>Description</u>: The vice president of customer experience is responsible for creating and implementing strategies to enhance the customer journey and improve satisfaction and loyalty. They work across departments to ensure a seamless and positive experience at every touchpoint.

- <u>Key Responsibilities</u>: Customer journey mapping, CX strategy, retention strategies, cross-functional collaboration, customer feedback analysis.

- <u>Why It's Emerging</u>: The rise of customer-centric business models, driven by SaaS and e-commerce, has made CX leadership critical for building long-term relationships and driving revenue growth.

6. Vice President of Ecosystem Partnerships

- <u>Description</u>: The vice president of ecosystem partnerships builds and manages strategic alliances with partners, resellers, and technology providers to expand the company's reach. They focus on developing mutually beneficial relationships that drive revenue and market expansion.

- <u>Key Responsibilities</u>: Partnership strategy, ecosystem development, channel sales, technology alliances, partner enablement.

- <u>Why It's Emerging</u>: As the tech industry becomes more interconnected, the ability to create strong partnerships in a broader ecosystem is essential for growth, innovation, and market reach.

Example: *Head of partnerships* is number twenty-four on LinkedIn's fastest-growing jobs list.[26]

7. Head of AI-Driven Marketing

- <u>Description</u>: This role focuses on leveraging artificial intelligence (AI) to create personalized and predictive marketing strategies. The head of AI-driven marketing uses AI tools to analyze customer data, automate campaigns, and optimize marketing spend.

---

[26] LinkedIn, Jobs on the Rise 2024: The 25 Fastest-growing Roles in the U.S. https://www.linkedin.com/pulse/linkedin-jobs-rise-2024-25-fastest-growing-roles-us-linkedin-news-dxmie/

- **Key Responsibilities**: AI-powered customer segmentation, marketing automation, predictive analytics, personalized content creation, campaign optimization.

- **Why It's Emerging**: AI is transforming marketing by enabling highly targeted, real-time engagement strategies. This role capitalizes on AI to improve campaign effectiveness and customer personalization.

8. Director of Influencer Marketing

- **Description**: The director of influencer marketing leads strategies to engage influencers and advocates who can promote the company's products or services. They manage partnerships with key influencers to build brand credibility and expand reach.

- **Key Responsibilities**: Influencer engagement, campaign management, content creation, partnership development, brand advocacy.

- **Why It's Emerging**: As social media becomes a dominant channel for consumer engagement, influencer marketing is increasingly important for tech companies looking to tap into new markets and build brand trust.

Example: *Influencer marketing manager* is number seventeen on LinkedIn's fastest-growing jobs list.[27]

9. Vice President of Brand and Culture Marketing

- **Description**: This role involves creating marketing strategies that not only promote products but also emphasize the company's culture, values, and mission. The vice president of brand and culture marketing leads initiatives that highlight the company's social responsibility, sustainability, and inclusiveness.

- **Key Responsibilities**: Brand strategy, culture marketing, corporate social responsibility (CSR), storytelling, internal and external communications.

- **Why It's Emerging**: As customers and employees place greater importance on a company's values and culture, brands that can communicate their mission and purpose effectively are more likely to attract loyal customers and talented, prospective employees.

10. Chief Customer Officer (CCO)

- **Description**: The CCO is responsible for overseeing the end-to-end customer experience, from acquisition to retention. This role ensures that all customer-facing departments (sales, marketing, support, and success) work together to create a seamless and positive experience.

- **Key Responsibilities**: Customer experience strategy, cross-functional collaboration, customer feedback, customer journey mapping, retention strategies.

---

[27] LinkedIn, Jobs on the Rise 2024: The 25 Fastest-growing Roles in the U.S. https://www.linkedin.com/pulse/ linkedin-jobs-rise-2024-25-fastest-growing-roles-us-linkedin-news-dxmie/

- <u>Why It's Emerging</u>: As customer expectations continue to rise, the need for a unified customer experience across all touchpoints is becoming increasingly important for long-term business success.

These emerging sales and marketing leadership roles in the technology industry reflect the growing need for data-driven strategies, customer-centric leadership, and integration of new technologies, such as AI and automation. These positions are becoming vital as companies scale, adopt digital transformation, and seek innovative ways to engage customers and drive sustainable growth.

Scaling Customer Success and Customer Support

A significant percentage of tech company revenues are recurring revenues, which means customers must be satisfied with tech companies' products or services, or they are at risk of not renewing their subscriptions.

Customer success and customer support are critical functions in driving customer satisfaction, retention, and growth, as well as in maintaining a competitive advantage. These teams are continuously challenged to create scale so tech companies don't have to invest linearly in customer success managers and customer support specialists as they bring on new customers or grow existing customers.

EMERGING ROLES TO CREATE SCALE

As customer success and customer support functions evolve in the technology industry, companies are creating new roles to ensure scalability, efficiency, and enhanced customer experiences. These emerging positions focus on leveraging automation, data analytics, and customer engagement strategies to meet growing demands and ensure customer retention. Here are some of the key emerging roles aimed at creating scale in these areas:

1. Customer Success Operations Manager

- <u>Description</u>: The customer success operations manager optimizes the tools, processes, and workflows used by customer success teams. They focus on implementing automation, improving data visibility, and ensuring that CSMs have the resources to efficiently manage growing customer bases.

- <u>Key Responsibilities</u>: Process automation, CRM management, customer success platform integration, reporting on success metrics (NPS, churn), cross-functional collaboration.

- <u>Why It's Emerging</u>: As customer success teams grow, operations managers ensure efficiency by streamlining processes and managing the tech stack used to deliver success at scale.

2. Customer Success Automation Specialist

- **Description:** This role is responsible for implementing and managing automation tools that streamline repetitive tasks in customer success, such as onboarding workflows, customer health tracking, and communication triggers. They leverage AI and machine learning to optimize customer interactions.

- **Key Responsibilities:** Automating onboarding processes, customer health monitoring, workflow optimization, CRM automation, AI-driven customer interactions.

- **Why It's Emerging:** Automation is key to scaling customer success operations, especially for companies managing a large number of customers across different touchpoints.

3. Digital Customer Success Manager

- **Description:** Digital customer success managers focus on engaging and supporting customers through digital channels, including chatbots, automated email campaigns, and self-service portals. They manage customer success at scale using a low-touch or tech-touch approach.

- **Key Responsibilities:** Digital engagement strategy, customer segmentation, self-service platform management, customer life cycle automation, proactive outreach through digital channels.

- **Why It's Emerging:** As tech companies scale, digital customer success management allows businesses to engage with customers in a scalable, cost-effective manner, especially for mid-market or small customers.

4. Head of Self-Service and Customer Enablement

- **Description:** The head of self-service and customer enablement focuses on developing self-service strategies to empower customers to resolve issues independently. They oversee the creation and management of knowledge bases, community forums, and video tutorials to reduce dependency on live support.

- **Key Responsibilities:** Self-service platform development, knowledge management, customer education strategies, community engagement, self-service content creation.

- **Why It's Emerging:** As more customers prefer to resolve issues themselves, investing in self-service tools helps scale support operations without increasing human resources.

5. AI-Powered Support Specialist

- **Description:** AI-powered support specialists oversee the implementation and management of AI-driven customer support systems, including chatbots, virtual assistants, and machine learning algorithms. They ensure that AI tools are optimized to handle routine inquiries and escalate complex issues.

- **Key Responsibilities**: AI implementation for support, chatbot management, machine learning optimization, training AI models, support automation.

- **Why It's Emerging**: AI is revolutionizing customer support by providing scalable, automated solutions for handling common issues, reducing the need for live agents, and improving response times.

6. Head of Customer Advocacy

- **Description**: The head of customer advocacy is responsible for building programs that turn satisfied customers into brand advocates. They manage customer feedback loops, create referral programs, and engage with customers to share their success stories through testimonials and case studies.

- **Key Responsibilities**: Building customer advocacy programs, managing referral and testimonial initiatives, creating customer success stories, engaging brand ambassadors.

- **Why It's Emerging**: As businesses seek to scale through word of mouth and community-driven marketing, customer advocacy is a scalable way to leverage existing customers for new customer acquisition.

7. Customer Success Enablement Manager

- **Description**: Customer success enablement managers provide training, tools, and resources for customer success teams to improve their performance. They ensure that CSMs have the skills and knowledge to engage customers effectively and that processes are standardized for scale.

- **Key Responsibilities**: CSM training and onboarding, process standardization, knowledge sharing, sales and success alignment, performance coaching.

- **Why It's Emerging**: As customer success becomes more integral to revenue generation, there's a growing need for specialized enablement roles to equip teams with the skills and tools needed to manage larger customer bases efficiently.

8. Customer Experience (CX) Designer

- **Description**: CX designers focus on mapping the entire customer journey and designing experiences that ensure a smooth and seamless interaction with the company. They work on optimizing touchpoints, ensuring that customers receive consistent and personalized experiences at scale.

- **Key Responsibilities**: Customer journey mapping, CX optimization, cross-channel experience design, feedback loop creation, data-driven personalization.

- **Why It's Emerging**: As customer expectations rise, companies are focusing on providing frictionless experiences across all touchpoints, making CX design critical for scaling personalized support and success strategies.

9. Head of Customer Engagement Platforms

- <u>Description</u>: This role is responsible for managing the platforms used to engage customers, including CRM systems, marketing automation tools, and customer communication tools. The head of customer engagement platforms ensures that these systems are integrated and scalable.

- <u>Key Responsibilities</u>: Platform management, CRM integration, automation tool optimization, customer engagement analytics, cross-functional collaboration.

- <u>Why It's Emerging</u>: As businesses look to scale customer success and support, the technology stack managing customer interactions becomes increasingly important, requiring dedicated leadership.

10. Customer Success Data Scientist

- <u>Description</u>: Customer success data scientists analyze vast amounts of customer data to identify trends, predict behavior, and suggest actions that CSMs can take to enhance customer success. They build models that help in customer segmentation, retention strategies, and upsell opportunities.

- <u>Key Responsibilities</u>: Data analysis, customer behavior modeling, churn prediction, upsell opportunity identification, reporting.

- <u>Why It's Emerging</u>: With increasing access to customer data, data scientists are becoming critical in helping customer success teams focus on the most important areas for growth and retention.

11. AI-Driven Customer Success Manager

- <u>Description</u>: AI-driven CSMs leverage AI and machine learning tools to automate customer interactions, predict customer needs, and optimize the success journey. They work with AI-powered tools to drive engagement, reduce churn, and improve the customer experience at scale.

- <u>Key Responsibilities</u>: AI implementation for customer success, predictive analytics for engagement, automation of success workflows, customer health scoring.

- <u>Why It's Emerging</u>: AI-driven approaches are increasingly important for managing large customer bases, automating routine tasks, and providing personalized, scalable customer success.

These emerging customer success and support positions are driven by the need to scale operations efficiently, reduce manual workloads, and provide proactive, data-driven customer experiences. The focus on automation, self-service, and predictive analytics is transforming how companies engage with and support their customers, ensuring long-term success and retention at scale.

There are so many incredibly exciting growth areas projected for the tech industry. I hope you are energized after reviewing this chapter. Which high-growth and emerging roles in the tech industry are most interesting to you? Which areas will you explore further?

Exercises

Please document below the areas that interest you.

HOT SPOTS TO EXPLORE

Please document which of the eight hot spots in the tech industry you will explore further (e.g., evolving roles of sales and marketing leaders). And note to the right of the hot spot which of the roles sound interesting to you (e.g., chief growth officer). The role could be a position you are interested in holding for yourself, or it could be a role you would like to add to your team if you are a people leader.

High-Growth Hot Spots to Explore	Roles to Explore
•	•
•	•
•	•
•	•
•	•
•	•
•	•

SKILL DEVELOPMENT

For each of the roles listed above, please use your favorite AI engine to conduct some quick research on the skills you will need to invest in. For example, let's research the key skills required for an AI product manager working in the technology industry.

The prompt I used in ChatGPT was: "Please tell me the skills required to be a successful artificial intelligence product manager in the technology industry."

ChatGPT's response was comprehensive. Below is a *subset* of the response from ChatGPT:

Technical Knowledge

- <u>Understanding of AI/ML Concepts</u>: You need a strong grasp of AI and machine learning (ML) fundamentals, including algorithms, model training, neural networks, natural language processing (NLP), computer vision, and reinforcement learning. While you don't need to be a data scientist, familiarity with these technologies helps in discussions with engineering teams.

Product Management Skills

- <u>Product Strategy and Road Map Development</u>: As an AI product manager, you need to align AI capabilities with business goals. You should define clear product strategies that focus on delivering measurable value through AI, and you should be able to create a product road map that considers both technical complexity and customer needs.

AI-Specific Product Challenges

- <u>Model Evaluation and Experimentation</u>: AI products require frequent experimentation. You should be comfortable running A/B tests, analyzing model results, and understanding key performance metrics, such as loss functions and confusion matrices. You also need to balance trade-offs between precision, recall, and other metrics based on business priorities.

Strategic Vision and Innovation

- <u>Long-Term Vision</u>: AI product managers need to stay ahead of trends in AI and understand how emerging technologies—like GPT-4, reinforcement learning, or transfer learning—could shape future product capabilities. A long-term vision helps you anticipate new opportunities for AI in your product line and business model.

Pretty amazing insights from ChatGPT, don't you think?

Once you generate the list of skills required to be successful in the roles you are interested in, evaluate your current skills and experience against the list of skills provided by AI. Below, document the skills you will build or expand to become successful in this new role. Conduct this skills research for each role you are interested in and log the skills below.

Exercise: Role-Related Skills to Build or Expand

•
•
•

-
-
-
-
-
-
-
-

TRAINING

A significant percentage of workers' skills will be disrupted in the next five years in the tech industry. Investing in continuous learning in the high-demand areas will be your friend. It's critical to commit to lifelong learning and make it a priority to schedule (and complete) training that will help you stay relevant and marketable.

For each of the roles you documented above, please conduct some quick research on the training and resources that are available to help you build key skills.

The prompt I used in ChatGPT was:

"Please tell me the training, certification programs, and resources available to build the following skills as an Artificial Intelligence Product Manager in the technology industry:" [Copy and paste the prior response from Chat GPT here so ChatGPT can see the skills you need to build.]

ChatGPT responded with a comprehensive list of resources. Below are just a few examples:

Technical Knowledge

- Understanding of AI/ML Concepts

    - Udacity – AI Product Manager Nanodegree: Focused specifically on AI product managers, providing practical understanding of AI/ML concepts, how to work with data, and deploying models. ◦

AI-Specific Product Challenges

- Model Evaluation and Experimentation

    - Coursera – AI for Business Leaders (University of California, Berkeley): Covers how to evaluate machine learning models, run experiments, and measure performance using key AI metrics.

Business and Market Understanding

- Market Research and Competitive Analysis

    - Udemy – Competitive Market Research: Learn the fundamentals of competitive analysis, market research, and identifying AI-driven product opportunities.

Strategic Vision and Innovation

- Long-Term Vision

    - MIT OpenCourseWare – The Future of AI: A forward-looking course that explores how emerging AI technologies can impact industries and products.

Again, I think ChatGPT did an amazing job of aggregating training resources for the skills I asked it about.

Below, please log the training you will invest in to build or expand key skills for the roles you are interested in.

Exercise: Training Investments to Build or Expand Skills

•
•
•
•

-
-
-
-
-

The tech industry is a dynamic place to navigate your career. As mentioned earlier, continuously evolving your skills to stay marketable is a critical success factor for longevity in the tech industry.

Nice work on identifying hot spots in the tech industry that interest you, along with the roles, skills, and training to help you stay marketable.

While the insights from this chapter are fresh in your mind, please flip to Chapter 8 and log the high-growth hot spots in tech and the roles that interest you, the skills you will focus on, and the training you will invest in. Please log these on the second page of the Putting It All Together forms.

If you are feeling stuck or unfulfilled in your current role, identifying new areas in this chapter to focus on can bring new energy to your work. In parallel to building these new skills, look for projects or initiatives to get involved with at your company to start moving in this new direction. In Chapter 9, you will build career action plans. Getting involved in these new areas can be incorporated into your short-term action plan to bring more meaning to your career, hopefully rather quickly.

That wraps up the review of high-growth career options in the tech industry.

Exploring adjacent industries to the tech industry could create an even broader set of career opportunities to evaluate. There are so many great companies doing amazing things! I hope you will take the time to explore them in the next chapter.

CHAPTER 6

TECH-ADJACENT INDUSTRIES WHERE YOUR TECH EXPERIENCE COULD BE VALUED

*"Whenever you find yourself on the side of the majority,
it is time to reform (or pause and reflect)."*

– Mark Twain

Many labor market watchers predict it will be challenging for professionals to manage career changes in the technology industry over the next several years for a number of reasons:

- There are professionals who were laid off and are still seeking their next full-time, fully employed position.

- There is growing sentiment among employees of technology companies to look for a new position, resulting in even more competition.

- Slower hiring is predicted for technology companies.

- Across-the-board headcount cuts of over 20 percent are projected in tech companies due to efficiencies from AI.

If you are interested in exploring industries that are adjacent to the technology industry, you may find that many companies value the skills and competencies you have developed in the tech industry. The tech industry tends to be on the bleeding edge of implementing new technologies, investing in leadership training, and implementing best practices with customer-facing processes. Many of the industries listed below are a step or two behind the tech industry. So they may value your experience of having 'been there and done that' when it comes to applying innovative technologies, building a high-performance employee culture, or developing a best-in-class customer experience, as examples. Don't underestimate the experiences you've had and the competencies you've built by being in the tech industry!

This chapter will provide a broad perspective of adjacent industries and high-growth jobs for you to explore. I worked with companies in all of these industries when I was vice president of research and advisory services at TSIA. There are so many fascinating companies doing amazing work in these tech-adjacent industries. I hope you will take some time to explore the content in this chapter. You will likely see high-growth job titles in this chapter that are aligned with your experience in tech.

Much like Chapter 5, this chapter has a lot of content, so feel free to dive into the sections that interest you the most and skim the sections that are less interesting to you.

List of Tech-Adjacent Industries to Explore

As an experienced employee of a tech company, you can consider adjacent industries for career opportunities that align with your strengths, values, and interests. Some adjacent industries that are closely related to the technology industry and offer potential career paths include:

1. Automotive and Transportation

2. Healthcare and Biotechnology

3. Fintech (Financial Technology)

4. Medical Device

5. Education and EdTech

6. Entertainment and Media

7. Manufacturing and Industry 4.0/Industrial Automation

8. Agriculture and AgTech

9. Telecommunications

Let's take a deeper dive into the types of roles you might find in each of these industries that could leverage your experience in the tech industry.

Below is a list of technical roles and a list of customer-facing roles for each industry. It is amazing how many roles we commonly see in tech companies that are also deployed in tech-adjacent industries. Software and other technologies have been widely deployed in tech-adjacent industries, and that is only expected to increase.

HIGH-GROWTH ROLES IN ADJACENT INDUSTRIES

Automotive and Transportation

The automotive industry is undergoing a digital transformation and is rapidly evolving with advancements in technology. Most automotive companies have a software business unit, but they don't have many employees who understand how to optimize software business models; thus, they need to hire from other industries for this expertise.

TECHNICAL ROLES

Advancements in technology include electric vehicles (EVs), autonomous driving technology, connected car technology, and smart transportation systems. Employees of technology companies with technical skills have a wealth of opportunities in this dynamic sector. Here are the top ten high-growth jobs in the automotive and transportation industry for tech professionals:

1. Autonomous Vehicle Engineer

- Description: Autonomous vehicle engineers develop and refine software and hardware systems for self-driving cars. Their focus areas include sensor fusion, computer vision, machine learning, and robotics.

- Key Skills: Programming (C++, Python), robotics, AI, machine learning, computer vision.

2. Electric Vehicle Engineer

- Description: Electric vehicle engineers design and develop electric powertrains, battery systems, and charging infrastructure. They work on improving the efficiency, performance, and sustainability of electric vehicles.

- Key Skills: Electrical engineering, battery technology, power electronics, renewable energy systems.

3. Connected Car Developer

- Description: Connected car developers create software for vehicle-to-everything (V2X) communication, including infotainment systems, telematics, and advanced driver-assistance systems (ADAS).

- Key Skills: Embedded systems, software development, network protocols, cybersecurity.

4. Data Scientist/Analyst

- Description: Data scientists/analysts analyze data from connected cars, autonomous vehicles, and transportation systems to optimize performance, enhance safety, and improve user experience.

- Key Skills: Data analysis, machine learning, statistical modeling, Python/R, SQL.

5. Cybersecurity Specialist

- Description: Cybersecurity specialists protect automotive systems and connected vehicles from cyber threats. They implement security measures, conduct vulnerability assessments, and ensure data integrity.

- Key Skills: Network security, encryption, risk assessment, penetration testing.

6. Software Engineer

- <u>Description</u>: Software engineers develop embedded systems and software applications for automotive control units, infotainment systems, and vehicle management systems.

- <u>Key Skills:</u> Programming (C/C++, Python), embedded systems, real-time operating systems (RTOS).

7. AI and Machine Learning Engineer

- <u>Description</u>: AI and machine learning engineers implement AI and machine learning models for applications, such as autonomous driving, predictive maintenance, and intelligent transportation systems.

- <u>Key Skills:</u> Machine learning, deep learning, neural networks, TensorFlow/PyTorch.

8. Systems Engineer

- <u>Description</u>: Systems engineers oversee the integration of complex automotive systems, ensuring that hardware and software components work seamlessly together.

- <u>Key Skills</u>: Systems engineering, integration, project management, requirements analysis.

9. Robotics Engineer

- <u>Description</u>: Robotics engineers develop robotic systems for autonomous vehicles and manufacturing automation in the automotive industry.

- <u>Key Skills</u>: Robotics, automation, control systems, kinematics, programming.

10. Cloud Solutions Architect

- <u>Description</u>: Cloud solutions architects design and implement cloud-based solutions to support automotive operations, including connected car services, data storage, and analytics.

- <u>Key Skills</u>: Cloud computing, AWS/Azure/Google Cloud, DevOps, microservices architecture.

These roles leverage tech employees' technical skills to drive innovation, improve efficiency, and enhance the user experience in the automotive and transportation industry. As the industry continues to evolve with new technologies and innovations, these positions will play a crucial role in shaping the future of transportation.

CUSTOMER-FACING ROLES

For technology company employees with customer-facing skills, the automotive and transportation industry offers numerous high-growth job opportunities. These roles leverage their ability to interact effectively with customers, manage relationships, and provide technical support and insights. Here are the top ten high-growth jobs in this sector:

1. Customer Success Manager

- Description: Customer success managers ensure that customers are satisfied with their automotive and transportation solutions, helping them maximize the value of the products and services. They proactively manage relationships, address issues, and identify opportunities for upselling.

- Key Skills: Relationship management, problem-solving, communication, product knowledge.

2. Technical Account Manager

- Description: Technical account managers act as the main point of contact for key accounts, providing technical support, managing implementations, and ensuring customer satisfaction.

- Key Skills: Account management, technical knowledge, customer service, project management.

3. Sales Engineer

- Description: Sales engineers support the sales team by providing technical expertise during the sales process. They explain product features, address technical questions, and help design solutions that meet customer needs.

- Key Skills: Technical knowledge, sales skills, communication, solution design.

4. Field Service Engineer

- Description: Field service engineers install, maintain, and repair automotive and transportation equipment at customer locations. They provide technical support and ensure that devices are functioning correctly.

- Key Skills: Technical troubleshooting, customer service, hands-on skills, communication.

5. Product Manager (Customer-Focused)

- Description: Customer-focused product managers oversee the development and life cycle of automotive and transportation products with a focus on customer needs and satisfaction. They gather customer feedback, define product requirements, and work with cross-functional teams.

- Key Skills: Product management, customer research, communication, cross-functional collaboration.

6. Implementation Specialist

- Description: Implementation specialists assist customers with the implementation and integration of automotive and transportation solutions. They ensure a smooth onboarding process and provide training and support as needed.

- Key Skills: Project management, technical knowledge, customer training, communication.

7. Technical Support Specialist

- Description: Technical support specialists provide technical support to customers using automotive and transportation technologies. They troubleshoot issues, guide users through problem resolution, and ensure a positive customer experience.

- Key Skills: Technical troubleshooting, customer service, communication, patience.

8. Training and Education Specialist

- Description: Training and education specialists develop and deliver training programs for customers on the use of automotive and transportation products and systems. They ensure that users are proficient and comfortable with the technology.

- Key Skills: Training development, public speaking, product knowledge, communication.

9. Customer Experience Manager

- Description: Customer experience managers enhance the overall customer journey by analyzing feedback and implementing improvements. They focus on increasing customer satisfaction and loyalty.

- Key Skills: Customer feedback analysis, project management, communication, problem-solving.

10. Sales Representative

- Description: Sales representatives promote and sell automotive and transportation products and services to businesses and individuals. Build and maintain customer relationships, provide product demonstrations, and drive sales growth.

- Key Skills: Sales skills, customer relationship management, communication, negotiation.

These roles leverage tech employees' customer-facing skills to drive customer satisfaction, engagement, and business growth in the automotive and transportation industry. Tech professionals in these positions play a crucial role in ensuring a positive customer experience and fostering long-term relationships with clients.

Healthcare and Biotechnology

Technology plays a crucial role in healthcare, including electronic medical records, telemedicine, medical devices, and health informatics.

TECHNICAL ROLES

The healthcare and biotechnology industries are rapidly evolving with the integration of advanced technologies, creating numerous high-growth job opportunities for technology company employees with technical skills. Here are the top ten high-growth jobs in this sector:

1. Bioinformatics Scientist

- Description: Bioinformatics scientists combine biology, computer science, and information technology to analyze and interpret biological data. They develop algorithms and tools to understand genetic and molecular data.

- Key Skills: Bioinformatics, programming (Python, R), data analysis, genomics.

2. Health Informatics Specialist

- Description: Health informatics specialists implement and manage information systems in healthcare settings. These professionals develop and maintain electronic health records (EHR), ensure data interoperability, and improve data management practices.

- Key Skills: Health informatics, database management, data analysis, healthcare IT.

3. Software Engineer (Medical Devices)

- Description: Software engineers design and develop software for medical devices and healthcare applications, including embedded systems and user interfaces.

- Key Skills: Embedded systems, programming (C++, Python), software development, medical device regulations.

4. Data Scientist

- Description: Data scientists analyze healthcare data to provide insights that improve patient outcomes, optimize operations, and support medical research.

- Key Skills: Data analysis, machine learning, statistical modeling, Python/R, SQL.

5. AI and Machine Learning Engineer

- Description: AI and machine learning engineers develop AI and machine learning models for applications in diagnostics, treatment planning, drug discovery, and patient monitoring.

- Key Skills: Machine learning, deep learning, neural networks, TensorFlow/PyTorch.

6. Cybersecurity Specialist

- Description: Cybersecurity specialists ensure the security of healthcare information systems and protect sensitive patient data from cyber threats.

- Key Skills: Network security, encryption, risk assessment, penetration testing.

7. Clinical Systems Analyst

- Description: Clinical systems analysts manage and optimize clinical information systems and applications. They work closely with healthcare professionals to ensure that clinical software meets their needs.

- **Key Skills**: Clinical information systems, healthcare IT, project management, data analysis.

8. Robotics Engineer

- **Description**: Robotics engineers design and develop robotic systems for surgical procedures, rehabilitation, and other medical applications.

- **Key Skills**: Robotics, automation, control systems, kinematics, programming.

9. Cloud Solutions Architect

- **Description**: Cloud solutions architects design and implement cloud-based solutions for storing, analyzing, and sharing healthcare data.

- **Key Skills**: Cloud computing, AWS/Azure/Google Cloud, DevOps, data security.

10. Quality Assurance Engineer

- **Description**: Quality assurance engineers test and validate software and hardware components of medical devices and healthcare applications to ensure that they meet quality and safety standards.

- **Key Skills**: Quality assurance, testing, medical device regulations, documentation.

These roles leverage tech employees' technical skills to drive innovation, improve patient outcomes, and support the rapid growth of the healthcare and biotechnology industries. Tech professionals in these positions play a crucial role in advancing medical research, developing new treatments, and enhancing healthcare delivery.

CUSTOMER-FACING ROLES

For technology company employees with customer-facing skills, the healthcare and biotechnology industries offer numerous high-growth job opportunities. These roles leverage their ability to interact effectively with customers, manage relationships, and provide technical support and insights. Here are the top ten high-growth jobs in this sector:

1. Customer Success Manager

- **Description**: Customer success managers ensure that healthcare providers are satisfied with their healthcare and biotechnology products and services, helping them maximize value. They proactively manage relationships, address issues, and identify opportunities for upselling.

- **Key Skills**: Relationship management, problem-solving, communication, product knowledge.

2. Clinical Support Specialist

- **Description**: Clinical support specialists provide on-site support and training to healthcare professionals using medical devices and biotechnology products. These professionals ensure proper device usage, troubleshoot issues, and gather feedback to improve product performance.

- **Key Skills**: Clinical knowledge, technical support, training, communication.

3. Technical Account Manager

- **Description**: Technical account managers act as the main point of contact for key healthcare and biotech accounts, providing technical support, managing implementations, and ensuring customer satisfaction.

- **Key Skills**: Account management, technical knowledge, customer service, project management.

4. Sales Engineer

- **Description**: Sales engineers support the sales team by providing technical expertise during the sales process. They explain product features, address technical questions, and help design solutions that meet customer needs.

- **Key Skills**: Technical knowledge, sales skills, communication, solution design.

5. Field Service Engineer

- **Description**: Field service engineers install, maintain, and repair medical devices and biotech equipment at customer locations. They provide technical support and ensure that devices are functioning correctly.

- **Key Skills**: Technical troubleshooting, customer service, hands-on skills, communication.

6. Implementation Specialist

- **Description**: Implementation specialists assist customers with the implementation and integration of healthcare and biotech solutions. They ensure a smooth onboarding process and provide training and support as needed.

- **Key Skills**: Project management, technical knowledge, customer training, communication.

7. Clinical Account Manager

- **Description**: Clinical account managers manage relationships with key clinical accounts, ensuring that they are satisfied with their medical devices and biotech products. These managers provide ongoing support, address any issues, and work to expand business in existing accounts.

- **Key Skills**: Account management, clinical knowledge, communication, customer service.

8. Technical Support Specialist

- Description: Technical support specialists provide technical support to customers using healthcare and biotech technologies. They troubleshoot issues, guide users through problem resolution, and ensure a positive customer experience.

- Key Skills: Technical troubleshooting, customer service, communication, patience.

9. Training and Education Specialist

- Description: Training and education specialists develop and deliver training programs for healthcare providers and biotech users on the use of products and systems. They ensure that users are proficient and comfortable with the technology.

- Key Skills: Training development, public speaking, product knowledge, communication.

10. Product Manager (Customer-Focused)

- Description: These product managers oversee the development and life cycle of healthcare and biotech products with a focus on customer needs and satisfaction. They gather customer feedback, define product requirements, and work with cross-functional teams.

- Key Skills: Product management, customer research, communication, cross-functional collaboration.

These roles leverage tech employees' customer-facing skills to drive growth, enhance customer satisfaction, and ensure the successful adoption and use of healthcare and biotechnology products. Tech professionals in these positions play a crucial role in ensuring a positive customer experience and fostering long-term relationships with clients.

Fintech (Financial Technology)

The financial technology industry is rapidly expanding, driven by innovations in technology and changing consumer preferences. Fintech companies leverage technology to improve financial services, including banking, payments, lending, and investment management.

TECHNICAL ROLES

Technology company employees with technical skills have a wealth of opportunities in this dynamic sector. Here are the top ten high-growth jobs in the fintech industry for tech professionals:

1. Blockchain Developer

- Description: Blockchain developers design and implement blockchain solutions for secure and transparent financial transactions. They develop smart contracts, work with decentralized applications (dApps), and ensure the integrity and security of blockchain networks.

- Key Skills: Blockchain technology, smart contracts, cryptography, Solidity, Ethereum.

2. Data Scientist

- Description: Data scientists analyze large datasets to extract actionable insights, improve financial products, and enhance decision-making processes. These scientists work on projects such as fraud detection, customer analytics, credit scoring, and risk management.

- Key Skills: Data analysis, machine learning, statistical modeling, Python/R, SQL.

3. Cybersecurity Specialist

- Description: Cybersecurity specialists protect fintech platforms from cyber threats and ensure the security of sensitive financial data. They implement security protocols, conduct vulnerability assessments, and respond to security incidents.

- Key Skills: Network security, encryption, risk assessment, penetration testing, incident response.

4. AI and Machine Learning Engineer

- Description: These engineers develop AI and machine learning models to improve financial services, such as credit scoring algorithms, personalized financial advice, and automated trading systems.

- Key Skills: Machine learning, deep learning, natural language processing, TensorFlow/PyTorch.

5. Full-Stack Developer

- Description: Full-stack developers build and maintain fintech applications, including front-end user interfaces and back-end services. They ensure seamless integration of various components and create scalable and secure financial platforms.

- Key Skills: HTML, CSS, JavaScript, Python, Ruby, PHP, database management.

6. DevOps Engineer

- Description: DevOps engineers manage the deployment and operation of fintech applications, automating processes and ensuring continuous integration and delivery of software updates.

- Key Skills: CI/CD, Docker, Kubernetes, scripting (Python, Bash), monitoring tools.

7. Cloud Solutions Architect

- Description: Cloud solutions architects design and implement cloud-based solutions to support fintech operations. They ensure that cloud infrastructure is secure, scalable, and compliant with financial regulations.

- Key Skills: Cloud computing, AWS/Azure/Google Cloud, DevOps, microservices architecture.

8. Mobile Application Developer

- **Description**: Mobile application developers produce mobile applications for fintech services, ensuring that they are user-friendly, secure, and performant on both iOS and Android platforms.

- **Key Skills**: Swift, Kotlin, React Native, mobile UI/UX design, API integration.

9. Product Manager (Technical)

- **Description**: These product managers oversee the development and life cycle of fintech products, working closely with engineering and design teams to deliver user-centric solutions.

- **Key Skills**: Agile methodologies, product life cycle management, market research, technical writing, project management.

10. Financial Software Developer

- **Description**: These experts develop and maintain financial software solutions, such as trading platforms, payment systems, and investment management tools.

- **Key Skills**: Software development, financial markets, programming (C++, Java, Python), algorithm development.

These roles leverage tech employees' skills to drive innovation, enhance security, improve user experiences, and support the rapid growth of the fintech industry. Tech professionals in these positions play a crucial role in shaping the future of financial services.

CUSTOMER-FACING ROLES

For technology company employees with customer-facing skills, the fintech industry offers numerous high-growth job opportunities. These roles leverage their ability to interact effectively with customers, manage relationships, and provide technical support and insights. Here are the top ten high-growth jobs in the fintech sector for tech professionals with customer-facing skills:

1. Customer Success Manager

- **Description**: Customer success managers ensure that customers are satisfied and derive maximum value from fintech products and services. They proactively manage customer relationships, address issues, and identify opportunities for upselling and cross-selling.

- **Key Skills**: Relationship management, problem-solving, communication, product knowledge.

2. Technical Account Manager

- **Description**: A technical account manager acts as the main point of contact for key fintech accounts, providing technical support, managing implementations, and ensuring customer satisfaction.

- Key Skills: Account management, technical knowledge, customer service, project management.

3. Sales Engineer

- Description: These engineers support the sales team by providing technical expertise during the sales process. They explain product features, address technical questions, and help design solutions that meet customer needs.

- Key Skills: Technical knowledge, sales skills, communication, solution design.

4. Implementation Specialist

- Description: Implementation specialists assist customers with the implementation and integration of fintech solutions. They ensure a smooth onboarding process and provide training and support as needed.

- Key Skills: Project management, technical knowledge, customer training, communication.

5. Technical Support Specialist

- Description: Technical support specialists provide technical support to customers using fintech products. They troubleshoot issues, guide users through problem resolution, and ensure a positive customer experience.

- Key Skills: Technical troubleshooting, customer service, communication, patience.

6. Product Manager (Customer-Focused)

- Description: These product managers oversee the development and life cycle of fintech products with a focus on customer needs and satisfaction. They gather customer feedback, define product requirements, and work with cross-functional teams.

- Key Skills: Product management, customer research, communication, cross-functional collaboration.

7. Customer Experience Manager

- Description: Customer experience managers enhance the overall customer journey by analyzing feedback and implementing improvements. They focus on increasing customer satisfaction and loyalty.

- Key Skills: Customer feedback analysis, project management, communication, problem-solving.

8. Training and Education Specialist

- Description: Training and education specialists develop and deliver training programs for customers on the use of fintech products. They ensure that users are proficient and comfortable with the technology.

- Key Skills: Training development, public speaking, product knowledge, communication.

9. Business Development Manager

- Description: Business development managers identify new business opportunities, build relationships with potential clients, and develop strategies to expand market presence.

- Key Skills: Business development, relationship building, market research, negotiation.

10. Account Executive

- Description: These account executives promote and sell fintech products and services to businesses and individuals. They build and maintain customer relationships, provide product demonstrations, and drive sales growth.

- Key Skills: Sales skills, customer relationship management, communication, negotiation.

These roles leverage tech employees' customer-facing skills to drive customer satisfaction, engagement, and business growth in the fintech industry. Tech professionals in these positions play a crucial role in ensuring a positive customer experience and fostering long-term relationships with clients.

Medical Device

The medical device industry is experiencing robust growth driven by an aging population, increasing prevalence of chronic diseases, and advancements in medical technology.

TECHNICAL ROLES

The medical device industry offers numerous high-growth job opportunities for technology company employees with technical skills. Here are the top ten high-growth jobs in this sector:

1. Biomedical Engineer

- Description: Biomedical engineers design and develop medical devices and equipment. This role involves research, design, testing, and evaluation of medical devices to ensure that they meet regulatory standards and patient needs.

- Key Skills: Biomedical engineering, CAD software, materials science, medical device regulations.

2. Software Engineer

- Description: These software engineers develop software for medical devices, including embedded systems and user interfaces. They ensure compliance with medical industry regulations and standards.

- Key Skills: Embedded systems, programming (C++, Python), software development, real-time operating systems (RTOS).

3. Data Scientist

- <u>Description</u>: Data scientists analyze clinical data, patient data, and operational data to support product development, improve device performance, and ensure regulatory compliance.

- <u>Key Skills</u>: Data analysis, machine learning, statistical modeling, Python/R, SQL.

4. Regulatory Affairs Specialist

- <u>Description</u>: Regulatory affairs specialists ensure that medical devices comply with all regulatory requirements and standards. They prepare and submit documentation for regulatory approvals, manage compliance audits, and stay updated on regulatory changes.

- <u>Key Skills</u>: Regulatory knowledge, technical writing, quality assurance, project management.

5. Quality Assurance Engineer

- <u>Description</u>: Quality assurance engineers test and validate software and hardware components of medical devices to ensure that they meet quality and safety standards.

- <u>Key Skills</u>: Quality assurance, testing, ISO standards, FDA regulations.

6. Clinical Systems Analyst

- <u>Description</u>: Clinical systems analysts manage and optimize clinical information systems and applications. They work closely with healthcare professionals to ensure that clinical software meets their needs and supports efficient patient care.

- <u>Key Skills</u>: Clinical information systems, healthcare IT, data analysis, project management.

7. AI and Machine Learning Engineer

- <u>Description</u>: These engineers develop AI and machine learning models for applications in diagnostics, treatment planning, and patient monitoring.

- <u>Key Skills</u>: Machine learning, deep learning, neural networks, TensorFlow/PyTorch.

8. Cybersecurity Specialist

- <u>Description</u>: Cybersecurity specialists protect medical devices and healthcare information systems from cyber threats. They implement security measures, monitor for vulnerabilities, and respond to security incidents.

- <u>Key Skills</u>: Network security, encryption, risk assessment, penetration testing.

9. Systems Engineer

- <u>Description</u>: These systems engineers oversee the integration of hardware and software components in complex medical devices. They ensure that all parts work together seamlessly and meet regulatory standards.

- **Key Skills**: Systems engineering, integration, project management, requirements analysis.

10. Robotics Engineer

- **Description**: These engineers develop robotic systems for surgical procedures, rehabilitation, and other medical applications. They integrate advanced robotics with medical technologies to improve patient care.

- **Key Skills**: Robotics, automation, control systems, kinematics, programming.

These roles leverage tech employees' technical skills to drive innovation, improve patient outcomes, and support the rapid growth of the medical device industry. Tech professionals in these positions play a crucial role in advancing medical research, developing new treatments, and enhancing healthcare delivery.

CUSTOMER-FACING ROLES

For technology company employees with customer-facing skills, the medical device industry offers numerous high-growth job opportunities. These roles leverage their ability to interact effectively with customers, manage relationships, and provide technical support and insights. Here are the top ten high-growth jobs in this sector:

1. Sales Representative

- **Description**: Sales representatives promote and sell medical devices to healthcare providers, hospitals, and clinics. They build and maintain relationships with customers, provide product demonstrations, and drive sales growth.

- **Key Skills**: Sales skills, customer relationship management, product knowledge, communication.

2. Clinical Support Specialist

- **Description**: Clinical support specialists provide on-site support and training to healthcare professionals using medical devices. They ensure proper device usage, troubleshoot issues, and gather feedback to improve product performance.

- **Key Skills**: Clinical knowledge, technical support, training, communication.

3. Customer Success Manager

- **Description**: Customer success managers ensure that healthcare providers are satisfied with their medical devices, helping them maximize the value of the products. They manage customer relationships, address concerns, and identify opportunities for upselling and cross-selling.

- **Key Skills**: Relationship management, problem-solving, communication, product knowledge.

4. Field Service Engineer

- Description: Field service engineers install, maintain, and repair medical devices at customer locations. They provide technical support, perform preventative maintenance, and ensure that devices are functioning correctly.

- Key Skills: Technical troubleshooting, customer service, hands-on skills, communication.

5. Product Manager (Customer-Focused)

- Description: These product managers oversee the development and life cycle of medical devices with a focus on customer needs and satisfaction. They gather customer feedback, define product requirements, and work with cross-functional teams.

- Key Skills: Product management, customer research, communication, cross-functional collaboration.

6. Technical Support Specialist

- Description: Technical support specialists provide technical support to customers using medical devices. They troubleshoot issues, guide users through problem resolution, and ensure a positive customer experience.

- Key Skills: Technical troubleshooting, customer service, communication, patience.

7. Training and Education Specialist

- Description: These specialists develop and deliver training programs for healthcare providers on the use of medical devices. They create instructional materials, conduct training sessions, and assess the effectiveness of training programs.

- Key Skills: Training development, public speaking, product knowledge, communication.

8. Clinical Account Manager

- Description: Clinical account managers manage relationships with key clinical accounts, ensuring that they are satisfied with their medical devices. They provide ongoing support, address any issues, and work to expand the business in existing accounts.

- Key Skills: Account management, clinical knowledge, communication, customer service.

9. Customer Experience Manager

- Description: These managers enhance the overall customer journey by analyzing feedback and implementing improvements. They focus on increasing customer satisfaction and loyalty.

- Key Skills: Customer feedback analysis, project management, communication, problem-solving.

10. Implementation Specialist

- <u>Description</u>: Implementation specialists assist customers with the implementation and integration of medical devices. They ensure a smooth onboarding process and provide training and support as needed.

- <u>Key Skills</u>: Project management, technical knowledge, customer training, communication.

These roles leverage tech employees' customer-facing skills to drive growth, enhance customer satisfaction, and ensure the successful adoption and use of medical devices in healthcare settings. Tech professionals in these positions play a crucial role in ensuring a positive customer experience and fostering long-term relationships with clients.

Education and EdTech

Educational technology (EdTech) companies develop digital learning platforms, educational content, online courses, and learning management systems. They have partnerships and alliances with large tech companies like Microsoft, Google, Apple, and CDW-G. EdTech is rapidly applying best practices from traditional SaaS tech companies to modernize their capabilities to serve educators better. Particular areas of growing focus for K-12 and higher ed educators are security, student safety, mental health, productivity, learning outcome drivers, and interoperability between systems.

TECHNICAL ROLES

The education and EdTech industry is rapidly evolving with the integration of advanced technologies, creating numerous high-growth job opportunities for technology company employees with technical skills. Here are the top ten high-growth jobs in this sector:

1. EdTech Software Developer

- <u>Description</u>: These developers design and develop educational software and platforms. This includes learning management systems (LMS), educational games, and apps.

- <u>Key Skills</u>: Programming (JavaScript, Python, Ruby on Rails), software development, UX/UI design, API development.

2. Data Scientist

- <u>Description:</u> Data scientists analyze educational data to provide insights into student performance, optimize educational content, and improve learning outcomes.

- <u>Key Skills</u>: Data analysis, machine learning, statistical modeling, Python/R, SQL.

3. AI and Machine Learning Engineer

- <u>Description</u>: These engineers develop AI-driven solutions for personalized learning, adaptive learning platforms, and automated grading systems.

- Key Skills: Machine learning, natural language processing, deep learning, TensorFlow/PyTorch.

4. Cybersecurity Specialist

- Description: Cybersecurity specialists ensure the security of EdTech platforms and protect sensitive student data from cyber threats. They implement security measures and monitor for vulnerabilities.

- Key Skills: Network security, encryption, risk assessment, penetration testing.

5. Cloud Solutions Architect

- Description: Cloud solutions architects design and implement cloud-based solutions for scalable and secure EdTech platforms. They ensure compliance with data privacy regulations.

- Key Skills: Cloud computing (AWS, Azure, Google Cloud), DevOps, microservices architecture, data security.

6. Learning Experience Designer (LXD)

- Description: LXDs create engaging and effective digital learning experiences by integrating technology, pedagogy, and user experience design.

- Key Skills: UX/UI design, instructional design, multimedia development, e-learning tools.

7. Full-Stack Developer

- Description: These professionals develop both the front end and back end of EdTech applications, ensuring a seamless user experience and robust functionality.

- Key Skills: HTML, CSS, JavaScript, Node.js, Python, database management.

8. Virtual Reality/Augmented Reality Developer

- Description: Virtual reality/augmented reality developers create immersive learning experiences using VR and AR technologies to enhance engagement and understanding.

- Key Skills: Unity, Unreal Engine, 3D modeling, VR/AR development, C#.

9. Product Manager

- Description: These product managers oversee the development and life cycle of EdTech products, working closely with engineering and design teams to deliver user-centric solutions.

- Key Skills: Product management, agile methodologies, market research, project management.

10. Educational Content Developer

- <u>Description</u>: Educational content developers create and curate digital educational content, including interactive lessons, quizzes, and multimedia resources. They ensure that content aligns with learning objectives and standards.

- <u>Key Skills</u>: Content creation, instructional design, multimedia development, subject matter expertise.

These roles leverage tech employees' technical skills to drive innovation, enhance learning experiences, and support the rapid growth of the EdTech industry. Tech professionals in these positions play a crucial role in transforming education through technology and improving educational outcomes for learners.

CUSTOMER-FACING ROLES

For technology company employees with customer-facing skills, the education and EdTech industry offers numerous high-growth job opportunities. These roles leverage their ability to interact effectively with customers, manage relationships, and provide technical support and insights. Here are the top eleven high-growth jobs in this sector:

1. Customer Success Manager

- <u>Description</u>: These customer success managers ensure that educational institutions and learners are satisfied with EdTech products and services. They proactively manage relationships, address issues, and identify opportunities for upselling.

- <u>Key Skills</u>: Relationship management, problem-solving, communication, product knowledge.

2. EdTech Sales Engineer

- <u>Description</u>: These engineers support the sales team by providing technical expertise during the sales process. They explain product features, address technical questions, and help design solutions that meet customer needs.

- <u>Key Skills</u>: Technical knowledge, sales skills, communication, solution design.

3. Account Manager

- <u>Description</u>: They manage relationships with key educational accounts, ensuring that they are satisfied with their EdTech solutions. The account manager provides ongoing support, addresses any issues, and works to expand the business in existing accounts.

- <u>Key Skills</u>: Account management, customer service, communication, negotiation.

4. Implementation Specialist

- <u>Description</u>: Implementation specialists assist educational institutions with the implementation and integration of EdTech solutions. They ensure a smooth onboarding process and provide training and support as needed.

- <u>Key Skills</u>: Project management, technical knowledge, customer training, communication.

5. Technical Support Specialist

- <u>Description</u>: Technical support specialists provide technical support to educators and learners using EdTech products. They troubleshoot issues, guide users through problem resolution, and ensure a positive customer experience.

- <u>Key Skills</u>: Technical troubleshooting, customer service, communication, patience.

6. Product Manager (Customer-Focused)

- <u>Description</u>: These product managers oversee the development and life cycle of EdTech products with a focus on customer needs and satisfaction. They gather customer feedback, define product requirements, and work with cross-functional teams.

- <u>Key Skills</u>: Product management, customer research, communication, cross-functional collaboration.

7. Customer Experience Manager

- <u>Description</u>: These customer experience managers enhance the overall customer journey by analyzing feedback and implementing improvements. They focus on increasing customer satisfaction and loyalty.

- <u>Key Skills</u>: Customer feedback analysis, project management, communication, problem-solving.

8. Training and Education Specialist

- <u>Description</u>: Training and education specialists develop and deliver training programs for educators and administrators on the use of EdTech products. They ensure that users are proficient and comfortable with the technology.

- <u>Key Skills</u>: Training development, public speaking, product knowledge, communication.

9. Business Development Manager

- <u>Description</u>: These business development managers identify new business opportunities, build relationships with potential clients, and develop strategies to expand market presence.

- <u>Key Skills</u>: Business development, relationship building, market research, negotiation.

10. Community Manager

- <u>Description</u>: Community managers build and manage online communities around EdTech products and services. They engage with educators and learners, moderate discussions, and foster a sense of community and brand loyalty.

- <u>Key Skills</u>: Community management, social media, communication, content creation.

11. Head of Revenue Operations:

- <u>Description:</u> The head of revenue operations oversees the alignment of sales, marketing, and customer success operations. A key focus area is modernizing and automating systems, data capture, and processes with the deal desk and RFP processes to drive efficient revenue growth.

- <u>Key Skills</u>: Transformational leadership, agility, sales enablement, revenue forecasting, advanced analytics.

These roles leverage tech employees' customer-facing skills to drive customer satisfaction, engagement, and business growth in the education and EdTech industry. Tech professionals in these positions play a crucial role in ensuring a positive customer experience and fostering long-term relationships with clients.

Entertainment and Media

The entertainment and media industry is rapidly evolving with the integration of advanced technologies, such as streaming platforms, virtual reality, augmented reality, and data analytics. Technology influences content creation, streaming services, gaming, virtual reality (VR), augmented reality (AR), and digital advertising in the entertainment and media industries.

TECHNICAL ROLES

For technology company employees with technical skills, there are numerous high-growth job opportunities in this sector. Here are the top ten high-growth jobs in the entertainment and media industry:

1. Software Engineer (Media Platforms)

- <u>Description</u>: Software engineers develop and maintain software for streaming services, content management systems, and media distribution platforms.

- <u>Key Skills</u>: Programming (JavaScript, Python, Ruby on Rails), software development, cloud computing, API development.

2. Data Scientist

- <u>Description</u>: These scientists analyze audience data, content performance, and user behavior to provide insights that drive content strategy, advertising, and personalized recommendations.

- <u>Key Skills</u>: Data analysis, machine learning, statistical modeling, Python/R, SQL.

3. AI and Machine Learning Engineer

- <u>Description</u>: These engineers develop AI and machine learning models for content recommendation engines, predictive analytics, and automated content generation.

- <u>Key Skills</u>: Machine learning, natural language processing, deep learning, TensorFlow/PyTorch.

4. Cybersecurity Specialist

- <u>Description</u>: Cybersecurity specialists ensure the security of media platforms and protect content from piracy and cyber threats. They implement security measures and monitor for vulnerabilities.

- <u>Key Skills</u>: Network security, encryption, risk assessment, penetration testing.

5. Cloud Solutions Architect

- <u>Description</u>: Cloud solutions architects design and implement cloud-based solutions for scalable and secure media delivery. They ensure compliance with data privacy regulations.

- <u>Key Skills</u>: Cloud computing (AWS, Azure, Google Cloud), DevOps, microservices architecture, data security.

6. Full-Stack Developer

- <u>Description</u>: Full-stack developers build both the front end and back end of media applications, ensuring a seamless user experience and robust functionality.

- <u>Key Skills</u>: HTML, CSS, JavaScript, Node.js, Python, database management.

7. Virtual Reality/Augmented Reality Developer

- <u>Description</u>: Virtual reality/augmented reality developers create immersive media experiences using VR and AR technologies for entertainment, gaming, and interactive content.

- <u>Key Skills</u>: Unity, Unreal Engine, 3D modeling, VR/AR development, C#.

8. Digital Media Product Manager

- <u>Description</u>: A digital medial product manager oversees the development and life cycle of digital media products, working closely with engineering and design teams to deliver user-centric solutions.

- <u>Key Skills</u>: Product management, agile methodologies, market research, project management.

9. Video Engineer

- Description: Video engineers develop and maintain video encoding, streaming, and playback systems. They optimize video quality and performance across different devices and platforms.

- Key Skills: Video encoding, streaming protocols, compression techniques, cloud computing.

10. Interactive Content Developer

- Description: Interactive content developers create interactive media content, such as web-based applications, mobile apps, and interactive videos. They enhance user engagement through interactive elements.

- Key Skills: HTML5, JavaScript, CSS, interactive design, user experience (UX).

These roles leverage tech employees' technical skills to drive innovation, enhance user experiences, and support the rapid growth of the entertainment and media industry. Tech professionals in these positions play a crucial role in transforming how content is created, distributed, and consumed.

CUSTOMER-FACING ROLES

For technology company employees with customer-facing skills, the entertainment and media industry offers numerous high-growth job opportunities. These roles leverage their ability to interact effectively with customers, manage relationships, and provide technical support and insights. Here are the top ten high-growth jobs in this sector:

1. Customer Success Manager (Media Platforms)

- Description: These managers ensure that clients and subscribers are satisfied with media services and platforms, helping them maximize the value of the products. They proactively manage relationships, address issues, and identify opportunities for upselling.

- Key Skills: Relationship management, problem-solving, communication, product knowledge.

2. Media Sales Engineer

- Description: Media sales engineers support the sales team by providing technical expertise during the sales process. They explain product features, address technical questions, and help design solutions that meet customer needs.

- Key Skills: Technical knowledge, sales skills, communication, solution design.

3. Account Manager

- Description: These professionals manage relationships with key accounts, ensuring they are satisfied with their media services. They provide ongoing support, address any issues, and work to expand the business in existing accounts.

- **Key Skills**: Account management, customer service, communication, negotiation.

4. Field Service Engineer

- **Description**: Field service engineers install, maintain, and repair media equipment at customer locations. They provide technical support and ensure that devices are functioning correctly.

- **Key Skills**: Technical troubleshooting, customer service, hands-on skills, communication.

5. Implementation Specialist

- **Description**: Implementation specialists assist customers with the implementation and integration of media solutions. They ensure a smooth onboarding process and provide training and support as needed.

- **Key Skills**: Project management, technical knowledge, customer training, communication.

6. Technical Support Specialist

- **Description**: Technical support specialists provide technical support to customers using media platforms and services. They troubleshoot issues, guide users through problem resolution, and ensure a positive customer experience.

- **Key Skills**: Technical troubleshooting, customer service, communication, patience.

7. Product Manager (Customer-Focused Media)

- **Description**: These product managers oversee the development and life cycle of media products with a focus on customer needs and satisfaction. They gather customer feedback, define product requirements, and work with cross-functional teams.

- **Key Skills**: Product management, customer research, communication, cross-functional collaboration.

8. Customer Experience Manager

- **Description**: Customer experience managers enhance the overall customer journey by analyzing feedback and implementing improvements. They focus on increasing customer satisfaction and loyalty.

- **Key Skills**: Customer feedback analysis, project management, communication, problem-solving.

9. Training and Education Specialist

- **Description**: Training and education specialists develop and deliver training programs for customers on the use of media technologies. They ensure that users are proficient and comfortable with the technology.

- **Key Skills**: Training development, public speaking, product knowledge, communication.

10. Business Development Manager

- Description: These managers identify new business opportunities, build relationships with potential clients, and develop strategies to expand market presence.

- Key Skills: Business development, relationship building, market research, negotiation.

These roles leverage tech employees' customer-facing skills to drive customer satisfaction, engagement, and business growth in the entertainment and media industry. Tech professionals in these positions play a crucial role in ensuring a positive customer experience and fostering long-term relationships with clients.

Manufacturing and Industry 4.0/Industrial Automation

The integration of technology in manufacturing processes, robotics, automation, IoT (Internet of Things), and data analytics is driving the Industry 4.0 revolution. Similar to automotive and transportation, most of these companies have a software business unit that could leverage your experience with optimizing software business models.

TECHNICAL ROLES

The manufacturing and Industry 4.0 sectors are rapidly evolving with the integration of advanced technologies, such as automation, IoT, artificial intelligence, and data analytics. For technology company employees with technical skills, there are numerous high-growth job opportunities in this sector. Here are the top ten high-growth jobs in manufacturing and Industry 4.0:

1. Automation Engineer

- Description: Automation engineers design, develop, and implement automated systems and processes to improve efficiency and productivity in manufacturing. They work with robotics, PLCs, and control systems.

- Key Skills: Robotics, PLC programming, control systems, electrical engineering.

2. IoT Solutions Architect

- Description: IoT solutions architects develop and implement IoT solutions to connect machinery and devices, enabling real-time data collection and analysis for predictive maintenance and operational efficiency.

- Key Skills: IoT platforms, sensor technology, cloud computing, data analytics.

3. Data Scientist

- Description: These scientists analyze manufacturing data to optimize processes, improve product quality, and enhance decision-making. They work on projects related to predictive maintenance, supply chain optimization, and quality control.

- Key Skills: Data analysis, machine learning, statistical modeling, Python/R, SQL.

4. Cybersecurity Specialist (Industrial)

- Description: Cybersecurity specialists protect industrial control systems and manufacturing infrastructure from cyber threats. They implement security measures, conduct vulnerability assessments, and respond to security incidents.

- Key Skills: Network security, encryption, risk assessment, penetration testing.

5. Industrial Engineer

- Description: Industrial engineers optimize manufacturing processes to improve efficiency, reduce waste, and increase productivity. They use data and technology to streamline operations and implement lean manufacturing principles.

- Key Skills: Process optimization, lean manufacturing, Six Sigma, data analysis.

6. Additive Manufacturing Engineer

- Description: Additive manufacturing engineers develop and implement 3D printing and additive manufacturing technologies to produce complex parts and prototypes. They focus on material selection, process optimization, and quality control.

- Key Skills: 3D printing, CAD software, materials science, mechanical engineering.

7. AI and Machine Learning Engineer

- Description: These engineers develop AI and machine learning models for applications, such as predictive maintenance, quality control, and process optimization in manufacturing.

- Key Skills: Machine learning, AI, data analysis, Python/R, TensorFlow/PyTorch.

8. Cloud Solutions Architect (Industrial)

- Description: Cloud solutions architects design and implement cloud-based solutions to support smart manufacturing, data storage, and real-time analytics. They ensure that cloud infrastructure is secure and scalable.

- Key Skills: Cloud computing (AWS, Azure, Google Cloud), DevOps, microservices architecture, data security.

9. Full-Stack Developer

- Description: Full-stack developers build both the front end and back end of industrial applications, ensuring seamless integration and robust functionality for manufacturing operations.

- Key Skills: HTML, CSS, JavaScript, Node.js, Python, database management.

10. Quality Assurance Engineer

- Description: These engineers develop and implement quality control processes and systems to ensure that manufactured products meet industry standards and specifications.

- Key Skills: Quality assurance, testing, ISO standards, statistical process control.

These roles leverage tech employees' technical skills to drive innovation, enhance efficiency, and support the transition to smart manufacturing solutions in the Industry 4.0 era. Tech professionals in these positions play a crucial role in shaping the future of manufacturing through technology integration and data-driven decision-making.

CUSTOMER-FACING ROLES

For technology company employees with customer-facing skills, the manufacturing and Industry 4.0 sectors offer numerous high-growth job opportunities. These roles leverage their ability to interact effectively with customers, manage relationships, and provide technical support and insights. Here are the top ten high-growth jobs in this sector:

1. Customer Success Manager

- Description: Customer success managers ensure that manufacturing clients are satisfied with their Industry 4.0 solutions, helping them maximize the value of products and services. They proactively manage relationships, address issues, and identify opportunities for upselling.

- Key Skills: Relationship management, problem-solving, communication, product knowledge.

Example: I know a top-notch customer success leader, Samantha, who pivoted from a SaaS company into the industrial automation industry, and she is enjoying much success. Samantha joined Rockwell Automation. Rockwell Automation is a well-managed company with over a hundred years of history and has many smart people in their organization. However, knowledge of how to optimize software business models is not an organic core competency—they have hired this expertise from the software industry.

2. Sales Engineer (Manufacturing Technologies)

- Description: These engineers support the sales team by providing technical expertise during the sales process. They explain product features, address technical questions, and help design solutions that meet customer needs.

- Key Skills: Technical knowledge, sales skills, communication, solution design.

3. Account Manager

- Description: These professionals manage relationships with key manufacturing accounts, ensuring that they are satisfied with their solutions. They provide ongoing support, address any issues, and work to expand the business in existing accounts.

- <u>Key Skills</u>: Account management, customer service, communication, negotiation.

4. Field Service Engineer

- <u>Description</u>: Field service engineers install, maintain, and repair industrial equipment at customer locations. They provide technical support and ensure that devices are functioning correctly.

- <u>Key Skills</u>: Technical troubleshooting, customer service, hands-on skills, communication.

5. Implementation Specialist

- <u>Description</u>: Implementation specialists assist manufacturing clients with the implementation and integration of Industry 4.0 solutions. They ensure a smooth onboarding process and provide training and support as needed.

- <u>Key Skills</u>: Project management, technical knowledge, customer training, communication.

6. Technical Support Specialist

- <u>Description</u>: Technical support specialists provide technical support to manufacturing clients using Industry 4.0 technologies. They troubleshoot issues, guide users through problem resolution, and ensure a positive customer experience.

- <u>Key Skills</u>: Technical troubleshooting, customer service, communication, patience.

7. Product Manager (Customer-Focused)

- <u>Description</u>: These managers oversee the development and life cycle of Industry 4.0 products with a focus on customer needs and satisfaction. They gather customer feedback, define product requirements, and work with cross-functional teams.

- <u>Key Skills</u>: Product management, customer research, communication, cross-functional collaboration.

8. Customer Experience Manager (Industrial Solutions)

- <u>Description</u>: Customer experience managers enhance the overall customer journey by analyzing feedback and implementing improvements. They focus on increasing customer satisfaction and loyalty.

- <u>Key Skills</u>: Customer feedback analysis, project management, communication, problem-solving.

9. Training and Education Specialist

- <u>Description</u>: Training and education specialists develop and deliver training programs for manufacturing clients on the use of Industry 4.0 technologies. They ensure that users are proficient and comfortable with the technology.

- <u>Key Skills</u>: Training development, public speaking, product knowledge, communication.

10. Business Development Manager

- <u>Description</u>: Business development managers identify new business opportunities, build relationships with potential clients, and develop strategies to expand market presence.

- <u>Key Skills</u>: Business development, relationship building, market research, negotiation.

These roles leverage tech employees' customer-facing skills to drive customer satisfaction, engagement, and business growth in the manufacturing and Industry 4.0 sectors. Tech professionals in these positions play a crucial role in ensuring a positive customer experience and fostering long-term relationships with clients.

Agriculture and AgTech

AgTech companies utilize technology for precision farming, crop monitoring, agricultural drones, smart irrigation systems, and supply chain management in agriculture.

Many people are not familiar with agriculture and AgTech, so I'm providing some context about this industry, which I think is solving some important problems.

Over the past two hundred years, the human population has grown from about 1 billion people to nearly 8 billion today. The average diet has also changed dramatically over this same period.

AgTech is defined as the technologies the agriculture industry uses to help transform agriculture production to keep up with food demand and provide solutions for labor shortages while also not destroying the planet. This could be a great career pivot if you are passionate about these real-world challenges. (Or if you are passionate about gardening and growing food like I am!)

Startups in the AgTech industry raised $5.7 billion from venture investors in 2023, per CropLife. AgTech companies "leverage advancements in data analytics in biotechnology, sensors, machinery, AI, indoor farming equipment, and automation," per PitchBook. Two specific areas of innovation are precision agriculture and indoor vertical farms:

- Precision agriculture technologies optimize planting methods and reduce organic inputs, such as fertilizer and pesticides, with drone aerial imaging, data analytics, and robotics for optimal decision-making.

- Indoor vertical farms provide year-round harvests using hydroponic and aeroponic techniques, which reduce the need for scarce land, reduce water consumption, and reduce negative effects of pests.

TECHNICAL ROLES

The agriculture and AgTech industry is rapidly evolving with the integration of advanced technologies, such as IoT, AI, robotics, and data analytics. For technology company employees with technical skills, there are numerous high-growth job opportunities in this sector. Here are the top ten high-growth jobs in agriculture and AgTech:

1. Precision Agriculture Specialist

- Description: Precision agriculture specialists develop and implement precision agriculture technologies that use data analytics, IoT, and GPS to optimize crop yields and resource use.

- Key Skills: GIS, remote sensing, data analysis, IoT, agronomy.

2. AgTech Software Developer

- Description: AgTech software developers design and develop software solutions for agriculture applications, such as farm management systems, mobile apps, and data analytics platforms.

- Key Skills: Programming (JavaScript, Python, Ruby on Rails), software development, API development, UX/UI design.

3. Data Scientist

- Description: Data scientists analyze agricultural data to provide insights that improve crop management, optimize resources, and enhance decision-making processes.

- Key Skills: Data analysis, machine learning, statistical modeling, Python/R, SQL.

4. AI and Machine Learning Engineer

- Description: These engineers develop AI and machine learning models for applications such as predictive analytics, crop monitoring, and automated farming equipment.

- Key Skills: Machine learning, computer vision, deep learning, TensorFlow/PyTorch.

5. IoT Solutions Architect

- Description: IoT solutions architects design and implement IoT solutions for smart farming, including sensor networks for monitoring soil health, weather conditions, and crop status.

- Key Skills: IoT platforms, sensor technology, cloud computing, data analytics.

6. Robotics Engineer

- Description: These engineers develop robotic systems for agricultural applications, such as automated harvesting, planting, and weed control.

- Key Skills: Robotics, automation, control systems, mechanical engineering, programming (C++, Python).

7. Agricultural Drone Specialist

- **Description**: Agricultural drone specialists design, operate, and maintain drones for precision agriculture, including crop monitoring, aerial imaging, and spraying.

- **Key Skills**: Drone technology, remote sensing, GIS, data analysis, UAV operation.

8. Cloud Solutions Architect

- **Description**: Cloud solutions architects design and implement cloud-based solutions to support smart farming, data storage, and real-time analytics.

- **Key Skills**: Cloud computing (AWS, Azure, Google Cloud), DevOps, microservices architecture, data security.

9. Sustainability Analyst

- **Description**: Sustainability analysts develop and implement sustainable farming practices and technologies to reduce environmental impact and improve resource efficiency.

- **Key Skills**: Environmental science, data analysis, sustainable agriculture, project management.

10. Full-Stack Developer

- **Description**: Full-stack developers build both the front end and back end of AgTech applications, ensuring seamless integration and robust functionality for agricultural operations.

- **Key Skills**: HTML, CSS, JavaScript, Node.js, Python, database management.

These roles leverage tech employees' technical skills to drive innovation, enhance efficiency, and support the transition to smart agriculture solutions. Tech professionals in these positions play a crucial role in advancing the agriculture industry through technology integration and data-driven decision-making.

CUSTOMER-FACING ROLES

For technology company employees with customer-facing skills, the agriculture and AgTech industry offers numerous high-growth job opportunities. These roles leverage their ability to interact effectively with customers, manage relationships, and provide technical support and insights. Here are the top ten high-growth jobs in this sector:

1. Customer Success Manager

- **Description**: Customer success managers ensure that agricultural clients are satisfied with their AgTech products and services. They proactively manage relationships, address issues, and identify opportunities for upselling.

- **Key Skills**: Relationship management, problem-solving, communication, product knowledge.

2. AgTech Sales Engineer

- Description: AgTech sales engineers support the sales team by providing technical expertise during the sales process. They explain product features, address technical questions, and help design solutions that meet customer needs.

- Key Skills: Technical knowledge, sales skills, communication, solution design.

3. Account Manager

- Description: These professionals manage relationships with key agricultural accounts, ensuring that they are satisfied with their AgTech solutions. They provide ongoing support, address any issues, and work to expand the business in existing accounts.

- Key Skills: Account management, customer service, communication, negotiation.

4. Field Service Engineer

- Description: Field service engineers install, maintain, and repair AgTech equipment at customer locations. They provide technical support and ensure that devices are functioning correctly.

- Key Skills: Technical troubleshooting, customer service, hands-on skills, communication.

5. Implementation Specialist

- Description: Implementation specialists assist agricultural clients with the implementation and integration of AgTech solutions. They ensure a smooth onboarding process and provide training and support as needed.

- Key Skills: Project management, technical knowledge, customer training, communication.

6. Technical Support Specialist

- Description: Technical support specialists provide technical support to farmers and agricultural businesses using AgTech products. They troubleshoot issues, guide users through problem resolution, and ensure a positive customer experience.

- Key Skills: Technical troubleshooting, customer service, communication, patience.

7. Product Manager (Customer-Focused)

- Description: These managers oversee the development and life cycle of AgTech products, with a focus on customer needs and satisfaction. They gather customer feedback, define product requirements, and work with cross-functional teams.

- Key Skills: Product management, customer research, communication, cross-functional collaboration.

8. Customer Experience Manager

- **Description**: Customer experience managers enhance the overall customer journey by analyzing feedback and implementing improvements. They focus on increasing customer satisfaction and loyalty.

- **Key Skills**: Customer feedback analysis, project management, communication, problem-solving.

9. Training and Education Specialist

- **Description**: Training and education specialists develop and deliver training programs for farmers and agricultural businesses on the use of AgTech products. They ensure that users are proficient and comfortable with the technology.

- **Key Skills**: Training development, public speaking, product knowledge, communication.

10. Business Development Manager

- **Description**: Business development managers identify new business opportunities, build relationships with potential clients, and develop strategies to expand market presence.

- **Key Skills**: Business development, relationship building, market research, negotiation.

These roles leverage tech employees' customer-facing skills to drive customer satisfaction, engagement, and business growth in the agriculture and AgTech industry. Tech professionals in these positions play a crucial role in ensuring a positive customer experience and fostering long-term relationships with clients.

Telecommunications

The telecommunications industry is rapidly evolving with the advent of 5G, IoT, cloud computing, and other advanced technologies. With the convergence of telecommunications and technology, opportunities exist in areas such as network infrastructure, mobile technology, and communication services.

TECHNICAL ROLES

For technology company employees with technical skills, there are numerous high-growth job opportunities in this sector. Here are the top ten high-growth jobs in telecommunications for tech professionals:

1. 5G Network Engineer

- **Description**: 5G network engineers design, implement, and manage 5G network infrastructure. They work on the deployment and optimization of 5G technology to enhance connectivity and performance.

- **Key Skills**: Network design, RF engineering, telecommunications protocols, 5G technology.

2. IoT Solutions Architect

- Description: IoT solutions architects develop and implement IoT solutions for connected devices and smart networks. They ensure seamless integration and security of IoT devices in the telecommunications network.

- Key Skills: IoT platforms, sensor technology, cloud computing, network security.

3. Cloud Solutions Engineer

- Description: Cloud solutions engineers design and manage cloud infrastructure for telecommunications services. They implement cloud solutions to support scalable and reliable network operations.

- Key Skills: Cloud computing (AWS, Azure, Google Cloud), DevOps, virtualization, cloud security.

4. Network Security Specialist

- Description: Network security specialists protect telecommunications networks from cyber threats and vulnerabilities. They implement security measures, conduct risk assessments, and respond to security incidents.

- Key Skills: Network security, encryption, risk assessment, cybersecurity.

5. Data Scientist

- Description: These scientists analyze large datasets to optimize network performance, enhance customer experiences, and drive business insights. They work on predictive analytics and machine learning models.

- Key Skills: Data analysis, machine learning, statistical modeling, Python/R, SQL.

6. Telecommunications Software Developer

- Description: Telecommunications software developers build software solutions for telecommunications applications, including network management systems, customer portals, and communication tools.

- Key Skills: Programming (Java, Python, C++), software development, APIs, telecommunications protocols.

7. DevOps Engineer

- Description: DevOps engineers manage the deployment, operation, and optimization of telecommunications applications. They automate processes to improve efficiency and reliability.

- Key Skills: CI/CD, Docker, Kubernetes, scripting (Python, Bash), monitoring tools.

8. RF Engineer

- **Description**: RF engineers design and optimize radio frequency (RF) systems for telecommunications networks. They work on improving signal strength, coverage, and network capacity.

- **Key Skills**: RF engineering, signal processing, wireless communication, network optimization.

9. AI and Machine Learning Engineer

- **Description**: These engineers develop AI and machine learning models to improve network management, predictive maintenance, and customer service automation.

- **Key Skills**: Machine learning, AI, data analysis, Python/R, TensorFlow/PyTorch.

10. Full-Stack Developer

- **Description**: Full-stack developers build both the front end and back end of telecommunications applications, ensuring seamless integration and robust functionality.

- **Key Skills**: HTML, CSS, JavaScript, Node.js, Python, database management.

These roles leverage tech employees' technical skills to drive innovation, enhance network performance, and support the transition to advanced telecommunications solutions. Tech professionals in these positions play a crucial role in shaping the future of connectivity and communication.

CUSTOMER-FACING ROLES

For technology company employees with customer-facing skills, the telecommunications industry offers numerous high-growth job opportunities. Here are the top ten high-growth jobs in the telecommunications industry for tech professionals with customer-facing skills:

1. Customer Success Manager

- **Description**: Customer success managers ensure that clients are satisfied with their telecommunications services and products. They proactively manage relationships, address issues, and identify opportunities for upselling.

- **Key Skills**: Relationship management, problem-solving, communication, product knowledge.

2. Sales Engineer

- **Description**: Sales engineers support the sales team by providing technical expertise during the sales process. They explain product features, address technical questions, and help design solutions that meet customer needs.

- **Key Skills**: Technical knowledge, sales skills, communication, solution design.

3. Account Manager

- Description: These professionals manage relationships with key accounts, ensuring they are satisfied with their telecom services. They provide ongoing support, address any issues, and work to expand the business in existing accounts.

- Key Skills: Account management, customer service, communication, negotiation.

4. Field Service Engineer

- Description: Field service engineers install, maintain, and repair telecommunications equipment at customer locations. They provide technical support and ensure that devices are functioning correctly.

- Key Skills: Technical troubleshooting, customer service, hands-on skills, communication.

5. Implementation Specialist

- Description: Implementation specialists assist customers with the implementation and integration of telecom solutions. They ensure a smooth onboarding process and provide training and support as needed.

- Key Skills: Project management, technical knowledge, customer training, communication.

6. Technical Support Specialist

- Description: Technical support specialists provide technical support to customers using telecom products and services. They troubleshoot issues, guide users through problem resolution, and ensure a positive customer experience.

- Key Skills: Technical troubleshooting, customer service, communication, patience.

7. Product Manager (Customer-Focused)

- Description: Product managers oversee the development and life cycle of telecom products with a focus on customer needs and satisfaction. They gather customer feedback, define product requirements, and work with cross-functional teams.

- Key Skills: Product management, customer research, communication, cross-functional collaboration.

8. Customer Experience Manager

- Description: Customer experience managers enhance the overall customer journey by analyzing feedback and implementing improvements. They focus on increasing customer satisfaction and loyalty.

- Key Skills: Customer feedback analysis, project management, communication, problem-solving.

9. Training and Education Specialist

- <u>Description</u>: Training and education specialists develop and deliver training programs for customers on the use of telecom products and services. They ensure that users are proficient and comfortable with the technology.

- <u>Key Skills</u>: Training development, public speaking, product knowledge, communication.

10. Business Development Manager

- <u>Description</u>: Business development managers identify new business opportunities, build relationships with potential clients, and develop strategies to expand market presence.

- <u>Key Skills</u>: Business development, relationship building, market research, negotiation.

These roles leverage tech employees' customer-facing skills to drive customer satisfaction, engagement, and business growth in the telecommunications industry. Tech professionals in these positions play a crucial role in ensuring a positive customer experience and fostering long-term relationships with clients.

That completes the list of tech-adjacent industries and the high-growth jobs that are projected, many of which can be filled by professionals who currently work in the tech industry. Did an industry or role spark your interest? Before we get to the exercises for this chapter, I'll cover one more topic—employee happiness ratings.

Happiness Ratings by Industry

I came across an interesting survey on employee happiness conducted by BambooHR. Below are the survey findings where they report on declining or increasing employee happiness ratings by industry. Not all of the tech-adjacent industries listed above are represented in the survey below, but there are interesting trends in the survey, along with some industries you may not have considered before.

Below are the highlights.[28]

1. **Construction industry** is the happiest industry on the list and experienced an 8 percent increase. "Construction continues to remain an anomaly as the only industry with an employee net promoter score (eNPS) over 50." Its rating has been trending up due in part to the high demand for this industry's services and the labor shortage it is experiencing; this results in higher wages for employees.

2. **Travel and hospitality industry** is experiencing rising happiness with an impressive recovery from the 2020 pandemic period. There is renewed optimism in the industry and a surge in demand for jobs. Companies are creating more flexibility with work hours and work locations, which is a welcome change for employees.

---

[28] BambooHR, What Industries Have the Happiest (and Unhappiest) Employees? Q1 2024.

3. **Education industry** has experienced a bumpy ride with employee happiness over the past three years, but it is trending up with the steepest rise (9 percent increase) versus all industries. Significant challenges still remain with teacher burnout, leadership credibility, testing requirements, and teachers spending too much time explaining their jobs to other adults. We need fresh leadership in the education system to turn this around!

4. **Finance industry** employee happiness has reached a new four-year low of 34.4 eNPS. "Failure of many financial institutions to meet evolving compensation and benefits expectations of their employees" is stated as one of the key reasons. High interest rates have created challenges for institutions to manage and grow their earnings.

5. **Restaurants, food, and beverage industry** experienced a modest 4 percent increase recently and an 11 percent increase over the past year. "The National Restaurant Association reports that sales are up in 2024—the food industry is forecast to reach $1 trillion in sales this year, a first in history. And they project 200,000 jobs will be added by the end of this year."

6. **Tech industry** employee happiness has been on a steep decline and "recorded its lowest eNPS in the last four years, with a score of 35." It has dropped 19 percent. Massive layoffs and return-to-office mandates are cited as key dissatisfiers.

Figure: Tech Industry Employee Happiness

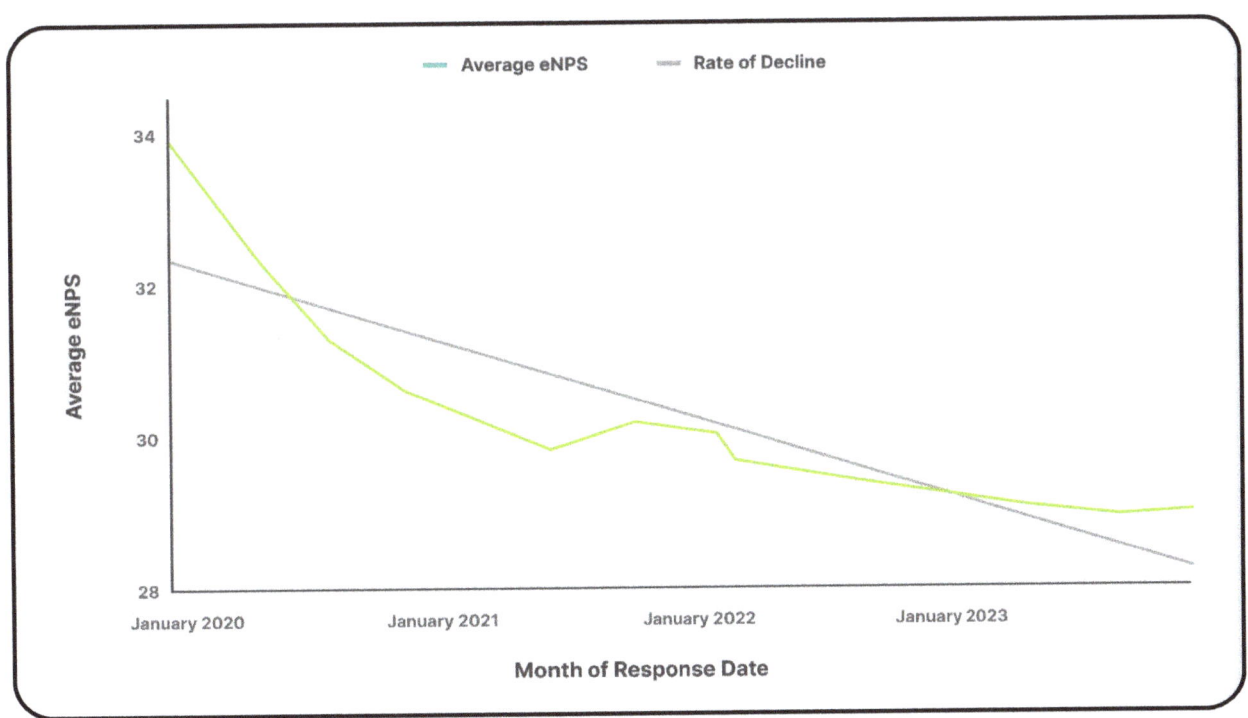

7. **Nonprofit industry** experienced a notable increase of 13 percent over the past six months after experiencing a four-year low. "More than half (56%) of survey respondents believed their nonprofit's overall circumstances improved in 2023, and they also predicted their situation would improve in 2024." Employment has grown three times faster than the

for-profit sector since 2008 (33 percent for nonprofit industry and 9 percent in for-profit companies) as professionals seek more meaning in their work. Many nonprofits would welcome the skills you have built in the tech industry.

8. **Healthcare industry** has been experiencing improving employee happiness, but it holds last place for overall ratings, so there is much to do here. "One of three healthcare workers are experiencing burnout and exhaustion." Interestingly, employees aren't leaving the field. Instead, they are finding new jobs in the same industry. Underappreciation, from both management and patients, is cited as the core reason for burnout. This is a problem since these employees can be in life-and-death situations with their patients every day. Healthcare employees are drawn to organizations that are more values-driven and that prioritize high-quality, patient-centered care.

Some industries are focusing more on employee retention and happiness than other industries. It is especially disconcerting that layoffs are continuing in the tech industry and that many large tech companies are requesting employees to come back to the office five days a week. I've talked with many tech professionals, including executives, who are not fans of this in-office policy and will look outside the company if they lose their flexibility to work from home at least part of the time. Some large tech companies are very draconian. They tell employees that maybe they should work for another company if they don't want to be in the office five days a week. Other large tech companies are stating that remote employees are not allowed to be promoted. Yikes! No wonder the employee happiness ratings have plummeted. I have to believe this will come back to bite these large tech companies, especially when their competitors begin to increase their hiring. The silver lining is the small to midsize tech companies. Many of these companies, which were my clients when I was an executive recruiter, embrace remote work since they care most about hiring the best talent. It will be a competitive advantage for them if they continue this practice.

That rounds out the insights on tech-adjacent industries and roles to explore. Below, please document the areas that interest you most and that you will explore.

Exercises: Adjacent Industries, Roles, and Fast-Growing Companies to Explore

- Identify two or three adjacent industries that are interesting for you to explore, then document them below.

- Identify roles in these adjacent industries that are interesting for you to explore, then document them below.

- Leverage ChatGPT to identify fast-growing companies in the adjacent industries (see sample AI prompt below). Document the fast-growing companies below.

- You can review the websites of fast-growing companies for career opportunities or search job posting sites, such as LinkedIn, Glassdoor, Indeed, etc.

Adjacent Industries:	Roles:	Fast-Growing Companies:
•	•	•
•	•	•
•	•	•
•	•	•
•	•	•
•	•	•
•	•	•
•	•	•
•	•	•
•	•	•
•	•	•
•	•	•
•	•	•
•	•	•

Sample ChatGPT Prompt to Identify Fast-Growing Companies:

"Please provide a list of fast-growing companies in the medical device industry."

ChatGPT Response:

Here are some of the fast-growing companies in the medical device industry:

Insulet

- Sector: Diabetes care

- **Growth Drivers**: Known for its Omnipod® Insulin Management System, Insulet has revolutionized diabetes care with wearable, tubeless insulin delivery systems, including the recently FDA-approved Omnipod GO™.

Zynex

- **Sector**: Pain management and monitoring

- **Growth Drivers**: Zynex focuses on pain management with electrotherapy devices and cardiac monitoring solutions, expanding rapidly through strategic acquisitions and innovative product development.

CMR Surgical

- **Sector**: Robotic surgery

- **Growth Drivers**: CMR Surgical's Versius system for minimally invasive surgeries is gaining traction in operating rooms globally, positioning the company as a leader in robotic surgical solutions.

LightPoint Medical

- **Sector**: Cancer detection

- **Growth Drivers**: LightPoint Medical is pioneering precision-guided robotic cancer surgery, developing innovative imaging tools for intraoperative cancer detection.

These companies are innovating across various medical fields, from diabetes management to robotic surgeries and cancer detection, positioning them for significant growth.

You can refine the AI prompt to include companies that are based in a specific country or specify whether you are interested in startups, midsize, or large companies. It's an efficient and effective way to research who the key players are in these tech-adjacent industries.

While the insights from this chapter are fresh in your mind, please flip to Chapter 8 and log the tech-adjacent industries you will explore, the roles that interest you, and the fast-growing companies you will research. Please log these on the second page of the Putting It All Together forms.

So, we have reviewed high-growth jobs in the tech industry and tech-adjacent industries. In the next chapter, we will explore out-of-the-box career possibilities for either the short term or down the road. These are business ownership opportunities. As mentioned earlier, don't underestimate the experiences you've had and the competencies you have built by being in the tech industry. Many of those skills can be applied to side hustles or full-time business ownership.

I hope you will keep an open mind and spend some time exploring the next chapter, "Is It Time to Start Your Own Business or Side Hustle?"

CHAPTER 7

IS IT TIME TO START YOUR OWN BUSINESS OR SIDE HUSTLE?

"Working hard for something we don't care about is called stress. Working hard for something we love is called passion."

— Simon Sinek

When I look back on my career in tech, I am very thankful for the income that allowed my family to have a wonderful lifestyle in a very expensive West Coast state. But I stayed too long as a tech executive. I didn't know how to re-architect my career into something more meaningful until much later in my career.

Speaking from personal experience, starting my own business has been the most fulfilling chapter of my career in terms of both meaningful work and financial achievements. It was an experience of complete freedom for me—freedom to operate my business according to my values, freedom to decide how to spend my time, freedom to make pivots based on market changes, and the list goes on.

What about you? Is business ownership something you think about? Full-time or part-time? Let's work through two common objections that cause some people to talk themselves out of business ownership before fully exploring the possibilities: Risk and Time.

Managing the Risks of Business Ownership

Business ownership has historically been perceived as higher risk and, therefore, a less secure income stream. Conversely, working for a large tech company was perceived to create a secure income stream, which was a safe bet. But in this day and age of chronic layoffs, how secure is it to work for a tech company? Might it be less risky to rely on your own skills, motivation, and abilities directed into your own business versus being someone else's employee? Something to ponder.

When it comes to business ownership, the risks are real—but they can also be managed. Here are three things I did to manage risk when I started my executive recruiting business:

First, I chose a business that played to my strengths. I parlayed my sales and management experience, my passion for helping others with their careers, and my broad network in the tech industry into my executive recruiting business.

Second, I hired Barb, a business advisor who taught me the recruiting business. For six months, I spent evenings and weekends going through her program to learn the business and set up all aspects of my recruiting business.

These two strategies helped me hit the ground running in the first year of my new business.

Third, my husband and I ensured we had enough money in savings to cover a year's worth of personal expenses. I'm thankful we never had to touch this, but it gave us both peace of mind, especially my husband, who was nervous about losing my consistent paycheck.

If you would like to explore opening a business while you are still employed, have you thought about starting a side hustle to test out the business model, verify market demand, and confirm your level of enjoyment in the business? That's yet another way to manage risk.

Those are some tips about managing risk. Next, let's talk about time.

Making Time for a Side Hustle

Side hustles are part-time gigs or supplementary income streams. They have become increasingly popular as people look for ways to supplement their primary income or pursue their passions outside of their main job. More than half of Gen Zers and millennials have a side hustle, according to a recent survey from LendingTree. Many side hustles can grow into very lucrative full-time businesses. I've provided some examples sprinkled throughout the balance of this chapter as inspiration.

And then there's this little question about time. You might be thinking, *I'm too busy to start a side hustle*. I get it. Many of you are going eighty miles per hour with your hair on fire, especially if you have a demanding job in tech right now. But if you are feeling stuck, unfulfilled, or in fear of the next wave of layoffs, what is your level of motivation to start a side hustle? If you are ready to take the next step, here are some tips on making time for a side hustle:

- **Set realistic goals**. Break down your side hustle into smaller, actionable tasks. Prioritize the tasks that will drive the most progress with your side hustle.

- **Start with small, manageable blocks of time**. Thirty to sixty minutes in the early morning or evening or a few hours on the weekends is a good starting point. Consistency is the key.

- **Set boundaries**. I learned early in my tech career that some of the B-level priorities, and certainly most of the C-level priorities, might never be completed. Initially, that was hard for me. But avoiding burnout was more important than clearing out the action item list. Embracing this reality might also free up time in your current full-time job. Tech companies are notorious for expecting employees to take on workloads of one-and-a-half to three people. Prioritizing, delegating, avoiding perfectionism, and learning to say 'no' (in a professional way) could free up blocks of time for a side hustle. The second set of boundaries to think about is with your personal time. How could you protect and invest your personal time better to create time for your side hustle?

- **Use automation and outsourcing**. Automate routine tasks, like social media scheduling or email management. Consider outsourcing less critical tasks to freelancers to free up your time for higher-value work in your side hustle. There are vibrant, talented, affordable global communities of freelancers ready to engage with entrepreneurs to help scale a side hustle.

Semiretirement Options

As you plan for the fall season of life, have you thought about semiretirement options to help you ease into the third season of life? Instead of giving up all of your income with full retirement, could you work part-time and also enjoy more free time to pursue activities outside of work? There is a plethora of part-time career opportunities that could provide supplemental income and allow you to engage with people in activities that are meaningful for you.

Seventeen Categories of Business Ownership, Side Hustles, and Semiretirement Options

In this chapter, we will explore a wide variety of options that are available for starting your own business, whether part-time or full-time, and help you decide if this is for you. The business ownership options are broken into seventeen categories as follows:

1. Financial and Business Services

2. Technology-centered Businesses

3. Coaching

4. Health and Wellness

5. Real Estate and Homes

6. Photography and Digital Products

7. Selling Artisan Products and Crafts

8. Marketing

9. If You Love to Cook

10. If You are an Expert Planner

11. If You are Mechanical or Good with Your Hands

12. If You Enjoy Working Outside

13. If You are Good with Children

14. If You Love Animals

15. If You are Creative

16. If You are a Good Writer

17. Boring Jobs that Pay Surprisingly Well

There is a lot of content in this chapter, so feel free to focus on the areas that are most interesting to you and skim the rest. I do encourage you to read the short success stories throughout the chapter since they might provide inspiration for you. I have provided quantitative income potential where possible. And you can get additional detail for the success stories by following the URLs in the footnotes.

FINANCIAL AND BUSINESS SERVICES

- **Business Consulting Services**: If you have expertise in a specific industry or field, starting a consulting business can be highly profitable. You could offer consulting services in management, finance, leadership, marketing, customer success, product management, human resources, or technology to businesses looking for expert advice and guidance. You could help new entities get started by helping them create a business plan, conduct market research, or organize a management structure. You could also help larger organizations through challenging periods of restructuring, help them increase value for their customers, or outline a successful exit strategy, just to name a few ideas. Some consultants also take on interim C-suite roles for smaller tech companies.

- **Accounting and Tax Services**: "At some point, most people seek the advice of a good bookkeeper or accountant, whether to prepare for tax season, get advice for starting a business, or simply plan for the future. You'll want to explore the recommended educational prerequisites and plan to obtain the appropriate credentials. Most tax preparation franchises offer courses, seminars, and training to get you ready to work for them."[29]

- **Financial Planning and Advising**: "Financial advisors help millions of Americans save for things like retirement and college funds while also helping them grow their wealth through various investments. If your goal is to become a Certified Financial Planner (CFP), you'll

---

[29] https://www.entrepreneur.com/starting-a-business/need-a-business-idea-here-are-55/201588

need to complete coursework and ultimately pass an exam. This will earn you a certificate that shows potential clients you have expertise and credibility."[30]

- **Notary Public Services**: "In most states, a notary public is a state officer who is authorized to witness and attest to the legalities of certain documents by stamping a seal and signing. Most states require that you pass an exam and a background check, but it costs very little to become a notary."[31] Mobile notary services are a great convenience, for example, when a real estate client is signing mortgage contracts to buy a new house.

Success Story: A retired UPS employee, William Zuniga, started a notary service business that grew into a document-signing service with an annual income of $500,000 over two years. His company locates the right notaries for his clients to get documents (e.g., loan contracts) signed quickly. This is a good example of a business that started small and grew into a nice-sized company.[32]

- **Executive Director for a Nonprofit**: Dedicate your time and skills to nonprofit organizations or community projects as an executive director, volunteer, board member, or consultant. Nonprofit work offers the opportunity to give back to the community while making a meaningful difference in the lives of others. Many executive director positions are paid positions.

- **Board of Directors**: Join the board of a nonprofit or a privately or publicly held company to share your expertise with other organizations. It's also an opportunity to forge collegial relationships with other board members. Often, there is annual compensation, travel reimbursement, and possibly equity in the company.

TECHNOLOGY-CENTERED BUSINESSES

- **Tech Setup Services**: Utilize your technical computer skills by offering to set up home networks, smart home devices, computers, and cell phones. Many small businesses need technology assistance as well. I have a technology expert I rely on for my businesses' computer needs, and I don't know what I'd do without them!

- **Software as a Service (SaaS) Business**: Developing and selling software solutions as a service can be highly profitable due to recurring subscription revenue. SaaS businesses can cater to various industries, such as project management, customer relationship management (CRM), accounting, marketing automation, and many more.

Success Story: GlossGenius started as a side hustle and now provides all-in-one booking, payments, and point-of-sale solutions for 65,000 beauty and wellness professionals (e.g., hair stylists). The company is now worth over $510 million.[33]

---

[30] https://www.entrepreneur.com/starting-a-business/need-a-business-idea-here-are-55/201588

[31] https://www.entrepreneur.com/starting-a-business/need-a-business-idea-here-are-55/201588

[32] https://www.entrepreneur.com/starting-a-business/a-retired-ups-employees-side-hustle-makes-over-500k-a-year/468099

[33] https://www.entrepreneur.com/starting-a-business/how-a-dorm-room-side-hustle-led-to-a-510-million-business/469736

- **Web Development**: Every business needs a website, and many small business owners don't have the time or interest to develop a professional-looking website. There are many courses available to teach you how to build websites. Or you can leverage platforms, like GoDaddy, to quickly and easily create websites for customers without needing to know a programming language. You may have clients who hire you to both create the website and then maintain it on a recurring basis.

- **E-commerce Store**: Launching an e-commerce store allows you to tap into the growing trend of online shopping. You can create your own niche products to sell online and reach a wide audience, generating sales twenty-four seven. You can also sell someone else's products that get drop-shipped to your customer; with this business model, you make a commission without the requirement to inventory products. Drop-shippers manufacture their products, you put them on your website for sale, and then you create demand that turns into orders.

Success Story: An entrepreneur, Katherine Watercutter, started a Shopify online store and created a website and Instagram account for her activewear brand, Gold Hinge. The brand went viral on TikTok. Her company's revenue has a monthly income of seven figures and an annual income of eight figures. Just be sure you have a plan to invest in cash flow to grow the business. This entrepreneur provides more insight in the full article referenced in the footnote.[34]

- **Sell Print-on-Demand Products**: If you like to create fun sayings or graphics and have a knack for illustration or photography, you can generate income by adding your creations to a wide array of print-on-demand products including T-shirts, mugs, pillows, wall décor, hats, and much more.

- **YouTube Channel**: Share your expertise by creating how-to video tutorials on YouTube and offer upsells for products or premium offerings, including subscriptions for online training or education. "You can monetize YouTube videos once you've reached at least 1,000 subscribers and average over 4,000 video watch hours per year. It's possible to earn many thousands each month. Many dedicated side hustlers have turned their YouTube channel into a highly profitable full-time gig."[35]

- **Remote Work Solutions**: With the rise of remote work, there is growing demand for products and services that support remote work environments. Consider starting a business offering remote work tools, ergonomic furniture, virtual team-building activities, or remote work consulting services.

- **Subscription Box Service**: Subscription box services have become increasingly popular, offering curated products delivered to customers' doorsteps on a recurring basis. Consider starting a subscription box service catering to a specific niche or interest, such as beauty products, snacks, or books.

---

[34] https://www.entrepreneur.com/starting-a-business/side-hustle-turned-full-time-has-7-figure-months-gold-hinge/470748

[35] https://www.forbes.com/advisor/business/best-side-hustle-ideas/#17_youtube_channel_section

COACHING

- **Career Coaching**: "Career coaches help people navigate professional transitions, establish business goals, and make the most of their skills. As a career coach, you might help people write cover letters and resumes, find new career opportunities, establish business plans and success strategies, or hone their niche in a crowded market." You could work with "recent graduates, people looking to start second careers, or someone who has been out of the workforce for years."[36]

- **Business Coach**: A business coach guides a businessperson in the pursuit of their work goals. The coach may help the client build leadership skills, create business strategies, or improve their mindset, as just a few examples.

Success Story: A coaching side hustle was started to pay back student loans, and the side hustle earned $300,000 annually. Dielle Charon saved a year's worth of expenses for business and personal needs before launching full-time into the business. Her coaching business income is now $1.5 million, which she has achieved consistently for the past two years. Dielle advises women of color who want to start a side hustle on how to master sales, adopt a successful mindset, and build a solid financial plan for success.[37]

- **Life Coaching**: "Life coaching has exploded in popularity over the past decade, as many people are looking to recreate or realign their personal goals. Life coaches do not provide clinical mental healthcare (a therapist does), but they help people create and use tools to move closer to their ultimate goals." A life coach can help "people with professional hurdles to clear, or help busy entrepreneurs looking to reclaim work/life balance," as just a few examples.[38]

- **Online Courses and Coaching**: Share your expertise by creating online courses that people are willing to pay for. There are user-friendly, low-cost online course platforms that make launching an online course easier. You can check out "Udemy, Thinkific, and Podia where they walk you through the course creation process and help you pair your courses with personalized coaching."[39] Creating and selling online courses or coaching services in your area of expertise, whether it's personal development, fitness, nutrition, business, or a specialized skill, can be a fulfilling endeavor.

- **Tutoring**: "If you have a background in education, you can make significant supplement income, or launch a full-fledged business, by offering tutoring services. Start by choosing the subject area that best fits your strengths." For example, "if you're skilled in math or sciences, you could help high schoolers with algebra or precalculus."[40] Or you could teach arts and crafts, music, or languages.

---

[36] https://www.entrepreneur.com/starting-a-business/need-a-business-idea-here-are-55/201588

[37] https://www.entrepreneur.com/starting-a-business/social-workers-side-hustle-skyrockets-to-300000-in-a-year/466544

[38] https://www.entrepreneur.com/starting-a-business/need-a-business-idea-here-are-55/201588

[39] https://www.forbes.com/advisor/business/best-side-hustle-ideas/#15_online_courses_and_coaching_section

[40] https://www.entrepreneur.com/starting-a-business/need-a-business-idea-here-are-55/201588

HEALTH AND WELLNESS

- **Fitness Studio**: The fitness industry continues to grow, with people prioritizing health and fitness. Starting a personal training studio or boutique fitness studio specializing in a specific niche can be a rewarding business opportunity.

- **Personal Training**: "Many people are looking to improve their overall fitness, and working with a personal trainer is one way to achieve their goals. You'll need to obtain a certification, which will help your clients trust that you know what you're doing and can help them avoid injury."[41] In addition to in-person training, there is a growing trend toward online health and fitness services.

- **Nutritional Advising**: "With so many different dieting trends and supplements, a nutritionist can help people better understand the landscape of healthy eating and living. Determine which type of nutrition service you want to provide, including pediatric, sports, holistic, etc."[42]

- **Private Athletic Coaching**: "Active children and adults alike often seek athletic instruction beyond what they've learned in group formats. If you're highly skilled in an athletic discipline, you can help take athletes to the next level. Common business options include golf, tennis, running, baseball pitching, and soccer."[43]

- **Senior Care Services**: With the aging population, there is growing demand for senior care services, such as home care, assisted living facilities, and senior transportation services. Starting a business that caters to the needs of seniors can be highly profitable and rewarding.

- **Health and Wellness Coaching**: As people become more health-conscious, there is a growing demand for health and wellness coaches who can provide guidance on nutrition, fitness, stress management, and overall well-being.

REAL ESTATE AND HOMES

- **Real Estate Investing**: Real estate investing can be highly profitable, especially in locations with high demand and appreciation potential. You can invest in rental properties, fix-and-flip opportunities, commercial real estate, or real estate investment trusts (REITs).

- **Real Estate Agent**: "Every community needs trusted real estate agents. Whether your clients are buying or selling property, there are many opportunities to launch your own business"[44] or work part-time or full-time for a real estate company.

---

[41] https://www.entrepreneur.com/starting-a-business/need-a-business-idea-here-are-55/201588

[42] https://www.entrepreneur.com/starting-a-business/need-a-business-idea-here-are-55/201588

[43] https://www.entrepreneur.com/starting-a-business/need-a-business-idea-here-are-55/201588

[44] https://www.entrepreneur.com/starting-a-business/need-a-business-idea-here-are-55/201588

- **Mortgage Broker**: Becoming a mortgage broker offers the opportunity to help individuals and families achieve homeownership by guiding them through complex financing options and securing the best possible mortgage terms. This career provides flexibility, with many brokers working independently or owning their own businesses, allowing for a balance of autonomy and client-focused work. Successful brokers can enjoy a lucrative income potential through commissions, particularly as they build a reputation and client base in the real estate and finance industry.

Success Story: My older son, Corey Stegman, is a mortgage broker with *The Mortgage Doctor*. He was drawn to the mortgage business for its strong income potential and the flexibility it provides to work in any location. This allows him to be present to both his family and his work, whether he's traveling, attending his kid's events, etc. To build his clientele as a new broker, he focused on tapping into markets that established brokers weren't interested in. Often, this included loans that were more challenging, such as qualifying self-employed people or working through the unique intricacies of condos and townhomes. A home is one of the most important assets a person can acquire. Homeownership can result in the creation of generational wealth, where one can pass on wealth to children and grandchildren. Corey finds this work very meaningful as he helps his clients achieve homeownership.

- **Property Management**: "Many people manage properties as a side hustle. Maybe you have a vacation home that you use for short-term rentals, or perhaps you have an additional property with a long-term lease. If you want to dive in full-time, you can acquire multiple properties and be a full-time landlord. Your job will be to ensure the property is running smoothly, ensure tenants are paying rent and honoring the lease terms, and be available in case of any issues. You can also contract with individual property owners to serve as their property manager, lightening their load by taking care of the landlord duties for them."[45]

- **Professional Organizing**: "Spatial planning is not everyone's strength. If it's yours, you can make good money as a professional organizer for individuals or businesses. For individuals, you can either do the organizing work, such as a kids' playroom or a cluttered garage, or consult with the homeowner to help them better organize themselves. Businesses, too, don't always know how to organize their office and maximize the efficiency of their spaces. You can consult on ways to better arrange furniture, desks, conference areas, stockrooms, and more."[46]

- **Home Inspection**: "To be a successful inspector, first establish contacts with real estate agents who can recommend your services to customers. Home inspection can be a competitive market so you will need to continuously update your education and knowledge. For example, builders are constantly introducing new materials."[47]

---

[45] https://www.entrepreneur.com/starting-a-business/need-a-business-idea-here-are-55/201588

[46] https://www.entrepreneur.com/starting-a-business/need-a-business-idea-here-are-55/201588

[47] https://www.entrepreneur.com/starting-a-business/need-a-business-idea-here-are-55/201588

- **Home Energy Audit**: "Homeowners look for ways to save on their utility bills. With some specialized training, you can help by conducting an audit of their homes and calculate how much they might save on heating, cooling, and electrical use by implementing new technology or upgraded appliances."[48]

- **Interior Decorating and Design**: "If you have an eye for design, market your interior decorating talents to building contractors. People purchasing new homes can often be overwhelmed with choices and possibilities. Create questionnaires for each major element and room in the house. You can help them purchase furniture, art, plans, and more. You can also work with businesses such as hotels and restaurants to design their spaces."[49]

PHOTOGRAPHY AND DIGITAL PRODUCTS

- **Photography**: There are a number of specialty areas that photographers have developed to run a successful business, including family portraits, high school photos, weddings, real estate listings, editorial shots for newspapers or magazines, or expert product pictures for a company's website. Creating a portfolio of work will show potential clients your expertise.

- **Digital Artwork and Logos**: This is a low- to no-cost side hustle through which you can sell digital artwork, photos, logos, website design templates, etc. It's a hot market. Check out Canva, Photopea, and the GarageBand app.

- **Videography**: "If you can do quality work behind a camera and edit footage as well, there are plenty of opportunities for videography work, from creating brand videos, to filming events, weddings, and interviews. Your clients could include outdoor brands, small nonprofits, and big corporations."[50]

- **Audio Editing**: "Audio storytelling is a growing industry, with countless podcasts being streamed daily by listeners all over the world. If you have experience recording and editing audio, you could shop your services to media brands, businesses or individuals who might want to launch their own podcasts."[51]

SELLING ARTISAN PRODUCTS AND CRAFTS

- **Art**: If one of your hobbies is creating art, you could sell your artwork for a profit. Many artists sell their artwork on sites, like Etsy and Shopify. A growing trend is brick-and-mortar establishments that house many artisans' works under one roof. Additional options are art shows, clients who commission you for a specific piece of art, or companies that need custom art or illustrations to add to their brand assets. Sharing your knowledge by teaching others is another avenue.

---

[48] https://www.entrepreneur.com/starting-a-business/need-a-business-idea-here-are-55/201588

[49] https://www.entrepreneur.com/starting-a-business/need-a-business-idea-here-are-55/201588

[50] https://www.entrepreneur.com/starting-a-business/need-a-business-idea-here-are-55/201588

[51] https://www.entrepreneur.com/starting-a-business/need-a-business-idea-here-are-55/201588

- **Sell at Local Markets and Festivals**: Create and sell unique goods, including gourmet foods and artisanal breads, at local markets, fairs, and festivals. You can also use these opportunities to build brand awareness for your online store and social media platforms to attract more sales.

- **Jewelry Making and Repair**: There are many options for creating your own line of custom jewelry. The materials are endless, including glass, gemstones, wood, and a wide variety of metals.

MARKETING

- **Influencer Marketing**: Pursuing a career in influencer marketing allows you to work creatively with social media and leverage digital platforms to build authentic connections between brands and audiences. This field is dynamic and growing fast. Influencers earn money using all types of content, such as product reviews and suggestions, entertaining videos, how-to tips and tricks, and much more.

- **Digital Marketing Agency**: With businesses increasingly relying on digital channels for marketing, a digital marketing agency can be lucrative. Offer services such as search engine optimization (SEO), pay-per-click (PPC) advertising, social media management, and content marketing.

IF YOU LOVE TO COOK

- **Private Chef Service**: "If you have experience working in restaurants or other areas of the food and beverage industry, you could tap into the growing private chef market. Whether potential customers are looking to accommodate specific dietary needs or an intimate event with friends, a positive experience should lead to client testimonials and referrals to help you grow your business."[52]

- **Bed and Breakfast or Airbnb**: "Do you own a property that could function as a small lodging establishment near a tourist area, sports stadium, or large venue? Maybe you own a charming home in the country. If so, you can turn your property into a bed and breakfast or Airbnb/VRBO rental and welcome guests into a home away from home."[53] Pair the B&B with an artisanal bakery, and you have two hot areas.

- **Catering**: "Are you experienced with managing large-scale food operations? Consider branching out into catering to serve large events like weddings and corporate banquets. You'll need strong project-management and personnel-management skills because catering requires you to lead a team and deliver exceptional service for clients."[54]

---

[52] https://www.entrepreneur.com/starting-a-business/need-a-business-idea-here-are-55/201588

[53] https://www.entrepreneur.com/starting-a-business/need-a-business-idea-here-are-55/201588

[54] https://www.entrepreneur.com/starting-a-business/need-a-business-idea-here-are-55/201588

- **Mobile Food Truck**: The food truck industry has experienced significant growth in recent years, offering flexibility and lower startup costs compared to traditional brick-and-mortar restaurants. Consider starting a mobile food truck that offers unique and high-quality cuisine.

- **Craft Brewery**: "Maybe you've been experimenting with brewing beer at home. If so, opening a craft brewery could be an option. You'll want to pursue training in brewing sciences and work as an apprentice to someone who knows the craft well."[55]

IF YOU'RE AN EXPERT PLANNER

- **Wedding Planning**: "You will need to be up to date on wedding trends, dress styles, popular colors, and every other facet of the wedding industry. You could offer your customers an à la carte menu of services, from helping to choose flowers, a wedding gown and bridesmaid dresses to picking the venue and hiring the caterer."[56]

- **Tourism or Hospitality**: Explore opportunities in the tourism or hospitality industry, such as working as a tour guide or travel consultant. These roles allow for flexibility and the opportunity to interact with people while exploring your interests.

Success Story: Entrepreneur Scott Goodfriend coordinates food tours all over New York City. Fortunately for him, this side hustle had gained traction and provided $30,000 of income as he worked on the weekends. He was laid off from his full-time job at Meta and subsequently pursued his thriving business full-time. He now earns $200,000 per year doing what he loves.[57]

- **Event Planning**: "There are a variety of ways to launch an event-planning business, particularly if you have a professional background in planning large gatherings. Possible options could include private parties at people's homes, kid's birthday parties, or corporate events."[58]

- **Vacation Planning**: "Some people take great joy in planning their vacations. However, if you're an experienced traveler and know how to save people money, you can be in high demand as a vacation planner for individuals or large groups. You can coordinate hotel and flight bookings, arrange transportation, provide daily itineraries, and help your client re-book in case of unforeseen travel crises."[59]

IF YOU ARE MECHANICAL OR GOOD WITH YOUR HANDS

- **The Trades**: Demand for electricians, plumbers, masons, welders, construction managers, etc. is growing at double-digit percentages. Working as an employee, these roles can earn between $100,000 to $175,000 per Mike Rowe, who is famously associated with the

---

[55] https://www.entrepreneur.com/starting-a-business/need-a-business-idea-here-are-55/201588

[56] https://www.entrepreneur.com/starting-a-business/need-a-business-idea-here-are-55/201588

[57] https://www.entrepreneur.com/starting-a-business/laid-off-from-meta-he-took-his-side-hustle-to-200k-a-year/472868

[58] https://www.entrepreneur.com/starting-a-business/need-a-business-idea-here-are-55/201588

[59] https://www.entrepreneur.com/starting-a-business/need-a-business-idea-here-are-55/201588

TV show 'Dirty Jobs'. Mike is an advocate of the trades and is educating people on the shortage of trades people. Also, if you *own* the trade business, you can make substantially more money. How do I know this? We have a vacation home on a lake and many of our neighbors are business owners of plumbing, electrical, or construction businesses—they are making a great living.

- **Handyman**: "If you have experience working in construction, you may be ready to start your own handyman business and take on projects of your own. From building a fence to hanging drywall or framing an addition, many people need skilled labor who can do quality work on time."[60]

- **Furniture Restoration and Flipping**: If you enjoy working with wood and upholstery, furniture restoration might be a good business for you. For inspiration and instruction, research online videos to get you started. Just think of all the materials you will prevent from being deposited in the dump!

Success Story: The need to pay off a $10,000 dental bill turned into a furniture-flipping business that now creates $250,000 per year. This side hustle is now Lilly Skjoldahl's full-time business.[61]

- **Home Renovation and Remodeling**: With the housing market booming and homeowners investing in home improvement projects, starting a small business offering home renovation, remodeling, or repair services can be profitable. Focus on a specific niche or specialization to stand out from competitors.

IF YOU ENJOY WORKING OUTSIDE

- **Landscaping**: "Put your green thumb to work. Most people want their yards tidied up in the spring, their lawns mowed in the summer, their leaves removed in the fall, and their shrubs and trees trimmed and cared for. You could also offer irrigation services including installation and repair of sprinkler lines."[62]

- **Homesteading**: Homesteading is a lifestyle of self-sufficiency. It is characterized by subsistence agriculture and home preservation of food, and it may involve small-scale production of textiles, clothing, food, or crafts for sale.

IF YOU ARE GOOD WITH CHILDREN

- **Open a Preschool**: Preschools can be home-based or housed in a separate building that is exclusively used for the preschool.

---

[60] https://www.entrepreneur.com/starting-a-business/need-a-business-idea-here-are-55/201588

[61] https://www.entrepreneur.com/starting-a-business/from-dental-debt-to-37k-monthly-side-hustle-success-story/465736

[62] https://www.entrepreneur.com/starting-a-business/need-a-business-idea-here-are-55/201588

Success Story: I have a friend, Tamara, in our county who built a separate building on her property to operate a preschool, and she has been very successful. She is well-known in the community and has a perpetual waiting list; thus, she is now opening a second preschool.

- **At-Home Day Care**: "Childcare needs continue to soar in the United States, and many people prefer for their child to be cared for in a home environment as opposed to a more institutional setting. These factors make the market ripe for a home-based childcare business. The regulations for a home-based childcare business vary by state, so you'll need to pursue appropriate certifications and training depending on where you live."[63]

IF YOU LOVE ANIMALS

The global pet industry has a booming annual growth rate of 11.6 percent and is valued at $232 billion. Two out of three Americans have at least one pet, and the average pet-owning household spends $1,120 per year on their pets. There are growing needs for pet care services and products.

- **Dog Walking**: "If you have a flexible schedule and can make multiple house calls, you can generate significant revenue as a dog walker." You can also offer additional services like "playing with and feeding pets, bringing in newspapers and mail, and turning lights on and off."[64]

- **Doggy Day Care**: Many workers have returned to the office or work in professions that require them to leave their dogs at home for long periods of time. Studies are showing that this isn't good for most dogs' mental and physical health. Doggy day care is a growing business in which dogs are dropped off at your facility, then you entertain and care for them until their pet parent is done with work for the day and swings back by to pick them up.

- **Mobile Pet Grooming**: Mobile pet grooming services are in high demand and are lucrative. Typical target clients include dual-income couples who are too busy to groom their dogs, elderly clients who don't want to lift their dogs and take them to a brick-and-mortar dog groomer, and successful business owners who don't have time to groom their dogs.

Success Story: My younger son, Josh Stegman, owns a mobile dog-grooming business. He has built up a client base of amazing people (and dogs!). Josh lives in a town with over three hundred wineries, so he has a lot of clients who are winemakers. Not only are they generous with tipping, but they also give him great wine! (People who own dogs must be nicer than the average person.) Mobile dog grooming is a local, relationship-oriented business in which word-of-mouth referrals can contribute to a loyal, regular client base.

- **Online Pet Store**: Online pet-related purchases lead the e-commerce markets in terms of revenue growth. Creating an online pet store allows you to tap into the thriving pet industry while offering convenient access to products pet owners need and love. This business model provides flexibility and the opportunity to cater to niche markets, whether through unique pet supplies, eco-friendly products, or personalized pet services.

---

[63] https://www.entrepreneur.com/starting-a-business/need-a-business-idea-here-are-55/201588
[64] https://www.entrepreneur.com/starting-a-business/need-a-business-idea-here-are-55/201588

IF YOU ARE CREATIVE

- **Graphic Design**: "Have an eye for design? Logos, fliers, newsletters, information sheets, and advertisements are just a few of the types of design materials that businesses hire independent designers to create for them. Websites and online advertising need graphic design services as well. You can offer clients a suite of services to take their project from beginning to end, including coordinating content creators and print shops and getting products ready to mail and present."[65]

- **Making Gift Baskets**: "Finding a niche is the best way to start out in the gift basket business. Are you a dog-lover, horse enthusiast, or exercise guru who could put together baskets that hold the things that people with this interest would like? You could create custom gift baskets that can be shipped across the country or sold in a local store."[66]

Success Story: Shari Fitzpatrick created Shari's Berries, a world-famous line of gourmet-dipped strawberries that are shipped in a pretty gift box. She now sells them under the brand Berried in Chocolate.[67] She started making chocolate-dipped strawberries for her clients when she was a mortgage broker in Los Angeles. The berries became so popular that she turned it into a multi-million-dollar business.

IF YOU ARE A GOOD WRITER

- **Self-Publish a Print-on-Demand Book**: The publishing industry has changed dramatically, providing great opportunities to write and publish a book without having to wait around for a traditional publisher to agree to publish your book. Print-on-demand technology enables you to publish a paperback or hardcover book without having to make a large investment to buy and resell your books. When a customer purchases your book, the print-on-demand company prints and ships the physical book and pays you a royalty.

- **Create a Podcast**: "Podcasts are a popular low- to no-cost side hustle that is easy to launch and build. Podcasts are pre-recorded audio files that you record, edit and upload to podcasting services so listeners can access them at their convenience. Podcasts can be monetized through ads, sponsored content, affiliate links in the podcast descriptions, and paid subscriptions."[68]

- **Content and Editorial Contracting**: "Almost every business or organization needs good writers and editors, and if you have the skills to go out on your own, you'll likely find a bevy of work. From copyediting to developmental editing, ghostwriting, and digital content production, freelance writers and editors can find clients in a host of industries including marketing, communications, journalism, and book publishing. You'll need to

---

[65] https://www.entrepreneur.com/starting-a-business/need-a-business-idea-here-are-55/201588

[66] https://www.entrepreneur.com/starting-a-business/need-a-business-idea-here-are-55/201588

[67] https://www.berriedinchocolate.com/pages/about-us

[68] https://www.forbes.com/advisor/business/best-side-hustle-ideas/#20_create_a_podcast_section

create a portfolio of your work that exemplifies your skills."[69] I hired a professional editor to help me with developmental editing and copyediting. She made my book better and was worth her weight in gold.

BORING JOBS THAT PAY SURPRISINGLY WELL

- **Storage Facility**: Some people acquire more things than they can store in their homes. According to Storeganise.com, owning a self-storage business could provide between $365,000 and $800,000 of annual income, depending upon the facility's location and size, as well as the services you provide.

- **Car Wash**: The car wash and detailing industry in America is a $15 billion business, per Kleen-Rite Car Wash, and annual income for a car wash varies between $40,000 for a small, self-serve car wash and $700,000 for tunnel car washes.

- **Laundry Facility**: According to Huebsch.com, laundromat facilities have a 95 percent success rate. Technology has automated the management of a laundromat by providing remote machine starts and system monitoring, service alerts via email or text, and cloud-based machine programming. And no more collecting cash out of the machine—it can all be digital currency. According to UpFlip.com, the laundromat industry in the US is worth $5 billion, with the average laundromat earning $238,000 annually.

Franchise Opportunities

Buying a franchise may accelerate your ability to open your own business and replace your existing income. Franchises typically have an established brand and successful products, and they provide business training, which is helpful for people who have never owned a business. The one area I hear dissatisfaction with consists of the fees that companies continue to take from franchisee owners on an ongoing basis, so it's wise to examine the up-front costs and ongoing costs very carefully.

See *Entrepreneur*'s article on "Franchise Basics," which includes the pros and cons of franchising versus opening your own business from scratch, as well as identification of franchises that might meet your criteria.

https://www.entrepreneur.com/franchises/basics-of-buying-a-franchise-business-for-entrepreneurs/36328

Determining the most profitable franchise opportunities in the US can depend on various factors, including industry trends, market demand, profitability margins, and franchisee satisfaction.

See *Entrepreneur*'s 2024 Franchise 500 Ranking at https://www.entrepreneur.com/franchise500

---

[69] https://www.entrepreneur.com/starting-a-business/need-a-business-idea-here-are-55/201588

Do You Have the DNA to Be an Entrepreneur?

Are you curious about whether you would be successful as an entrepreneur? How would you manage yourself and others if you decided to start your own business?

Psychology Today has a helpful entrepreneurial personality test that provides information about "which aspects of your personality are well-suited for owning a business, and which aspects could be problematic.[70] In addition, you will receive information about your entrepreneurial style, each of which is based on Bill Wagner's book, *The Entrepreneur Next Door*."

The assessment costs just under ten dollars and is insightful. It provides scoring in critical categories and helpful suggestions on improving skills for successful entrepreneurship.

Exercises

What did you learn about yourself in the entrepreneurial personality test? Please jot down your key observations and insights below.

From the summary, what was your overall score?

And from the assessment's perspective, what is your likeliness to succeed as an entrepreneur?

What are your key strengths?

What are your limitations?

---

[70] Psychology Today, https://www.psychologytoday.com/us/tests/personality/can-you-be-entrepreneur

Which advice will you prioritize to act on?

This chapter covered the tip of the iceberg in terms of common side hustles and businesses to start. But I hope it gave you a wide variety of specialty areas to consider. There are countless opportunities, depending on your skills, interests, and resources.

Did you find inspiration as you perused the business possibilities and success stories? Are you more comfortable opening your mind to business ownership opportunities and working through whatever may have been holding you back in the past? Are you considering a part-time business during semiretirement that could ease you out of full-time work without eliminating all your income? If so, the key is to find something that aligns with your strengths and passions, provides value to others, and fits into your schedule and lifestyle.

Exercises

Below, please identify and document two or three business ownership opportunities in the areas that are relevant for you, whether you are considering a side hustle, full-time business ownership, or part-time opportunities in semiretirement.

List two or three side hustles to explore:

List two or three full-time businesses to explore:

List two or three semiretirement options to explore:

While the insights from this chapter are fresh in your mind, please flip to Chapter 8 and log the side hustle or semiretirement options, as well as the full-time business ownership opportunities, you will explore. Please log these on the second page of the Putting It All Together forms.

That completes Phase 2! There was a lot of content to explore in Chapters 5, 6, and 7. Good job working through the areas that interested you the most. I hope you identified multiple career possibilities that you are excited about pursuing.

Also, congratulations on completing the Putting It All Together section. Great job! In the next chapter, we will discuss next steps you will take with the insights and decisions you have logged in the Putting It All Together section.

PHASE 3
CAREER PATH AND PLAN

Congratulations on putting in the work in Phase 1 and Phase 2.

To recap our progress thus far, in Phase 1, you spent time in self-reflection, assessing your life and career satisfaction, identifying how you're spending your time, and reconnecting with your strengths, values, and unique capabilities.

In Phase 2, you explored career options in the tech and tech-adjacent industries, as well as part-time and full-time business ownership opportunities.

Along the way, you logged insights and decisions into the two-page summary, Putting It All Together.

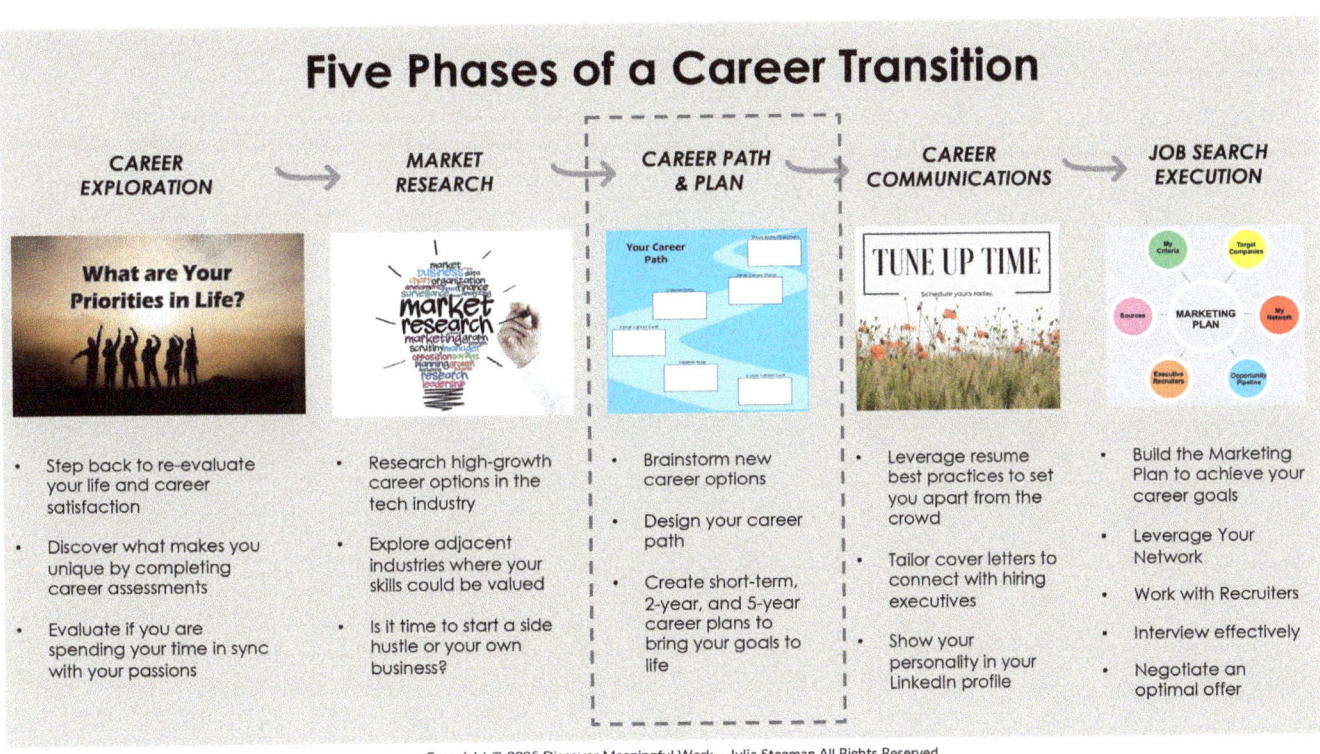

In Phase 3, you will build plans to act on these insights and decisions. This is an exciting phase during which you will:

- Review all the insights and decisions you logged on the two-page summary, Putting It All Together. You will look for patterns and combinations to identify how you can shape your career going forward.

- Craft a career path that will deliver more meaning in your career based on the criteria that are most important to you.

- Build a short-term action plan so you can build momentum quickly.

- Build two- and five-year action plans so you have a clear path to achieve your career goals.

We will start with the great work you have done throughout Phases 1 and 2, completing the Putting It All Together summary.

CHAPTER 8

CREATE YOUR CAREER PATH

"The things that excite you are not random.
They are connected to your purpose.
Follow them."

– Terri Davoll Hudson

At this point in the book, I hope you are excited about crafting the next phase of your career journey. There are so many fascinating careers and intriguing companies to consider.

This chapter is my favorite. It's an opportunity for you to pull the insights, decisions, and observations from the prior chapters into a single view. This will help you look for patterns and connections across these insights to identify what would bring you more fulfillment in your career and, therefore, your life.

Let's start by ensuring you have gathered up your insights, observations, and decisions from all the prior chapters into the two-page summary below. If you have any gaps, take some time now to go back to Chapters 2 through 7 and complete the Putting It All Together summary on the next pages.

You will use this summary as input to brainstorm your career path. This summary is also useful if you want to get input from a mentor, former boss, career coach, or anyone who could help you craft your career path. More on this later in this chapter.

Putting It All Together

Insights from Career Assessments *(Chapter 4)*

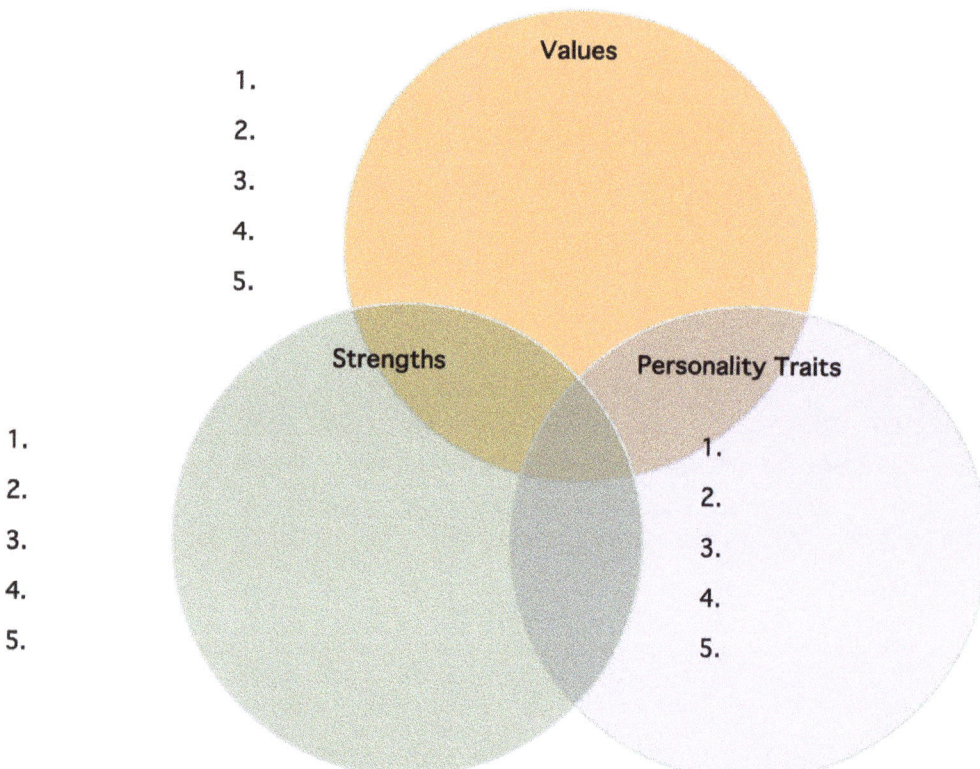

Values
1.
2.
3.
4.
5.

Strengths
1.
2.
3.
4.
5.

Personality Traits
1.
2.
3.
4.
5.

Life Satisfaction: *(Chapter 2)*

Top Dissatisfiers	Possible Solutions
•	•
•	•
•	•

Career Satisfaction: *(Chapter 2)*

Top Dissatisfiers	Possible Solutions
•	•
•	•
•	•

Seasons of Life: Observations and Decisions *(Chapter 3)*

•	•

Work-Life Balance: Observations and Decisions *(Chapter 3)*

•	•

Putting It All Together

If Money Wasn't an Issue: Passions to Explore *(Chapter 3)*

-
-

High-Growth Hot Spots in Tech to Explore: **Roles to Explore:** *(Chapter 5)*

•	•
•	•
•	•

Skills to Build or Expand for High-Growth Tech Hot Spots: *(Chapter 5)*

-
-
-

Training You Will Invest in for Skill Development: *(Chapter 5)*

-
-
-

(Chapter 6)

Adjacent Industries to Explore:	Roles to Explore:	Fast-Growing Companies:
•	•	•
•	•	•
•	•	•
•	•	•
•	•	•

Side Hustles You Will Explore: *(Chapter 7)*

-
-

Full-Time Business Ownership Opportunities You Will Explore: *(Chapter 7)*

-
-

Semiretirement Options You Will Explore: *(Chapter 7)*

-
-

Brainstorm Patterns and Combinations

As you review the summary above, what patterns, connections, or combinations do you see?

Do some of your strengths play well in specific tech-adjacent industries?

Did one of your passions become front and center in your mind? Could you turn it into a side hustle or business opportunity?

Also, to the degree that you can identify career options that leverage where the three circles of values, strengths, and personality intersect, there will be greater career satisfaction.

I encourage you to do some brainstorming of career ideas on your own first, before gathering others' input. Trust your instincts.

Below, jot down the patterns, connections, and combinations that you see.

Exercise: Career Path – My Idea Brainstorming

WITHIN THE TECH INDUSTRY:

Hot Spot and Role:	Life and Career Dissatisfiers to Improve:	Strengths/Values/Personality Traits to Leverage:
•	•	•
•	•	•
•	•	•
•	•	•
•	•	•
•	•	•

IN TECH-ADJACENT INDUSTRIES:

Industry and Role:	Life and Career Dissatisfiers to Improve:	Strengths/Values/Personality Traits to Leverage:
•	•	•
•	•	•
•	•	•
•	•	•
•	•	•
•	•	•

BUSINESS OWNERSHIP:

Business I'm Interested In:	Side Hustle, Full-time, or Semiretirement?	Which Season of Life?
•	•	•
•	•	•
•	•	•
•	•	•
•	•	•
•	•	•

Before proceeding to action planning, this is a good time to share the two-page summary with people who know you and whom you trust. It could be a significant other, former boss, friend, colleague or former colleague, spiritual leader, sibling, parent, career coach, etc. Explain to them that you are stepping back to evaluate a career path that plays to your strengths, leverages your passions, and is consistent with your values and life goals. Ask them what comes to mind for them as you share your two-page summary with them.

Below, jot down the patterns, connections, and combinations that others see.

Exercise: Career Path – Brainstorming with Others

WITHIN THE TECH INDUSTRY:

Hot Spot and Role:	Life and Career Dissatisfiers to Improve:	Strengths/Values/Personality Traits to Leverage:
•	•	•
•	•	•
•	•	•
•	•	•
•	•	•
•	•	•

IN TECH-ADJACENT INDUSTRIES:

Industry and Role:	Life and Career Dissatisfiers to Improve:	Strengths/Values/Personality Traits to Leverage:
•	•	•
•	•	•

•	•	•
•	•	•
•	•	•
•	•	•

BUSINESS OWNERSHIP:

Business I'm Interested In:	Side Hustle, Full-time, or Semiretirement?	Which Season of Life?
•	•	•
•	•	•
•	•	•
•	•	•
•	•	•
•	•	•

Now that you've brainstormed potential career opportunities, it's time to prioritize and sequence them.

Craft Your Career Path

Traditional career pathing, like the framework below, can cause frustration and disappointment. It locks us into a limited set of options for just taking the next stair step in one career job family. What happens when economic headwinds make it difficult to move up and to the right with this type of career path planning? Or maybe you work for a company with a high percentage of long-term employees, which limits the number of job openings that are up the career ladder.

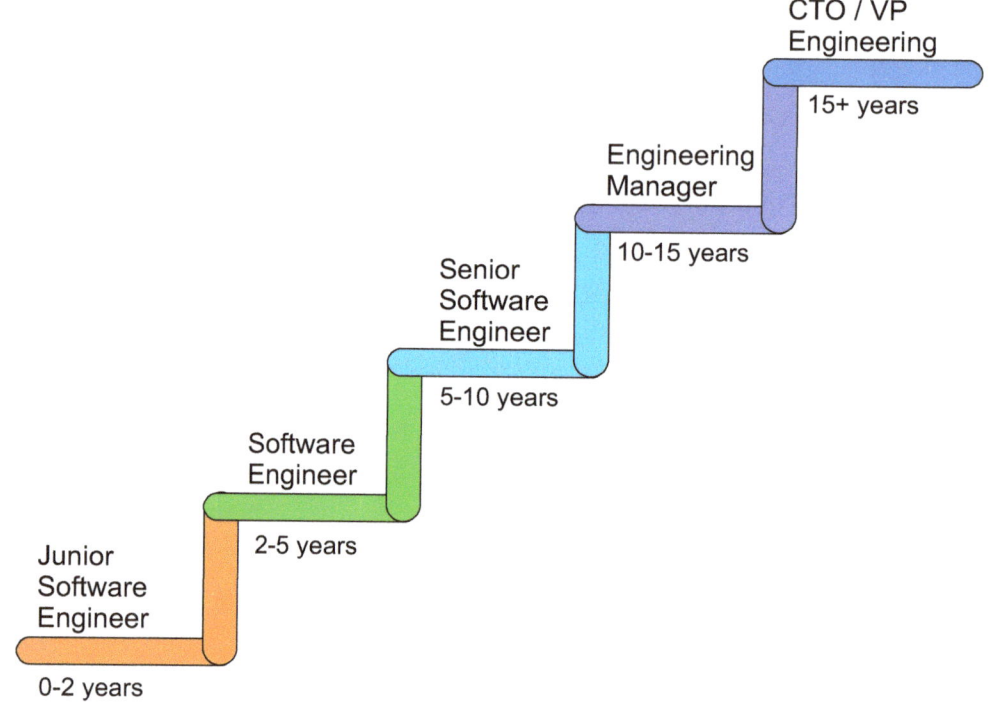

Your path does not have to be linear. By following the methodology in this book, you have been considering a wide variety of options where:

- The work intrigues you.

- The roles play to your strengths.

- You have the opportunity to build a broader set of skills.

What does your dream career look like?

Exercise

On the career path template below, craft your career path:

- List your short-term objectives that will enable you to derive more meaning from your career and position you to take your next career move.

- The next position you want to pivot to would be your next career move. What is your goal for your next career move?

- Is there an interim step that would position you to achieve your two-year career goal? It could be a lateral position to increase the breadth of your experience or gain critical skills. It could be taking on more responsibility to prepare you for your next career move. Or it could be an investment in training, education, or certifications.

- Document your two-year career goal.

- Is there an interim step that would position you to achieve your five-year career goal? It could be a lateral position to increase the breadth of your experience or gain critical skills. It could be taking on more responsibility to prepare you for your next career move. Or it could be an investment in training, education, or certifications.

- Document your five-year career goal.

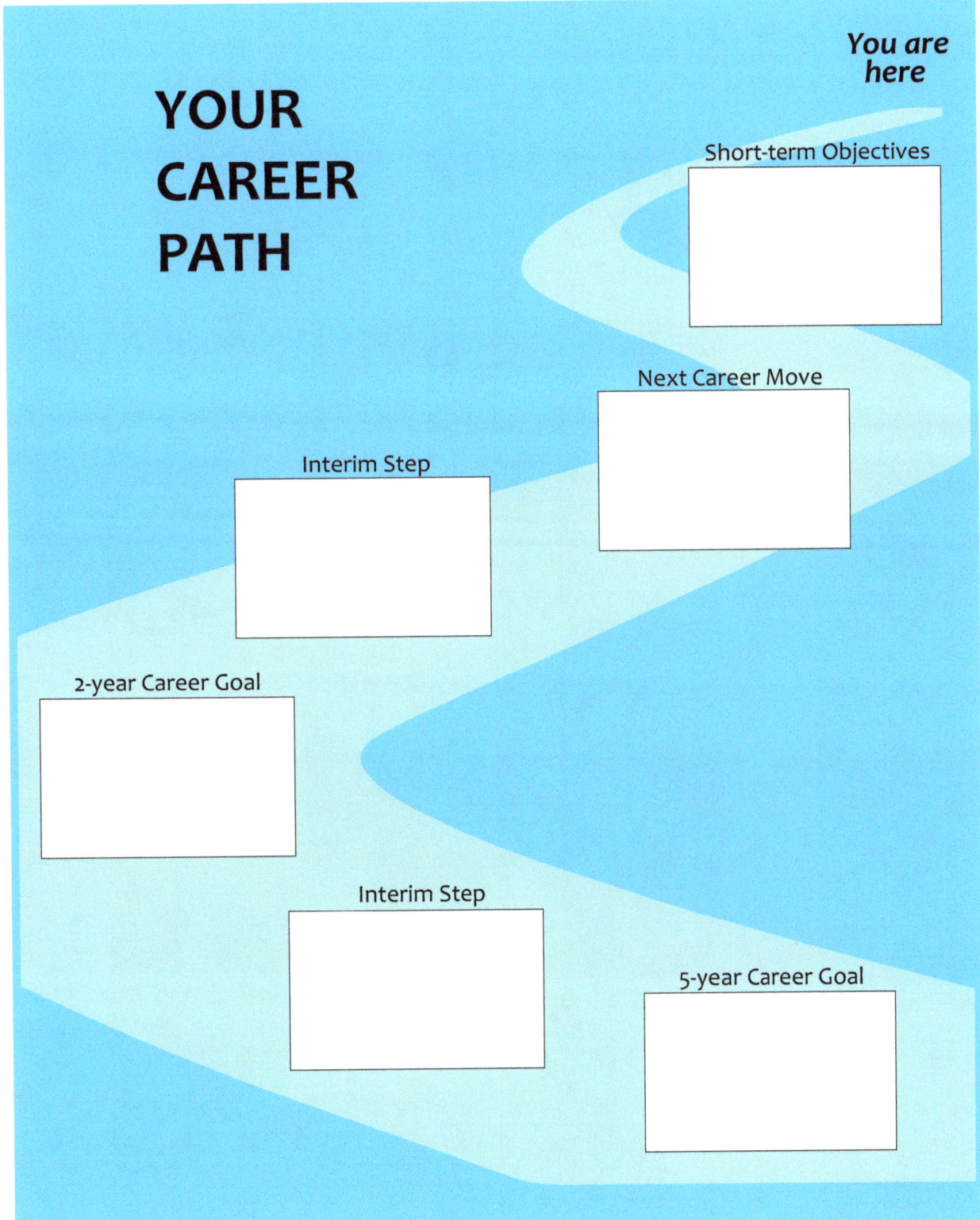

Doesn't it feel great to envision the next five years of your career? Way to go! In the next chapter, you will create an action plan to confirm your career path choices, make any revisions based on additional information, and then prepare yourself to take on these exciting roles in your future.

CHAPTER 9

CAREER ACTION PLANS

"Plan your work, and work your plan."

– Napolean Hill

Let's reiterate these powerful statements:

"People are 76% more likely to achieve goals

if they write action commitments and share weekly progress reports.

Writing down goals helps you achieve them

by providing clarity, commitment, and motivation."

The shocking fact is only 3 percent of people write down their goals.[71]

So, let's set you up to be in this elite category of people who write down and achieve their career goals.

Now that you have established a career path, it's time to document what it will take to accomplish it. Let's start with the short-term objectives.

Activities to Increase Meaningfulness in Current Role

Based on your summary of insights listed in Chapter 8, "Putting it All Together," what are the top areas you will focus on immediately to improve the meaningfulness in your current role?

Examples could be:

- Reduce the hours worked during the weekend and late evenings by setting boundaries, prioritizing more effectively, saying 'no', delegating more, or guarding against perfectionism.

---

[71] https://www.zippia.com/advice/goal-setting-statistics/

- Make your current job more interesting or increase your visibility to leaders in your organization by volunteering to lead or participate in a cross-functional project that is interesting to you. This is a great way to learn how other departments function.

- Ask your boss for a raise.

Activities to Explore Careers for Your Next Career Move, Two-Year Goal, and Five-Year Goal

Document the activities you will conduct to confirm each of your goals. This could include gathering additional insights on what it will take to accomplish each career goal.

Examples could be:

- Conduct one informational interview per week to gain more insight into each of the career goals in your career path. Understand the skills, experience, and training you will need to accomplish each goal; gain an understanding of what the job entails on a day-to-day basis.

- Spend one hour per week researching positions in tech or tech-adjacent industries that you logged on your summary in Chapter 8.

- Ask recruiters what the compensation ranges are for roles you are interested in. Be sure to obtain data points from multiple sources. It's best not to make financial decisions based on one data point.

- Spend one hour per week talking with business owners to understand the pros and cons of running your own business.

Set Goals for Next Career Move, Two-Year Goal, and Five-Year Goal

Once you have gathered enough intelligence, confirm and document your career goals for your next career move, two-year career goal, and five-year career goal.

Be sure to also include goals for side hustles or full-time business ownership, if appropriate.

Identify Skills, Training, and Experience Required to Achieve Each Goal

For each of your three career goals (next career move, two-year career goal, and five-year career goal), document the skills, training, and experience required to evolve to these roles.

Examples could be:

- Commit to education: Obtain a new certification, take AI classes, complete a professional degree, etc. Does your employer offer educational assistance?

- Improve performance metrics in your current role. This is always important if you want to be hired into a new role.

- Schedule one hour on Fridays to network and broaden the number of people you know in companies or industries that are interesting to you.

- Review the interim steps you documented on your career path and ensure you are committing to action items that help you achieve these.

- Hire a business advisor to teach you a business before launching a full-time business of your own.

- Create flexibility for a significant change. Will your two-year or five-year career goals necessitate a change to a lower-cost location? Will it require a reduction in your living expenses to provide flexibility for a career change that is more meaningful? Maybe the best path will be to take an interim career step that will pay off with the next career move?

Exercise: Career Action Plans – Document Goals and Activities

Short-Term Objectives:

Activities to Increase Meaningfulness in Current Role:	Start Date:	Completion Date:

Activities to Explore Careers for Next Career Move:	Start Date:	Completion Date:

Activities to Explore Careers for Two-Year Career Goal:	Start Date:	Completion Date:

Activities to Explore Careers for Five-Year Career Goal:	Start Date:	Completion Date:

Now that you have gathered additional information about your career goals, make any revisions and finalize your next career move goal, your two-year career goal, and your five-year career goal. Update your career path with your final goals. Then continue with the action planning below.

Goal for Next Career Move:

Goal for My Next Career Move:	Date:

Skills, Training, and Experience to Invest in to Achieve Next Career Move:	Start Date:	Completion Date:

Two-Year Career Goal:

Goal for My Career in Two Years:	Date:

Skills, Training, and Experience to Invest in to Achieve Two-Year Career Goal:	Start Date:	Completion Date:

Five-Year Career Goal:

Goal for My Career in Five Years:	Date:

Skills, Training, and Experience to Invest in to Achieve Five-Year Career Goal:	Start Date:	Completion Date:

Great job on confirming your career path and building your career action plans!

You are now in the elite category of 3 percent of people who document their goals! Fantastic achievement! I hope you will celebrate this milestone and do something special for yourself.

Keep your career path and career action plans front and center where you can see them every day. Block time on your calendar weekly to ensure you are moving your goals forward. And be sure to track your milestones and celebrate your wins!

Congratulations! You have completed Phase 3.

In Phase 4, we will focus on career communication documents that will help you:

- Articulate what makes you unique

- Clearly communicate your next career goal

- Enable you to connect with hiring executives

PHASE 4
CAREER COMMUNICATION DOCUMENTS

Effective career communication documents will help you stand out from the crowd. This takes some effort but will result in a competitive advantage for you.

In Phase 4, we will walk through:

- Best practices for articulating your personal brand in your resume

- Guidelines for adding personality to your LinkedIn profile

- Templates for tailoring cover letters to help you connect with hiring executives

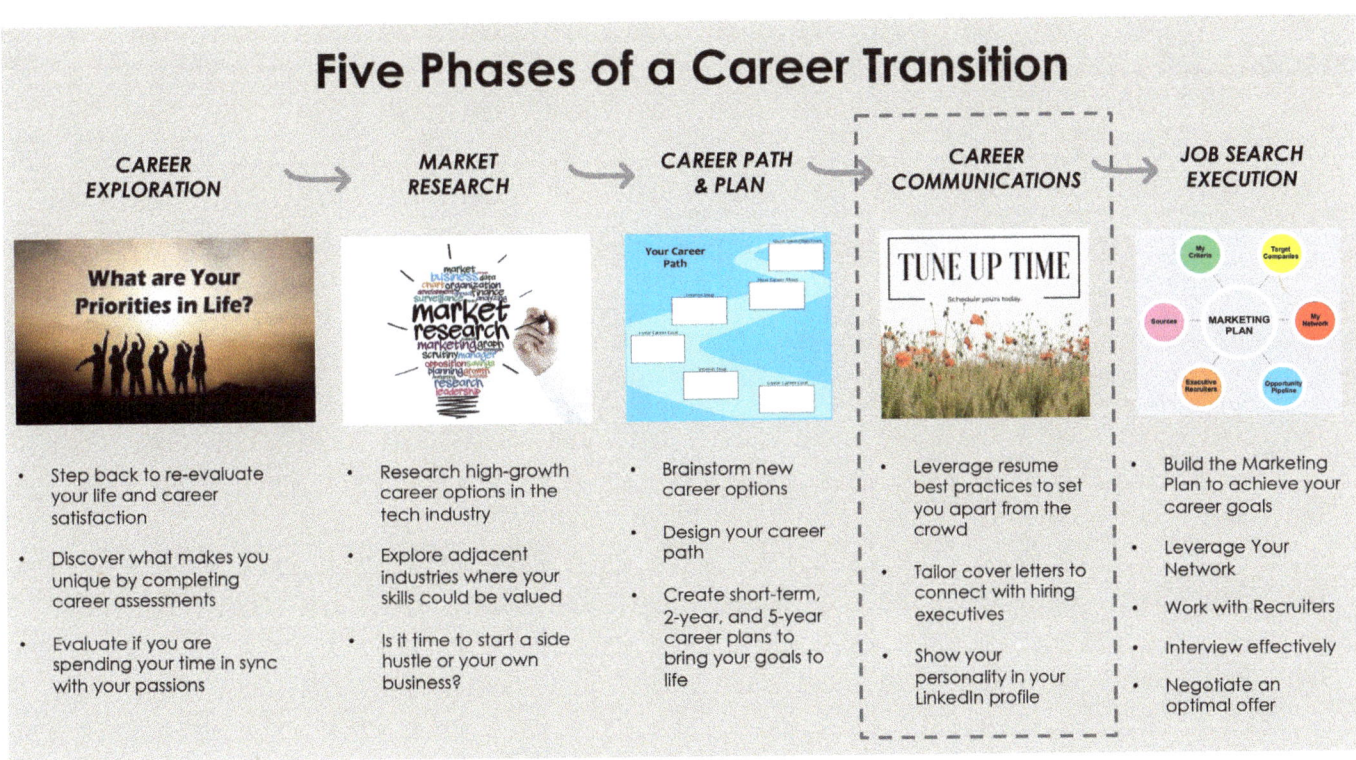

Five Phases of a Career Transition

CAREER EXPLORATION	MARKET RESEARCH	CAREER PATH & PLAN	CAREER COMMUNICATIONS	JOB SEARCH EXECUTION
What are Your Priorities in Life?	market research	Your Career Path	TUNE UP TIME	MARKETING PLAN
• Step back to re-evaluate your life and career satisfaction	• Research high-growth career options in the tech industry	• Brainstorm new career options	• Leverage resume best practices to set you apart from the crowd	• Build the Marketing Plan to achieve your career goals
• Discover what makes you unique by completing career assessments	• Explore adjacent industries where your skills could be valued	• Design your career path	• Tailor cover letters to connect with hiring executives	• Leverage Your Network
• Evaluate if you are spending your time in sync with your passions	• Is it time to start a side hustle or your own business?	• Create short-term, 2-year, and 5-year career plans to bring your goals to life	• Show your personality in your LinkedIn profile	• Work with Recruiters
				• Interview effectively
				• Negotiate an optimal offer

Your good work to this point will be leveraged in the next three chapters. In this phase, you will follow step-by-step guides, and the outcomes will be very tangible:

- A resume you will be proud of that will communicate your unique combination of skills, experiences, and talents

- A LinkedIn profile that is interesting for hiring executives and people in your network to read

- Cover letters that will connect with hiring executives

Let's start with the most important career document: your resume!

CHAPTER 10

CREATE YOUR PERSONAL BRAND IN YOUR RESUME

"A resume is a marketing document, not a historical record."

– Jacquelyn Smith

As mentioned in Chapter 1, some people would opt to visit the dentist rather than take time to write or update their resume. But having a well-crafted resume that reflects your uniqueness is an ante to the game.

If you want to be like the *average* tech employee:

- Don't update your resume.

- Have a passive LinkedIn profile that lacks personality.

- Don't bother writing cover letters.

I assure you, as an executive recruiter, I talked with *many* candidates who fell into the above category.

If, however, you want to take the offensive and set yourself apart with hiring executives:

- Write a resume that reflects what is unique about you so you stand out from the crowd.

- Add your personality to your LinkedIn profile.

- Put in the effort to write a tailored cover letter when reaching out about career opportunities.

Having effective career communication documents *will* set you apart from the typical person.

In this chapter, there are tools and templates to help you follow industry best practices and accelerate the development of your career communication documents.

You will start with templates and make them your own. You will build your resume one section at a time, much like eating one leg of the elephant at a time. Like any project, we will break this down into manageable components.

If you follow this process and are persistent in completing it, you will have a resume, LinkedIn profile, and cover letters you are proud of. It will give you the confidence to take the next steps in executing your job search.

Step-by-Step Instructions for Creating Your Personal Brand in Your Resume

Everyone has a short attention span these days. Research shows you have seven seconds to get the reader's attention with your resume, so the top two-thirds of the first page of your resume is critical. Therefore, it's more important than ever to remember to write your career communication documents *for the reader.* As the quote at the beginning of this chapter states, your resume should be not a sequential data dump of your entire career but rather a well-crafted document that helps connect your experience, skills, and unique talents with the hiring executive.

Creating your personal brand is about telling your story in your resume. You did a lot of good work earlier in this workbook to clarify your strengths, values, and capabilities. These are core to articulating your uniqueness since no one else has the same group of traits you have. We will use these insights when creating your resume.

So, let's begin building your resume. You can download a sample resume using the URL at the beginning of this workbook. There is also a sample resume in the appendix.

There are ten steps to building an effective resume. We will take it one step at a time and provide examples for each step.

Step 1: Your Contact Information

This is the first impression readers will have of your resume since it's on the top of the page.

List the following at the top of your resume:

- Your name

- City and state where you currently reside

- Personal email

- Cell phone number

- LinkedIn profile

I know this seems basic, but over the years as an executive recruiter, I saw a lot of people get this wrong. And this puts the reader on the defensive when reviewing your resume—if they continue reading at all.

Key Tips:

- **Name Placement**: Your name should be prominent, centered, and in a font that is easy to read. I use capital letters on my resume template to ensure that the reader clearly identifies whose resume this is.

- **City and State**: Recruiters and hiring managers need to know where you currently reside, so be transparent. If you are interested in relocating to another area, just address that in a cover letter. For privacy reasons, you should not include your street address. If an employer plans to make you an offer, they will likely ask for your street address then.

- **Email**: Use a personal email. Often, recruiters will send you information to complete prior to an interview. If you put your work email on your resume, that is where their requests will go.

- **Mobile**: List your personal cell phone number, not a shared phone number (like a landline) where someone else you live with could pick up the phone.

- **LinkedIn**: Recruiters and hiring managers spend a lot of time on LinkedIn when they are conducting a search for candidates, so make it easy for them to find your profile. Put the word *LinkedIn* on the top of your resume and hyperlink the word to your LinkedIn profile.

    - **How to Create a Hyperlink**: In MS Word, highlight the word *LinkedIn* on your resume, click on "Insert," then "Links," then "Link," and paste your LinkedIn profile URL into the box.

- **Length and Distinction**: Keep your contact information to three lines and use either dots or bars to separate them.

Examples:

JOHN SMITH

Santa Clara, CA

johnsmith@icloud.com | 415 345-2345 | LinkedIn

JOHN SMITH

Santa Clara, CA

johnsmith@icloud.com • 415 345-2345 • LinkedIn

Step 2: Your Professional Experience

A list of your work history is a core element of your resume. Gather the following information and sequence it, starting with the most current position, and continue down to the first position you held:

- Company name

- Title

- Month and year start date

- Month and year end date

- City and state where you were located

Example:

PROFESSIONAL EXPERIENCE

Citrix   Atlanta, GA
Senior Vice President, Global Technical Support (February 2021 – Present)
Vice President, Business Network Support (January 2019 – January 2021)

Dell Technologies   Santa Clara, CA
Senior Director, Global Support Services, Productivity Improvement Office (October 2015 – December 2018)
Chief of Staff, Global Support Services, Business Planning & Strategy (February 2012 – September 2015)

Travel Sabbatical
Explorer of the South Pacific (November 2011 – January 2012)
Explored the islands of the South Pacific to learn about Polynesian culture and understand what makes them so happy and appreciative.

Key Tips:

- **Gaps in Employment**: Recruiters get frustrated with resumes that state only the year. They want to see the month and year you started and ended a position. Don't try to hide gaps in employment due to layoffs, family leave, sabbaticals, etc. Gaps in employment are very common now due to the pandemic and tech layoffs. So, I suggest you be transparent in your resume and be prepared to verbally explain any employment gaps.

   You can either leave the gaps in employment blank or create an entry in your professional experience list that explains your gap. For example:

   - **Travel Sabbatical**: It's interesting if you write a short statement about what you learned on the sabbatical.

- **Family Leave**: Often, family leaves are quite personal, so a high-level statement works well. For example: "Time Off to Care for Family Member."

  - **Layoff**: If you worked part-time as a consultant or as an employee during the period of time you were laid off, you could list that here. If the part-time work isn't aligned with the direction you want to go, it's best to leave it off.

- **Mergers and Acquisitions**: Mergers and acquisitions are very common in the tech industry. If the company you worked for was acquired by another company, it's good to note that on your resume.

  - This is especially true if you worked for your employer for less than a year prior to the company being acquired.

  - You can note "Acquired by [New Company Name]" next to the name of the company that was acquired.

- **Titles**: Use the title your employer gave your position in case a reference call is made to your former employer. If your former employer used a title that doesn't conform to industry standards, it's okay to augment it on your resume so you can connect the dots for the reader. For example:

  - Account Manager | Customer Success Manager

  - If the company called the role "account manager" but the scope of your role aligned with a typical customer success manager, you can add "customer success manager" to your title.

Step 3: Your Education

Document the formal education you have completed.

Key Tips:

- **Formal Education**: Be honest! If you misrepresent your formal education, it can come up in your background check. If a company you lied to finds out later, it could be grounds for termination. It's not worth it! Be transparent. Also, be prepared to provide documentation as requested. When I was an executive recruiter, many of my clients verified formal education, even if the degree was acquired in a foreign country. I had an executive candidate who had to provide copies of his international degree and transcripts to verify a degree that was obtained in another country.

A word about incomplete college degrees: If you started a degree program but didn't finish it, it's okay to give yourself credit for the course work you did, but make it clear that you did not obtain a degree. (see the masters example below).

- **Certifications**: Hiring managers at tech companies often value certifications since technology evolves rapidly. It demonstrates you are staying current on developing new competencies or sharpening your skills. So do list any certifications you have received.

- **Dates**: It's best to leave dates off your formal education since it can indicate your age.

Example:

EDUCATION

Bachelor of Science Degree in Business Administration, San Jose State University.
Masters in Artificial Intelligence, Oxford University. One year of coursework completed.
Certifications:

- Certified Information Systems Security Professional (CISSP)
- AWS Certified Solutions Architect
- Project Management Professional (PMP)

Step 4: Honors, Professional Associations, Board Work, Volunteer Work

List any work you have done related to participation in professional associations (especially speaking engagements), honors or awards received, key volunteer work, or participation as a board member.

Example:

HONORS, PROFESSIONAL ASSOCIATIONS, BOARD WORK, VOLUNTEER WORK

Recipient of three TSIA STAR Awards for: "Excellence in Mission Critical Support," "Excellence in Continual Improvement," and "Best Knowledge Management Practices."

Conference attendee National Customer Service Association for seven years.

Member of the board of directors for Habitat for Humanity, 2014 – 2016.

Monthly volunteer at local food bank.

Key Tips:

- **Length**: Limit this section to three or four entries since it takes away space from other critical components of the resume.

- **Religious Affiliations**: Unfortunately, unconscious bias and conscious bias are alive and well during hiring processes. So, my advice is to be careful about listing work you have done related to a specific religious affiliation. If the work you did and the skills you utilized directly relate to the next role you want to land, then list it. If not, you might consider leaving it off to avoid the risk of being eliminated from the process due to bias. Sad state of affairs, but it's true.

Step 5: Keywords

Keywords are important for a number of reasons:

1. It's a quick way for a recruiter or hiring manager to get a feel for the competencies you have.

2. Many in-house recruiters (recruiters who are employed by one specific company) are often not familiar with the latest technologies, the impact of best practices you have implemented, or other descriptions on your resume that can set you apart. So it's important to give them common keywords that are used in the tech industry. Often, the hiring manager they are conducting the search for will give them a list of keywords to search for. So be sure your keywords are front and center on your resume.

3. Recruiters or hiring managers conduct keyword searches in databases, applicant tracking systems, etc., and are looking for specific competencies. The keywords you list on your resume will come up in their searches.

These keywords will be listed near the top of your resume and below your contact information and position title.

Key Tips:

-   **Length**:
    -   Use one- or two-word phrases. Occasionally, you can use a three-word phrase, but this makes it more difficult to read quickly.
    -   Create a list that fills two lines, and no more than that. The objective is for the reader to *quickly* gain a sense of your experience.

-   **Distinction**: Make the list readable by separating the list with dots or bars.

-   **Tailor**: In a separate document, you can make a comprehensive list of your core competency keywords, then whittle the list on your resume down to two lines when applying for a specific position. Choose your competencies that best match what the hiring manager is looking for. Connect the dots for them as to why you are a qualified candidate.

Example:

> Strategic Planning | Business Transformation | Enterprise Software | Customer Experience | Customer Success
> Cloud Services | SaaS | Application Support | Leadership | Managed Services | Digital Strategies | Global Operating Models
>
> Strategic Planning • Business Transformation • Enterprise Software • Customer Experience • Customer Success
> Cloud Services • SaaS • Application Support • Managed Services • Digital Strategies • Global Operating Models

Step 6: Short Description for Each Position Held

Write a two- or three-sentence description for each position you have held.

Example:

> *Vice President, Global Support Sales*
>
> Accountable for customer retention and renewal of $800M in support and subscription revenues. Led global team of 37 Support Sales Representatives in 44 countries. Leveraging a direct and channel partner go-to-market model, renewed 8,000 subscriptions.

Key Tips:

- **Word Economy**: Use as few words as possible; word economy is key in helping the reader understand the scope of the role you held and what you accomplished.

- **Long Work History**: If you have over twenty years of experience, you don't have to list the roles you held earliest in your career. Or you can list just the company and title without listing the dates or any other descriptions. See the example resume in the appendix.

Step 7: Key Business Results for Each Position Held

Many resumes are filled with lots of words that aren't relevant or helpful, especially fluffy adverbs. To avoid this, create a bullet list of key accomplishments for each role you have held, then name the competency you gained (listed in bold below).

Once you have created all of your business results under each position you have held, copy your most powerful line items to the Key Business Results section at the top of your resume so they can be highlighted. You should tailor this list of key business results to the specific role you are applying for.

Examples:

- **Global Operating Model Optimization**: Built and led the strategy to consolidate siloed support teams into a globally unified support model. Flexed from a product focus structure to a geography-aligned operation with a matrixed product overlay.

- **Proactive Service Transformation**: First-phase pilot executed on journey mapping, process engineering, videos, and knowledge base to build the foundation for proactive technical services, with the objective of reducing demand for labor by 20%.

- **Product Quality Improvements**: Improved tickets assigned to defects by 7 points. Formed partnership with Engineering and implemented Serviceability, Manageability, and Quality processes (including Product Trend Analysis) to drive product quality.

- **Improved Customer Experience**: Increased CSAT by 15 points. Improved the support experience by building a Customer First culture, offering real-time self-service capabilities, accommodating customer demands, and implementing best practices.

Key Tips:

- **Accomplishments**: Start by writing one or two sentences about what you accomplished and how you did it. Include quantitative measures of improvement in at least 50 percent of your accomplishments. For example:

  - Increased CSAT by 15 points. Improved the support experience by building a Customer First culture, offering real-time self-service capabilities and meeting changing customer demand.

- **Name the Competency**: Use as few words as possible to describe the competency (less is better, no more than four words). Include common terminology for your industry or profession so the reader identifies with the competency.

  - Artificial intelligence can be helpful with generating a list of competencies for the role you would like to have in your next career move.

  - For example, here is a ChatGPT prompt:

    - Please provide a list of competencies for chief customer officers in the technology industry.

  - The list ChatGPT returned was very accurate. You can review the ChatGPT response in the appendix.

  - Once you have the list of competencies for the role you are interested in for your next career move, use as many of these competencies as you can to tie to your experience, skills, and results. This helps the hiring executive see that you are a qualified candidate.

- **Tailor**: In a separate document, you can make a comprehensive list of your core competencies. When applying for a specific position, whittle the list in your resume down to two or three competencies for each position you held. Choose your competencies that best match what the hiring executive is looking for. Tech companies are looking for soft skills as well as hard skills (e.g., finance, specific technical skills), so be sure to include some soft skills in your descriptions (e.g., critical thinking, collaboration, and emotional intelligence).

- **Balance**: Include a balance of accomplishments across each of the following categories:
  - Customer-oriented competency
  - Revenue or profit-oriented competency
  - People- and employee-oriented competency
  - Operations-oriented competency
  - Technical competency

You want to show that you have a broad set of skills. For example, I typically see that sales leaders have a lot of revenue-oriented capabilities listed on their resumes, which is appropriate. But ensure that you also showcase your customer, employee leadership, and operations skill sets.

Step 8: Opening Paragraph

This is the most important component of your resume.

The opening paragraph is your elevator pitch about yourself. Giving this some thought and crafting a strong opening paragraph will give you a resume that makes you stand out from the rest. You can also use this short description to verbally communicate with others during your networking activities.

Let's bring the good work you did in earlier chapters front and center so it can be reflected in your communication documents.

Please flip to Chapter 8 and write below your top five God-given strengths, your top five values, and the top five characteristics that resonated with you from the personality type assessment.

Top Five God-Given Strengths:
1.
2.
3.
4.
5.

Top Five Values:
1.
2.
3.
4.
5.

Top Five Personality Traits:
1.
2.
3.
4.
5.

This opening paragraph will include three positioning statements (sentences) about your body of work and key characteristics. Each sentence should describe a different angle about you.

Customers: One statement should include a description of work you have done with customers and provide insight into how you think about them.

Technical: If your work has not been customer-facing, write a statement that showcases the technical work you have done.

Employees: One statement should include how you lead employees, whether you are a people leader or an individual contributor (we are all leaders, and hiring companies want to see this in your skill set).

Financial Result: One statement should include a financial result because hiring managers care about improving business performance.

Please take a few minutes to read the detailed descriptions from the career assessments—there are descriptions of your strengths, values, and capabilities that could be useful for your opening paragraph. Use these to help tell your story.

Key Tips:

- **Recognize Your Uniqueness**: Look across these three sets of insights about yourself (above) and take a few minutes to celebrate your uniqueness. No one else is just like you!

- **Play to Your Strengths**: Landing a role that allows you to utilize your strengths most of the time will result in a much higher degree of career satisfaction. So, be proud of who you are and what you have accomplished, and highlight your strengths.

Examples:

> High-impact executive, experienced general manager, and proven sales leader with a track record of consistent results and profitable revenue growth for software, hardware, and services companies. (financial result)
>
> Applies strong business acumen when working with customer executives, management, and boards to build trusting relationships that facilitate rapid discovery of customer needs, business/technical outcomes, solutions, and the mobilization of people to drive results. (customers) (financial result)
>
> A pragmatic leader who thinks broadly about business opportunities, engages with employees to bring out their best, and helps them achieve more than they think is possible. (employees)

Step 9: Key Skills Paragraph

The key skills paragraph describes *how* you have achieved your accomplishments. It's your bag of tricks you bring to the workforce.

It should include three sentences about how you get things done.

<u>Operational</u>: One statement should describe how you identify business problems, come up with solutions, and improve the operations of the business.

<u>Customers</u>: One statement should include a description of your angle on creating more value for customers. (Whether you are in a customer-facing role or not, hiring companies want to know you are keeping customers front and center.)

<u>Employees</u>: One statement should include how you help employees perform in their roles, develop and help them grow, and help them want to continue working for your employer.

Again, the detailed descriptions from the career assessments could be helpful here with telling your story and articulating your personal brand.

Examples:

> Has unique insights into relevant patterns and issues, making it easier to remove obstacles and execute on innovative solutions. (operational)
>
> Builds trusted customer relationships. Interested in each individual's capabilities and qualities, understands what makes people tick, and motivates teams to achieve higher performance levels. (employees) (customers)
>
> A transparent, engaging personality who communicates well, inspires others, and brings possibilities to challenging situations. (employees)

Step 10: Position Title

If you are applying for a specific position, put that title on your resume near the top. Your resume should be tailored for each position you apply to. The tailored changes can be minor, including the title, ensuring your keywords reflect what the hiring manager is looking for, putting the most relevant results in the Key Business Results section, and subtracting any line items that are not relevant to the reader. This small amount of time to tailor your resume can make a big difference with helping the recruiter or hiring executive understand that you are a qualified candidate.

If you are using your resume for networking and informational interviews, you can use a broader title so people understand the kind of roles you are looking for.

Examples of broader roles for networking and informational interviews are below:

President / General Manager

or

Sales, Operations, and Customer Success Executive

or

Global Executive – Customer Retention and Renewal Optimization

---

Julia's Top Resume Tips

1. Word economy will make you stand out. Edit, edit, edit your resume to remove as many words as possible. Make your statements short and punchy.

2. Do not use an MS Word resume template that has lines, boxes, or columns. Applicant Tracking Systems (ATS) don't know how to gather information from fancy formats. If you receive a rejection letter right away from a potential employer, it likely means their ATS system could not digest your resume or turn it into something they can analyze.

3. Less is more. Your resume should not contain your entire work history (drop off or shorten the experiences that were furthest away from today). Don't make the reader read nonrelevant items. By removing content from your resume that is not pertinent, you will create a resume that resonates with the reader.

4. Just the facts, Ma'am: Your resume should be factual in nature. Avoid using broad-based adjectives or adverbs wherever possible. This comes across as bragging. When you state the facts, they can't be refuted.

How Does Your Resume Look? Does It Reflect Your Uniqueness?

If you're not satisfied with it yet, share it with people who are familiar with your work experience—ideally, a former boss or colleague. Have them weigh in on what makes you unique and add their insights to your resume.

You know you're done when your resume reflects your unique combination of work experience, results, strengths, and capabilities--and you feel proud when you read it.

Now that your resume is up to date, it will be easy to keep it updated. You might consider updating your resume every year right after your performance evaluation so you can add relevant achievements, keywords, and enhancements to it. If you learned new competencies, be sure to reflect them in your resume too.

Doesn't it feel great to have an updated resume that is ready to go? You've completed the first of three career communication documents. Well done!

In the next chapter, the topic will be your LinkedIn profile. You will be able to leverage much of what is on your new resume, then just add your personality to a couple of areas. Let's get started with your LinkedIn profile in Chapter 11.

CHAPTER 11

ADD YOUR PERSONALITY TO YOUR LINKEDIN PROFILE:

"Social media is your opportunity to humanize your brand and let your personality shine through."

– Mari Smith

Having a strong LinkedIn profile is a *must-have* in the tech industry. LinkedIn has over 800 million members across two hundred countries. It gives you access to a vast pool of potential professional connections.

As we discussed in the prior chapter, a resume is a formal business document, so it is recommended that you limit personal information on the resume.

However, LinkedIn is different; it is less formal, so you can share more of your personality on your LinkedIn profile. In fact, adding your personality is how you can differentiate your profile from the typical profile.

For professionals in the tech industry, optimizing a LinkedIn profile is essential for showcasing expertise and for networking. It also enables the profile to be found by recruiters and hiring executives who are searching for candidates with specific expertise. Here's what to include for a strong and compelling LinkedIn profile:

Step-by-Step Instructions for Creating Your LinkedIn Profile

Professional Headline

The headline is prime real estate. This is the area right under your name. LinkedIn will automatically populate your headline with your current job title. But you should change your headline since it is the first impression hiring authorities have when they see your profile. When recruiters and hiring executives conduct searches on LinkedIn to identify candidates for their open positions, the LinkedIn search engines put a heavy weighting on the headline space. So, list keywords here (ideally three) to help people understand your expertise and the kind of work you are interested in.

For example:

Senior Software Engineer | AI Enthusiast | Cloud Architecture Expert

Profile Photo

Use a professional, high-quality photo. I don't recommend personal photos (e.g., you with your pet, you on vacation, etc.). LinkedIn is a professional social media networking platform, as opposed to Facebook, which is a personal platform. Your attire could be business professional or business casual. It does not have to be business formal.

The About Section

This is where you create a succinct summary about yourself. It should be written in the first person to help make you approachable. This is where you tell your story. It might be helpful to think about the verbal words you say when you introduce yourself to someone in a business setting. The more natural the language, the more inviting you become to the reader.

"Create a hook to grab the reader's attention in the first three sentences of your About summary. You could ask an intriguing question, share your point of view on a hot topic, or share a memorable moment from one of the jobs you held. You want others to feel comfortable engaging you."[72] The good work you did on the top part of your resume is a good place to start creating a hook since this is your elevator pitch about who you are as a professional.

The About section should also include a concise summary of your career journey thus far, your unique skills, career achievements, and what motivates you. Talk about what you're really good at! Focus on what sets you apart in the tech field, whether it's expertise with a specific technology, problem-solving approach, or product or process you built that creates a better customer experience.

Be sure to include keywords that are relative to your niche. For example, if you're a data scientist, mention skills like machine learning, Python, and big data. You can copy your keywords from your resume and list them in the body of your About section. This helps with the LinkedIn search engines as well.

Example Structure for Creating Content in The About Section:

- **Introduction**: Who you are, your current role, and your years of experience. Add an interesting hook here.

---

[72] Adapted from: https://www.briefcasecoach.com/linkedin-best-practices/

- **Expertise**: Key technologies or programming languages, tools, software expertise (e.g., Salesforce CRM), and skills.

- **Achievements**: Highlight significant projects or results you've delivered. Mention awards like President's Club achievement or patents.

- **Personal Values and Mission**: What excites you about your work or the tech industry. This one is key.

- **Call to Action**: State if you are open to collaborations, new career opportunities, or professional networking.

If your call to action includes an invitation for people to reach out to you, be sure to include your email or phone number so they know how to contact you.

To end the About section on a personal note, you can add a sentence at the bottom that talks about what you do outside work.

For example:

"When I'm not working, you can find me coaching my son's baseball team, hiking with my wife, or playing golf."

Experience Section

This is where you document your work history. I suggest you copy and paste your work history from your resume so it is the same in both places. As an executive recruiter, I found it confusing when a candidate had a work history on their resume that was different from their LinkedIn profile. It caused me to either pass on the candidate or ask the candidate why the LinkedIn work history was different from the resume.

Skills and Endorsements

Choose your top five skills for each of your roles. It is ideal if there is a good mix of skills across your work experience versus having the same five skills listed for every role. Keep the skills lists focused on the strengths you want to use in your next role.

Seek endorsements from colleagues or peers to boost your credibility.

Certifications and Courses

Given how fast the tech industry innovates, you definitely should list fresh certifications or completed courses on your LinkedIn profile. If you haven't taken any courses in a while, I suggest you identify courses or certifications that will increase your marketability and make it a priority to complete them. This will keep your skills fresh.

You can mention certifications, such as AWS Certified Solutions Architect, as well as tech courses from platforms like Coursera, Udemy, or edX that are relevant to the next role you want.

Education

Include degrees and diplomas with details about your field of study and any notable academic achievements. If you're a recent graduate, you can highlight relevant coursework or academic projects.

Volunteer Experience

Volunteering for tech-related causes or mentorship programs can add depth to your profile. It shows leadership, passion, and engagement beyond your job.

Recommendations

Ask for written recommendations from former bosses, colleagues, or clients. These provide social proof of your skills, work ethic, and ability to collaborate.

Publications and Patents

If applicable, showcase any research papers, articles, or patents you've contributed to. This is particularly important if you're in a cutting-edge field like artificial intelligence.

You can showcase your insights on an emerging technology, offer a detailed case study that demonstrates your problem-solving methodologies, or share a personal experience, such as what it is like to be a product manager.[73]

LinkedIn Articles and Posts

Publish thought leadership content or share insights about the tech industry. Writing articles on LinkedIn can boost your visibility as an expert in your field. In particular, executive recruiters look for thought leaders when they are sourcing candidates for open jobs. Recruiters specifically look for content that demonstrates your thought leadership.

"Exploring multimedia formats can elevate content. Incorporating videos for demonstrations or tutorials, along with audio formats like podcasts or interviews, caters to diverse learning preferences within the tech community."[74]

Also, when you see others posting interesting content, you can comment on their post and share your point of view. It is amazing to me how powerful LinkedIn is for helping you gain exposure to potential hiring executives. So, make a regular habit of posting and commenting on others' posts.

---

[73] Adapted from https://blog.get-merit.com/how-to-use-linkedin-a-guide-for-tech-professionals-to-stand-out-and-attract-opportunities/

[74] https://blog.get-merit.com/how-to-use-linkedin-a-guide-for-tech-professionals-to-stand-out-and-attract-opportunities/

Interests and Groups

Follow companies, influencers, and groups relevant to your industry. Engage in tech-related groups to stay updated and contribute to discussions.

There are thousands of LinkedIn Groups, which are private discussion boards you can join. Groups serve multiple purposes.

First, they are an opportunity to participate in a community where you share a common passion. You can comment on posts, keep an eye out for job postings that interest you, etc.

The second purpose is that they expand your LinkedIn network. If you ask to join a Group and they accept you, you are now connected to everyone in that LinkedIn Group, which enables recruiters and hiring executives on LinkedIn to find you more easily. It also broadens your ability to find people who are interesting to you. For example, I belong to Cloud Computing, SaaS, Data Centre & Virtualization, which has over one million users!

Custom URL

Personalize your LinkedIn URL to make it more professional and easier to share. For example, linkedin.com/in/your name. If you don't customize it, LinkedIn assigns a long list of numbers and letters, which isn't user-friendly.

- Go to your LI profile and click on your profile icon. Click on "Edit public profile & URL." Click the pencil icon next to your current URL. Enter your preferred URL: *linkedin.com/in/ your name*. If your first choice is taken, try variations, like adding your middle initial. Click on "Save."

By including the elements above, you can present a comprehensive, appealing, and impactful LinkedIn profile that resonates with potential employers, recruiters, and industry peers.

Whether your current goal is to find a new job, expand your network by making connections, or establish yourself as a thought leader, designing an inviting LinkedIn profile will be a helpful tool for you.

Sample LinkedIn Profile

Below is a LinkedIn profile that embodies many of the best practices listed in this chapter.

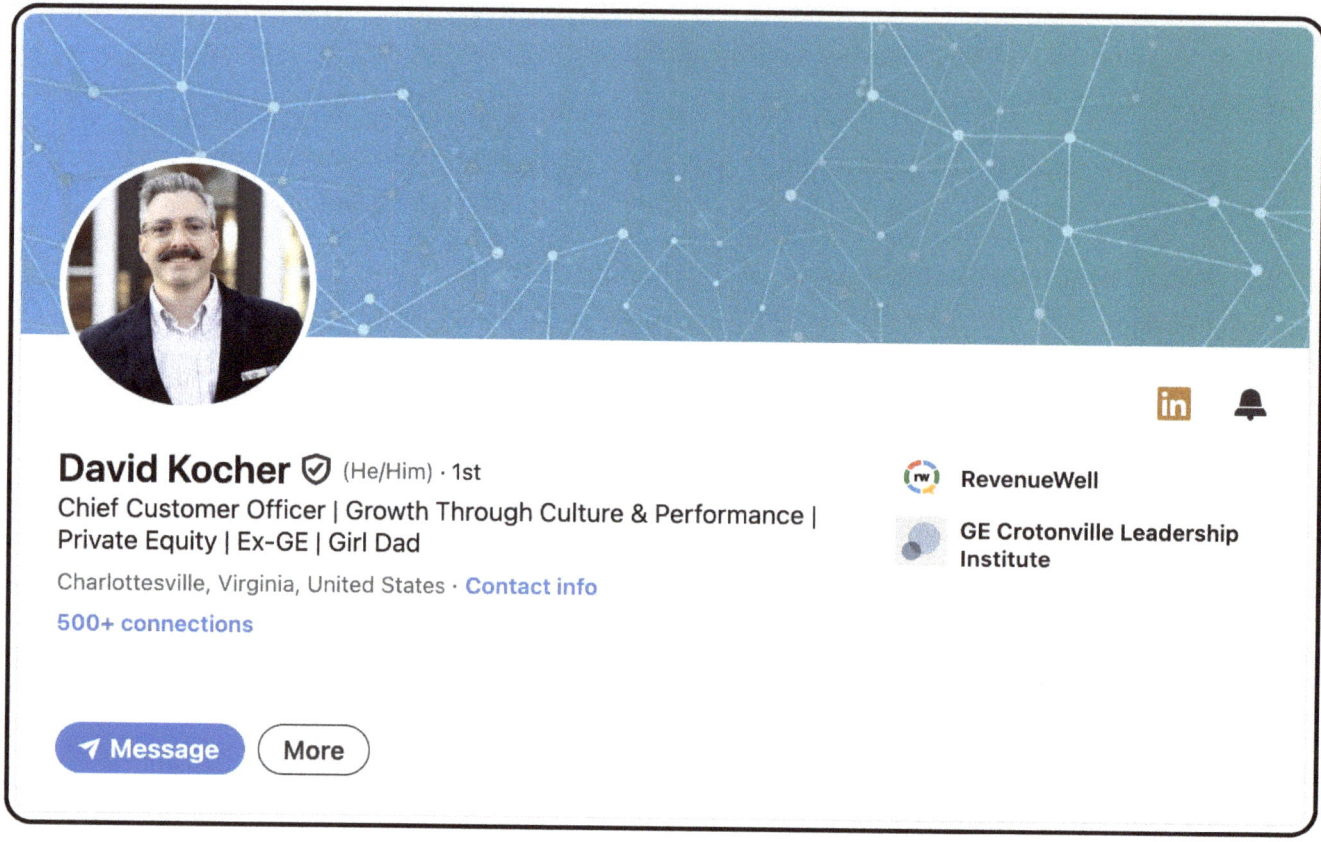

When you first land on David's profile,[75] you quickly learn a lot about who he is. He makes a strong first impression.

- David is currently a chief customer officer.

- He's known for growing revenue by building a strong culture and driving performance.

- He has experience working with private equity firms.

- He worked at GE—a company with a strong brand.

- He shares something personal—that he has a daughter.

That's a lot of insight in a small amount of real estate!

---

[75] Used with permission by David Kocher.

About

I'm a growth-focused technology executive with a passion for building high-performance teams and delivering transformative outcomes for customers and businesses alike. Throughout my 20+ years in technology and services, I've been called upon to solve complex challenges and lead turnaround efforts for businesses that are private start-ups, mid-market private equity backed, and Fortune 10 global entities.

As Chief Customer Officer at RevenueWell, I focus on optimizing the customer experience to increase retention and enable scalable growth. During my first year at the company, we realized a 26% improvement in churn, delivered a 12% reduction in costs, and generated millions in incremental up-sell/cross-sell revenue.

I thrive in environments that demand strategic thinking, data-driven insights, culture building, and a relentless focus on results. My leadership style centers around curiosity, commitment, candor, and collaboration ensuring that everyone is aligned toward a common goal.

As I look toward future leadership opportunities, including CEO roles, my mission is clear—create cultures that foster innovation, drive performance, and lead organizations to their full potential.

Let's connect if you're passionate about transforming companies, growing businesses, or fostering leadership cultures that deliver extraordinary outcomes.

His About section describes the kind of leader he is and the wide variety of experiences he has had. He talks about his current role and the improvements he is making to key KPIs. He describes the environments he thrives in, which shows good self-assessment, and he describes his leadership style.

One of the things I like the best about David's About summary is he talks about his future career goals. So many people are afraid to state their career goals in public. However, making your career goals clear to people can be so helpful in progressing toward those career goals.

David also offers a nice invitation to connect with him to discuss topics he is passionate about.

Fun fact--David told me he leveraged ChatGPT to refine his About paragraph. In your ChatGPT prompt, be sure to tell AI that this is for your LinkedIn profile and you would like to add your personality to it.

Now that we've broken down the component parts of a strong LinkedIn profile and provided an example, let's get to work on optimizing your profile.

Exercise: Your LinkedIn About Section

Below are questions from the Briefcase Coach[76] to help you get started with crafting an interesting summary for the About section of your LinkedIn profile. For now, jot down some notes in each section below:

What is it that you do?

Why do you do what you do?

What are the specialties and skills that set you apart?

What industries have you worked in?

---

[76] https://www.briefcasecoach.com/linkedin-best-practices/

Who is the target audience for what you do, and what do you do for them?

What do you want to do as your career progresses?

Once you have jotted down some answers to the above questions, turn them into sentences you can place in your About section. And then run it through AI to see how it can be refined.

Keeping Your LinkedIn Network Active

How frequently are you engaging on LinkedIn? When was the last time you created a post or commented on someone else's post? We will discuss the importance of this in Chapter 14, where we discuss the importance of networking. So, for now, I'll leave you with a couple of suggestions that are specific to LinkedIn:

- Set a goal to have over five hundred connections on LinkedIn, especially with people who are relevant to the industries you are interested in working in, whether that's tech or tech-adjacent industries. Break this goal into weekly goals (e.g., reach out to twenty people each week and request to connect with them).

- If you have more than five hundred connections on LinkedIn, set a goal to increase your connections by another five hundred people.

- Engage on LinkedIn at least twice a week. You can like others' posts, comment on a post, or congratulate people on their new jobs, anniversaries, or achievements. You can follow industry influencers or thought leaders in your area of expertise. You can reshare compelling content and add your point of view. It only takes a few minutes, and you will be pleasantly surprised by the exposure you will gain on LinkedIn by doing this.

- Create your own content to share on LinkedIn.

Some final thoughts and tips about utilizing LinkedIn:

1. It is a very powerful platform for expanding your network, demonstrating your thought leadership, and increasing your exposure to recruiters and hiring executives in the tech industry as well as in tech-adjacent industries.

2. It is a *professional* social media platform, not a personal social media platform. Your profile pictures and posts should be consistent with this.

3. Have some fun adding your personality to your LinkedIn profile; it can humanize your brand and make it interesting for people to read your profile.

You are moving your way through the career communications documents! Nice job on creating your resume and LinkedIn profile. The last career communication document is the cover letter. Let's delve into this next.

CHAPTER 12

TAILOR COVER LETTERS TO CONNECT WITH HIRING EXECUTIVES

"The difference between ordinary and extraordinary is that little extra."

– Jimmy Johnson

As mentioned earlier in the book, some people skip writing a cover letter because it takes some effort. If you want to be ordinary, don't write a tailored cover letter. However, you will differentiate yourself if you write a tailored cover letter when introducing yourself to a hiring executive, a networking contact, or someone who has agreed to meet with you for an informational interview. The objective of a cover letter is to net it out for the reader. In this context, you are connecting the dots for them about who you are as a professional, the skills, experiences, and strengths you bring to the table, and what you are looking for in your next career move.

Cover letters are typically an email. Or they can be an MS Word document that you upload or copy and paste into a company's career website when you are applying for a position.

When writing a cover letter, it's important to draft a message that highlights your specific strengths, whether that includes technical expertise, customer-facing skills, or leadership experience. Tailor each cover letter to the specific job description. Align your experience and skills with the company's needs. Include terminology from the job description in your cover letter so you can connect the dots for the reader that you have the skills and experience they are looking for.

Tips on Writing Cover Letters:

- Use quantifiable achievements wherever possible (e.g., "Improved system performance by 30%" or "Increased customer retention by 12 points").

- Keep your cover letter concise—aim for around three to four paragraphs and not more than one page.

- Avoid repeating content that is in your resume; instead, expand on key points with more context or insights that are relevant to the position you are applying for.

- Hiring executives want to hire candidates who are enthusiastic about their company and the position, so conduct some research on the company and communicate your passion for the role and the company.

Key Components of a Tailored Cover Letter

Salutation

- Address the letter to a specific person if possible, such as "Dear [First Name]."

- If the hiring executive's name is unavailable, "Dear Hiring Executive" is a good alternative.

Opening Paragraph – Introduction and Purpose

- State the position you are applying for and how you learned about the opportunity.

- Briefly mention what excites you about the role and why you believe you'd be a strong fit for both the position and the company.

Example: "I'm writing to express my interest in the [Job Title] position at [Company Name]. With [X years] of experience in [specific technology or role], I'm excited about the opportunity to contribute to [specific product, team, or project], especially given your company's focus on [relevant mission, technology, or innovation]."

Second Paragraph – Your Skills and Experience

- Highlight your technical skills, customer-facing experience, or leadership competencies, along with achievements that are most relevant to the position. Be specific about the technologies, tools, and frameworks you've worked with and how they align with the job requirements.

- Provide a concrete example of a past project or accomplishment that demonstrates the skills they are looking for.

Example: "In my previous role as a software engineer at [Previous Company], I led a project that reduced data processing time by 40% using [specific technology, e.g., Spark and Hadoop]. My expertise in [specific programming languages, frameworks, etc.] allows me to efficiently build scalable solutions that address complex challenges."

Third Paragraph – Why You're a Fit for the Role and Company

- Explain why you're drawn to this company in particular. Do some research on its mission, products, culture, or recent achievements and connect them with your personal values or professional goals.

- Illustrate how your unique combination of skills and experience will help the company achieve its goals. This is also a good place to mention any cultural fit (e.g., if you thrive in collaborative, innovative environments).

Example: "I'm particularly excited about [Company Name]'s innovative approach to [industry or technology], and I believe my experience in [specific area] will contribute to [company initiative or goal]. I'm passionate about working in agile teams that drive continuous improvement, and I'm eager to bring my skills in [specific expertise] to your growing engineering team."

Fourth Paragraph – Closing and Call to Action

- Express your enthusiasm for the next steps and your availability for an interview.

- Thank the hiring executive for considering your application and reiterate your interest in the role.

Example: "I would welcome the opportunity to discuss how my skills and experiences align with the needs of your team. I am available at your convenience for an interview and can be reached at [your phone number] or [your email]. Thank you for your time and consideration, and I look forward to the possibility of contributing to [Company Name]."

Closing

- Use a professional closing, such as:
  - "Sincerely,"
  - "Best regards,"
  - "Thank you,"

- Follow with your name, email, and phone number.

By addressing the hiring executive directly and focusing on your relevant skills, experience, and the value you can bring, your cover letter can make a strong impression and improve your chances of getting an interview.

Below are samples of cover letters.

Sample Cover Letter When Applying for a Specific Position

Dear [Hiring Executive's Name],

I am writing to express my enthusiasm for the Director of Customer Success position at [Company Name]. With 15 years of experience in Customer Success, I am confident my proven track record of driving customer retention and my alignment with your customer-first values would allow me to make a meaningful impact. I am particularly excited about the investments your company is making in artificial intelligence, as I believe AI will play a crucial role in enhancing customer experiences and improving success outcomes.

Throughout my career, I have been committed to fostering strong relationships with customers, improving retention, and driving long-term satisfaction. In my most recent role, I led initiatives that increased customer retention by 15 points over an 18-month period. Additionally, I've had the opportunity to share my insights as a speaker at leading conferences, including TSIA and Gainsight, where I've discussed best practices in customer success, AI-driven strategies, and creating scalable success teams.

I am impressed by [Company Name]'s dedication to innovation and customer-centricity. The values your team holds mirror my own approach to Customer Success—always putting the customer at the heart of every decision. I am confident that my ability to lead high-performing teams, coupled with my strategic use of AI tools to optimize the customer experience, would contribute significantly to your organization's goals.

I would welcome the opportunity to discuss how my skills and experience align with the needs of your team. I am available for an interview at your earliest convenience and can be reached at [your phone number] or [your email]. Thank you for considering my application. I look forward to the possibility of contributing to [Company Name]'s continued success.

Sincerely,

[Your Name]
[Email]
[Phone number]

This cover letter highlights the candidate's qualifications, excitement about the company, and alignment with its values while inviting further conversation through an interview.

Sample Cover Letter to a Person Who Has Agreed to an Informational Interview with You

Dear [Executive's Name],

I want to sincerely thank you for taking the time to meet with me for an informational interview. I appreciate your willingness to share insights about your experience and career trajectory, particularly as it relates to the Director of Customer Success role—a position I aspire to step into as my next career move.

With 15 years of experience in Customer Success, I've had the privilege of leading initiatives that have significantly impacted customer outcomes, including improving customer retention by 15 points over an 18-month period. I've also been fortunate to share best practices and industry trends as a speaker at conferences, like TSIA and Gainsight. As I look toward advancing into a director-level role, I'm eager to learn more about the strategic responsibilities, leadership challenges, and broader impact Customer Success can have on organizational growth.

Your guidance will be invaluable as I refine my career path and continue developing the skills needed to excel in this role. I look forward to having a conversation and gaining insights from your expertise. Thank you again for your time and consideration, and I'm excited about the opportunity to learn from your experiences.

Sincerely,

[Your Name]
[Email]
[Phone number]

This cover letter expresses gratitude, outlines relevant experience, and highlights the candidate's eagerness to learn from the executive during the informational interview.

Sample Cover Letter When Reaching Out to Someone in Your Network to Ask for a Phone Call

Dear [Recipient's Name],

I hope this message finds you well. I'm reaching out because I'm currently exploring opportunities to transition into a Director of Customer Success role, and I believe your insights and guidance would be invaluable as I navigate the next steps in my career.

With 15 years of experience in Customer Success, I've had the opportunity to drive significant improvements in customer outcomes, including increasing retention by 15 points over 18 months. Additionally, I've spoken at industry-leading conferences, like TSIA and Gainsight, where I've shared strategies for scaling customer success efforts and leveraging technology to improve retention and satisfaction.

Given your background and expertise, I would love the chance to schedule a call with you to discuss my career goals and gain your perspective on the current landscape for director-level roles in Customer Success. I greatly appreciate any advice or suggestions you may have.

Please let me know if you'd be open to a quick conversation. I am happy to work around your schedule and can be flexible with timing.

Thank you so much for your consideration—I look forward to the possibility of connecting!

Best regards,

[Your Name]
[Email]
[Phone number]

This cover letter is professional, concise, and respectful of the recipient's time while clearly outlining your request for a call to discuss career goals.

Exercise: Create the Building Blocks of Your Cover Letter When Applying for a Specific Position

This exercise will help you get started with your cover letter by creating the building blocks articulated earlier in this chapter. Once you start writing a couple of the components, I think you will find it comes together pretty quickly!

Introduction and Purpose: State the position you're applying for and how you learned about it. Briefly mention what excites you about the role and why you believe you'd be a strong fit.

Your Skills and Experience: Highlight your skills; include relevant achievements; be specific about technologies, tools, and frameworks; and provide a concrete example of a past project or accomplishment.

Why You're a Fit for the Role and Company: Explain why you're drawn to this company; what the company's mission, products, culture, or recent achievements are; connect these with your personal values or professional goals; and illustrate how your unique combination of skills and experience will help the company achieve its goals.

Closing and Call to Action: Express your enthusiasm for the next steps and your availability for an interview; thank the hiring executive for considering your application; reiterate your interest.

Now that you have jotted down some notes in each of the categories above, start drafting your first cover letter by turning your notes into sentences.

You will find that you can reuse your cover letter by changing just a few items to tailor it to your specific reader. This process can be efficient (not take much time) and can result in a cover letter that is customized to the reader.

That covers the third and final career communication document, tailored cover letters.

Now that you have a resume that reflects your personal brand, a LinkedIn profile that shows your personality, and cover letter templates in hand, you are ready to execute your job search.

PHASE 5
JOB SEARCH EXECUTION

Congratulations on completing Phases 1 through 4! The work you have done in the earlier chapters of this book will serve you well in Phase 5.

In this final phase, we will pull forward all of your good work and your decisions to execute your job search. At this point in the process, you should have:

- A clear goal for your next career move in terms of the industries and roles you will be targeting

- A well-crafted resume that communicates what makes you unique

- A LinkedIn profile that is interesting for readers to read

- A templated cover letter that is ready to be tailored for specific positions you will be applying to

With your prework completed, I hope you feel a greater degree of confidence and eagerness to take the next steps.

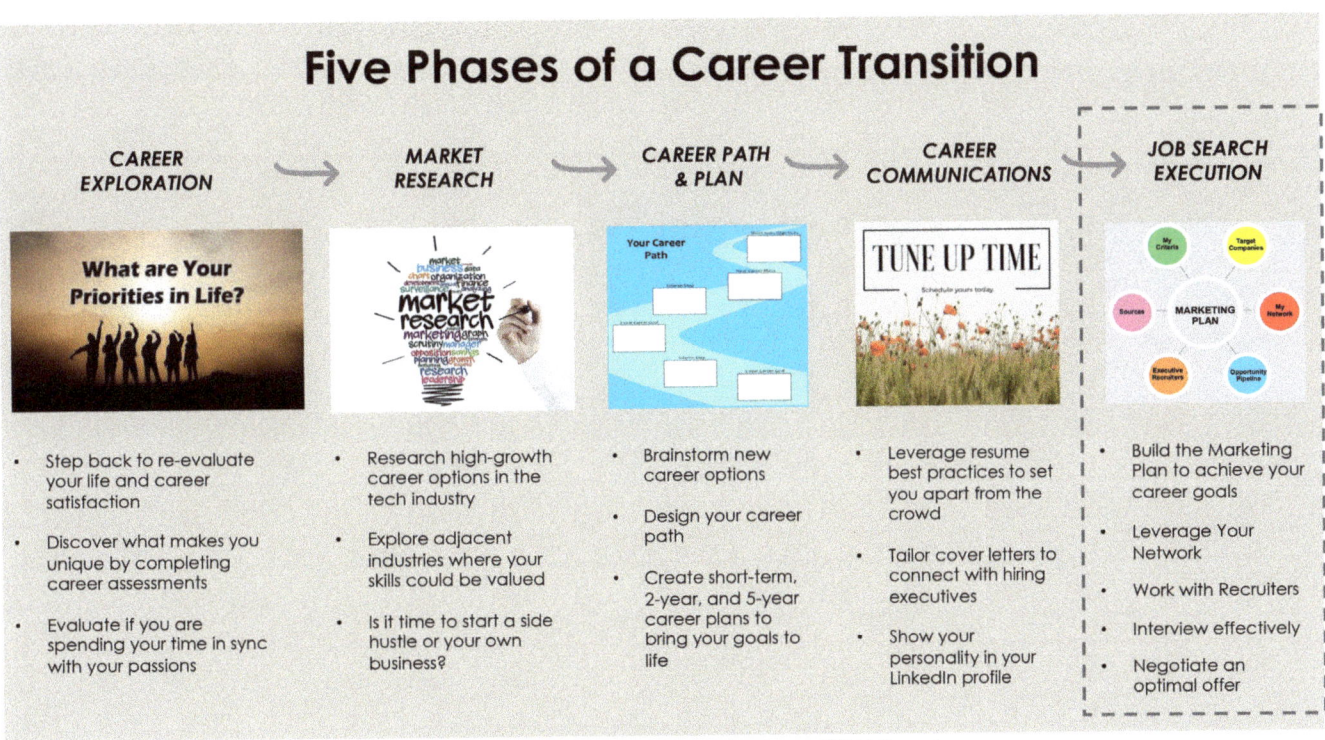

Executing your job search will require an investment of your time. I suggest you schedule blocks of time on your calendar so you can create momentum with your job search. For example, if you are currently working, schedule one-hour time blocks two or three days a week. It could be during your lunch break, at night, or on weekends. If you left or lost your job, I encourage you to spend five to six hours every day on your job search—your job is to find your next job.

In Phase 5, we will cover:

- Building and executing the marketing plan

- Leveraging your network

- Working with executive recruiters and in-house recruiters

- Interviewing effectively

- Negotiating offers and making a graceful exit

In the next chapter, we'll start with building and executing the marketing plan.

CHAPTER 13

THE MARKETING PLAN

"To be in business today, our most important job is to be head marketer for the brand called You."

– Tom Peters

When crafting a marketing plan for your job search, you're essentially marketing yourself to potential employers. The process resembles a sales and marketing process for a high-value product.

I recommend you utilize a spreadsheet to stay organized. House all the elements of your marketing plan in the spreadsheet and track the progress of your activities and career opportunities. You can download the marketing plan template via the URL at the beginning of this book. Below are the key components to include in your marketing plan. There is a tab in the marketing plan spreadsheet template for each of these key components:

- My criteria

- Companies to explore

- Sources of opportunities

- My network

- Executive recruiters

- Pipeline of opportunities

Your Criteria for Your Next Career Move

The first tab of your spreadsheet is My Criteria, which includes your criteria for your next career move.

You did good work earlier in this book when you thought through what is currently working for you and what is not. You have documented where the gaps in life and career satisfaction are, and you have crafted your career path. Let's bring those insights to this section and define the key criteria that will provide more meaning in your next career move.

Start by listing your criteria for each of the categories, then mark with an X if this criterion is nonnegotiable. If you are actively employed, you might have more nonnegotiables.

If you are currently in transition and need to find your next role sooner versus later, you might want to have fewer nonnegotiables. You can also consider taking a bridge position to get cash flowing in while you continue to evaluate other career options that check more of the boxes on your criteria list.

Reference the Putting It All Together summary as well as the career path you created in Chapter 8 to complete many of the criteria on the first tab.

MARKETING PLAN TAB: MY CRITERIA

YOUR CRITERIA FOR YOUR NEXT CAREER MOVE:

Borders

CATEGORY:	YOUR CRITERIA:	NON-NEGOTIABLE
Current Location:		
Geographic Locations You are Open to:		
Remote, In-Office, or Hybrid:		
Travel Percentage:		
Top Gaps in Work Life Balance to Satisfy:		
Your Industry Experience:		
Preferred Industries or Sectors:		
Preferred Technology Solutions:		
Size of Company:		
Exclude Industries or Companies:		
Culture Where You Thrive:		
Top 3 Gaps to Satisfy from Life Satisfaction Wheel:		
Top 3 Gaps to Satisfy from Career Satisfaction Wheel:		
Base Salary Range:		
Incentive Pay Range:		
Equity Range:		
Medical Benefits, 401K, Education Reimbursement, etc.		
Title #1:		
Title #2:		
Title #3:		

Location:

Document your current location (in case you share your marketing plan with a mentor, career coach, etc.).

What locations are you open to?

Work-Life Balance

In terms of work-life balance, do you prefer working from home 100 percent, working in the employer's office 100 percent, or a mix of the two (hybrid)? What percentage of time are you willing to travel? In the Putting It All Together summary, you noted any concerns about work-life balance. List those gaps in your work-life balance priorities here to keep them front and center.

Industries and Technology Solutions

Which industries have you worked in? And, if you work with customers, which industries are you familiar with based on the industries your customers are in? Industry experience is highly valued by employers because they're looking for employees who understand how the business models work, what KPIs are important, the industry terminology, etc.

From the Putting It All Together summary, list which industries you are open to exploring (tech or some of the tech-adjacent industries—be specific). Document these under your preferred industries.

Do you have preferred technology solutions? For example, if you like working with customers in sales and marketing roles, CRM and marketing automation might be interesting to you. However, working with very technical IT leaders may not be your strong suit.

Size of Company

What size company are you interested in working for? Startup, small, midsize, or large? Some people use revenue to classify a company's size while others use the number of employees.

Startups are often classified based on their annual revenue as a way to gauge their growth stage, funding needs, and market maturity. While classifications may vary depending on the source or industry, common classifications based on annual revenue include:

- **Pre-Revenue or Seed Stage**: Startups in this stage have not yet generated any significant revenue. They are typically focused on developing their product or service, building a customer base, and securing initial funding from investors, such as angel investors or venture capitalists. Depending on how much funding they have, these companies can be considered high risk since they have not typically achieved product-market fit. However, the equity component should be high since you are getting in on the ground floor. I see people take roles in these companies when they have already been successful in another startup or large corporation and have a financial cushion in case the company fails.

- **Early-Stage or Early Revenue**: Startups in this stage have begun generating some revenue, but it may not be consistent or substantial. They are still in the early growth phases and may be refining their business model, expanding their customer base, and seeking additional funding to scale operations. Some companies in this category have acquired Series A funding, which is typically larger than seed round and is often led by an institutional venture capital firm. The funding is used to fuel growth, expand the team, and invest in sales and marketing efforts to capture market share. Be sure to understand the company's current funding and how long it can sustain the operation.

- **Growth Stage**: Startups in the growth stage have achieved consistent revenue growth and are scaling their operations. They may have established a solid customer base, proven their product-market fit, and are focused on expanding into new markets or product lines. Revenue levels vary widely but typically range from several hundred thousand to several million dollars annually. Startups in this category might raise Series B funding.

- **Mature Stage**: Startups that have reached a mature stage have achieved significant revenue and market traction. They have a well-established business model and a large customer base, and they are generating substantial annual revenue, often in the tens of millions or even hundreds of millions of dollars. These companies may acquire additional rounds of funding, referred to as Series C and beyond, or they might be profitable and don't require additional funding rounds. These companies have built a foundation that could contribute to a higher success rate. The tradeoff is that equity might be less attractive for people who enter the company at this stage versus entering the company at an earlier stage.

In the technology industry, midsize companies typically have employee counts ranging from fifty to several thousand employees and annual revenue from several million to hundreds of millions of dollars. When it comes to midsize companies with hundreds of millions in revenue, many of these midsize companies have a goal to become a billion-dollar company, in terms of annual revenue.

Large companies in the technology industry tend to employ thousands to hundreds of thousands of employees and have billions to hundreds of billions of dollars in annual revenue.

Companies to Exclude

Next, ask yourself if there are any companies or industries you wish to exclude from your job search.

Culture and Gaps in Life Priorities and Career Priorities

When I was an executive recruiter, the majority of candidates I talked with mentioned how important culture is. If culture is important to you, list some elements of culture that you can test against once you are in interviews with a prospective employer. Reviewing your top five values from the Putting It All Together summary will provide clues for culture preferences as well.

Review the top three gaps from the Life Satisfaction Wheel and the Career Satisfaction Wheel that you placed in the Putting It All Together summary. Note them here so you can evaluate opportunities against these gaps. Closing these gaps can increase the meaningfulness and fulfillment you find in your next role.

Compensation

Compensation is always a factor, so note a range for the base salary, a range for incentive compensation, and a range for equity that would help you achieve your monetary goals. Also note what you are looking for with respect to medical benefits, 401(k) employer contributions, education reimbursement, etc. Evaluating an opportunity based on the full package is important.

Titles

From the work you did on your career path and career action plans, write down three titles that satisfy your career goal for your next career move. Consider that this role in a startup could be an executive vice president, but the role might be a director in a very large company. Titles are important to some people, which is completely fine. But be careful about walking away from an interesting role because the title doesn't suit you. If you stay in an interview process long enough and learn more about the company and the role, you might change your mind. Or you might be able to negotiate an upgrade in the title if you are the top candidate.

Here's a sample of the My Criteria tab.

MARKETING PLAN TAB: MY CRITERIA SAMPLE

YOUR CRITERIA FOR YOUR NEXT ROLE

CATEGORY:	YOUR CRITERIA:	NON-NEGOTIABLE
Current Location:	Boise, ID	X
Geographic Locations You are Open to:	Boise, ID	
Remote, In-Office, or Hybrid:	Hybrid	X
Travel Percentage:	30%	
Top Gaps in Work Life Balance to Satisfy:	Too much weekend work; cap needs to be 2 hrs on weekend	X
Your Industry Experience:	Software companies	
Preferred Industries or Sectors:	Software, Industrial Automation, EdTech	
Preferred Technology Solutions:	CRM and Marketing Automation, Education platforms. Software business unit in Industrial Automation company.	
Size of Company:	Midsize who wants to scale to $1 billion in revenue	
Exclude Industries or Companies:	Telecommunications	
Culture Where You Thrive:	Transparency in communication from senior executives; focus is on customers and growth; low internal politics	X
Top 3 Gaps to Satisfy from Life Satisfaction Wheel:	Health: need consistent exercise schedule. Friends: less weekend work, spend more time with friends. Finances: need higher base salary.	X
Top 3 Gaps to Satisfy from Career Satisfaction Wheel:	My Boss: someone who will appreciate my contributions. Professional Development: a role where I can expand my core competencies into AI. Meaning & Purpose: a company that I can get behind because the work they do is impactful.	X
Base Salary Goal:	$250,000 to $300,000	X
Incentive Pay:	20%	
Equity:	$100,000	
Medical Benefits, 401K, Education Reimbursement, etc.	401K employer match, good medical for family	X
Title #1:	Senior Vice President, Customer Success (mid size)	
Title #2:	Chief Customer Officer (smaller company)	
Title #3:	Chief Experience Officer (smaller company)	

Companies to Explore

There are many ways to identify interesting companies. It takes some time to review lists and identify companies that look interesting to you on the surface. Below are free sources of information:

- Computer Reseller News (CRN.com) has many helpful lists. Go to CRN.com and click on "Awards & Lists." Examples include:
  - Fast Growth 150
  - Cloud 100
  - Big Data 100
  - AI 100

- Deloitte publishes the Technology Fast 500 company list every year. You can find it via an internet search.

- TSIA conducts a quarterly webinar called the T&S 50, in which they provide information on the financial health of technology companies. You can register for their next public webinar via their website, tsia.com

- Leverage ChatGPT to identify high-growth companies that focus on specific technology platforms or any other criteria you wish to use. For example:

   - "Please provide a list of midsize high-growth companies in the technology industry that have heavily invested in artificial intelligence."

Also, add to the spreadsheet the tech-adjacent companies you identified in Chapter 6.

MARKETING PLAN TAB: COMPANIES TO EXPLORE

COMPANIES TO EXPLORE:

	INDUSTRY:	COMPANY:
1		
2		
3		
4		
5		
6		
7		
8		
9		
10		

Companies Explored and Removed from Consideration:

1. Review the lists of companies and add ten companies that interest you to the Companies to Explore tab and note which industry they are in.

2. Every week, after spending time exploring each company, decide on the status of each company:

   - If you aren't interested in the company, move it to the area below 'Companies Explored and Removed from Consideration' so you don't research the company more than once.

   - If you are interested in the company, move the company to the Pipeline of Opportunities tab and place it in the Top 10 Target Companies list.

3. Maintain a rolling list of ten companies to explore. Every week, as you remove companies or move companies from this list (Companies to Explore tab) into your pipeline (Pipeline of Opportunities tab), add new companies to explore so you have a continuous, rolling list of ten companies on the Companies To Explore tab.

Below is a sample of the Companies to Explore tab.

MARKETING PLAN TAB: COMPANIES TO EXPLORE SAMPLE

COMPANIES TO EXPLORE (SAMPLE):

	INDUSTRY:	COMPANY:
1	Industrial Automation	Rockwell Automation
2	Services	Accenture
3	EdTech	Coursera
4	AgTech	Bowery Farming
5	Healthcare IT	Olive
6	Software	Microsoft
7	Software	Freshworks
8	Hardware	Oura
9	Automotive	Ford Motor Company
10	Medical Device	Tempus

Companies Explored and Removed from Consideration:
IBM
Google Cloud

Sources of Opportunities

New career opportunities can come through many sources. So, the next tab is Sources of Opportunities. Here you will document a variety of sources where you could find possible career opportunities.

MARKETING PLAN TAB: SOURCES OF OPPORTUNITIES

SOURCES OF OPPORTUNITIES:

X	NETWORK:	Date:	LINKEDIN GROUPS:	Date:	JOB POSTING SITES:
	Former Colleagues		Professional Group #1		LinkedIn
	Former Bosses		Professional Group #2		Indeed
	Former Professors		Professional Group #3		Glassdoor
	Mentors		Professional Group #4		LinkUp (aggregates employer job postings)
	Friends		Professional Group #5		ZipRecruiter
	People You Have Met at Association Conferences/Workshops, etc.		Professional Group #6		CareerBuilder
	Anyone Else Who Can Potentially Make an Introduction For You		Professional Group #7		Monster
	Neighbors		Professional Group #8		JobCase
	Church Members		Professional Group #9		JustJobs
	People at the Gym		Professional Group #10		
	Family				
	School Classmates				
	Frieds of Friends				
	Industry Leaders				

- **Network**: Here is a list of potential sources of people in your network who might be helpful and provide a lead for your next career opportunity. Add any other sources that you should reach out to.

- **LinkedIn Groups**: Identify LinkedIn Groups where professionals in your field spend time.
  - Type in "Groups" in the LinkedIn main search and start exploring groups; ask the administrator to add you to the group. For example, there are 177,000 members in the Software-as-a-Service group. By connecting with this group, you connect with all 177,000 members. Being added to Groups can expand your LinkedIn network very quickly.

- **Job Posting Sites**: Spend time each week on various job posting sites since employers use a variety of job posting sites to post their open positions. LinkedIn is a must, and you can pick several other posting sites to see if positions you are interested in are posted there. You can also set up job alerts on the job posting sites so they send you new postings for titles you are interested in.

Keeping Track

As you engage with each category of people in your network, you can mark them off. Ensure to revisit the networking list occasionally to see if other people come to mind.

For LinkedIn Groups and job posting sites, note the last date you engaged so you know when to reengage. You should spend ongoing time in Groups and job posting sites.

Below is a sample of the Sources of Opportunities tab.

MARKETING PLAN TAB: SOURCES OF OPPORTUNITIES SAMPLE

SOURCES OF OPPORTUNITIES (SAMPLE):

X	NETWORK:	Date:	LINKEDIN GROUPS:	Date:	JOB POSTING SITES:
X	Former Colleagues	7/20/24	Customer Success	7/20/24	LinkedIn
X	Former Bosses	7/24/24	Revenue Operations (RevOps)	7/24/24	Indeed
	Former Professors	8/1/24	Association of Support Professionals	8/1/24	Glassdoor
X	Professional Mentors		Product Management		LinkUp (aggregates employer job postings)
	Friends	7/21/24	Women in Tech – TSIA	7/21/24	ZipRecruiter
	Associations	8/2/24	The Customer Success Forum	8/2/24	CareerBuilder
			On Startups – The Community for Entrepreneurs	7/2/24	Monster
		7/23/24	Generative AI Innovations and the human Experience		JobCase
		7/1/24	Technology Sales and Marketing Professional – Los Angeles and SOCAL	8/1/24	JustJobs
		7/5/24	Customer Experience Professionals		
			Cloud Computing		
		7/13/24	Professional Services Executive Forum		

Tapping Your Network

Let's specifically add detail now in terms of your network.

Begin by creating a list of all the people you know from various aspects of your life. These people might be helpful in providing leads for new opportunities for you, or they may know someone who could provide a lead. Don't limit the list to people who are in the industry you are targeting. You never know who they might know until you ask! Don't be shy.

MARKETING PLAN TAB: MY NETWORK

PERSON:	COMPANY:	CONTACT INFO: (phone & email)	HOW I KNOW THEM:	ACTIVITY #1:
1				
2				
3				
4				
5				
6				
7				
8				
9				
10				
11				
12				
13				
14				
15				
16				
17				
18				
19				
20				

People in your network could be:

- Former colleagues

- Former bosses

- Professors

- Mentors

- Friends

- Neighbors

- Church members

- People at the gym

- Family

- School classmates

- Friends of friends

- Industry leaders

- People you met at a professional association conference or workshop

- Anyone else who could potentially make an introduction for you

List each person, where they work, their contact info, and how you know them, then document each activity where you have engaged with them. See sample below.

MARKETING PLAN TAB: MY NETWORK SAMPLE

MY NETWORK (SAMPLE – all data is fictitious):

	PERSON:	TITLE:	COMPANY:	CONTACT INFO: (phone & email)	HOW I KNOW THEM:	ACTIVITY #1:
1	John Smith	VP Customer Experience	Microsoft	xxx xxx-xxxx; email	Former Boss	7/20/24: Sent LI msg asking for 15 min phone call
2	Joan Jones	Professor	University of St Paul	xxx xxx-xxxx; email	Professor from Graduate School	7/25/24: Sent email asking for 15 min phone call
3	Sally Superior	VP Customer Success	Proteus Digital Health	xxx xxx-xxxx; email	Former Colleague	7/25/24: Sent email asking for 15 min phone call
4	Julie Jones	Chief Operating Officer	Bowering Farming	xxx xxx-xxxx; email	Former Colleague	7/22/24: Sent LI msg asking for 15 min call to discuss vertical farming
5	Sandy Stapleton	Product Manager	Coursera	xxx xxx-xxxx; email	Neighbor	7/21/24: Chatted about EdTech industry.
6	Tanya Toledo	Chief Customer Officer	Rockwell Automation	xxx xxx-xxxx; email	Friend	7/20/24: Sent LI msg asking for 15 min call to discuss open position posted
7	Tom Tucker	Chief Product Officer	Tempus	xxx xxx-xxxx; email	Mentor	7/22/24: Called to discuss growth prospects in medical device industry
8	Dan Dime	Director Customer Success	Ford Motor Company	xxx xxx-xxxx; email	Uncle / Family	7/30/24: Called to discuss opening in Ford's software business unit
9	Steve Steiker	Management Consultant	Accenture	xxx xxx-xxxx; email	Classmate from Graduate School	8/1/24: Scheduled lunch to discuss management consulting industry
10	Sam Silor	Director of Sales	Freshworks	xxx xxx-xxxx; email	Friend of a Friend	7/20/24: Sent LI msg asking for 15 min call to discuss open position posted
11	Jane Jilly	VP Marketing	Oura	xxx xxx-xxxx; email	Industry Thought Leader	7/28/24: Reached out based on LI post & her industry expertise
12	Jean Johest	Director Marketing	Nuraphone	xxx xxx-xxxx; email	Met at Business Conference	7/25/24: Called to request 15 min call to discuss culture at Nuraphone

Executive Recruiters

Another group of people you should engage with are executive recruiters, otherwise known as headhunters.

Work with as many executive recruiters as possible since they all work with different clients and conduct different talent searches. Many recruiters specialize in certain types of roles, such as sales or technical roles.

Submit your information and resume via their website, which will place you into their database. I've had calls from recruiting firms years after my information was initially placed into their database. And reach out to them directly via email or LinkedIn to introduce yourself.

You can identify specific executive recruiters' names via company websites or conduct searches on LinkedIn and the internet to find recruiters in your specialty area. See Chapter 15 for more tips on working with executive recruiters.

MARKETING PLAN TEMPLATE: EXECUTIVE RECRUITERS

	RECRUITING AGENCY:	WEBSITE:	CONTACT:	TITLE:	RECRUITING SPECIALITY AREAS:	EMAIL:
EXECUTIVE RECRUITERS:						
1	20/20 Foresight Executive Search	https://2020-4.com/				
2	Amrop	https://www.amrop.com/				
3	Barbachano International	https://www.bipsearch.com/				
4	B. Brownson & Associates, L.P.	https://www.brownson.com/index.html				
5	BlueSteps	www.bluesteps.com				
6	Bonell Ryan	https://bonellryan.com/	John-Stuart Fauquet	VP & Senior Associate	FinTech, Payments, & SaaS	JSFauquet@bonellryan.com
7	Boyden	https://www.boyden.com/				
8	Caldwell Partners	https://www.caldwell.com/	Gina Barge	Consultant		gbarge@caldwellpartners.com
9	COIT Group	https://coitgroup.com/	Joe Belluomini	CEO		joe@coitgroup.com

Pipeline of Opportunities

As you start identifying career possibilities, list them in your pipeline. These potential career opportunities could be:

- Posted positions you have applied to

- Possible opportunities you are discussing with someone in your network

- Possible opportunities you are trying to cultivate with interesting companies on your top-ten list

Color code the status of each opportunity:

- Green = activity is underway

- Yellow = conversations have just begun or have stalled

- Red = opportunities which have not progressed in four weeks (move these below to the Closed Opportunities area)

MARKETING PLAN TAB: PIPELINE OF OPPORTUNITIES

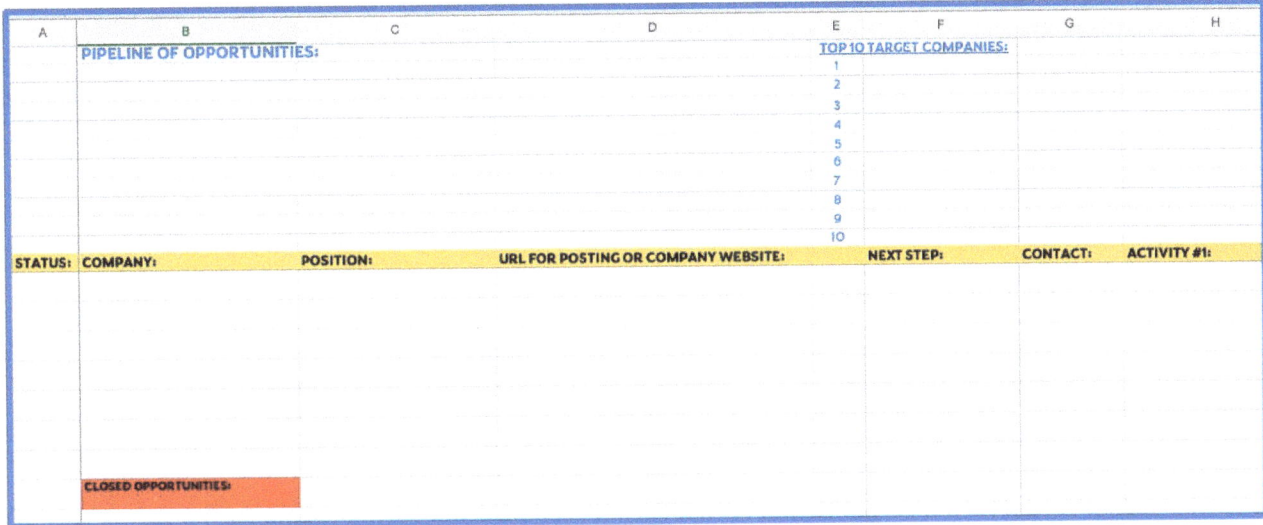

Continuously maintain a list of the top ten target companies to engage with to try to develop opportunities.

- You could reach out for an informational interview from a current executive or former executive for companies you are interested in.

- Or you can reach out to someone in your network who works there or used to work there.

Ensure that each green- and yellow-coded opportunity has a documented next step.

Track your job search activities and results. Monitor your progress, including the number of applications submitted, interviews attended, and networking connections made. Evaluate the effectiveness of your marketing efforts and adjust your strategy as needed to optimize your chances of success. See sample below.

MARKETING PLAN TAB: PIPELINE OF OPPORTUNITIES SAMPLE

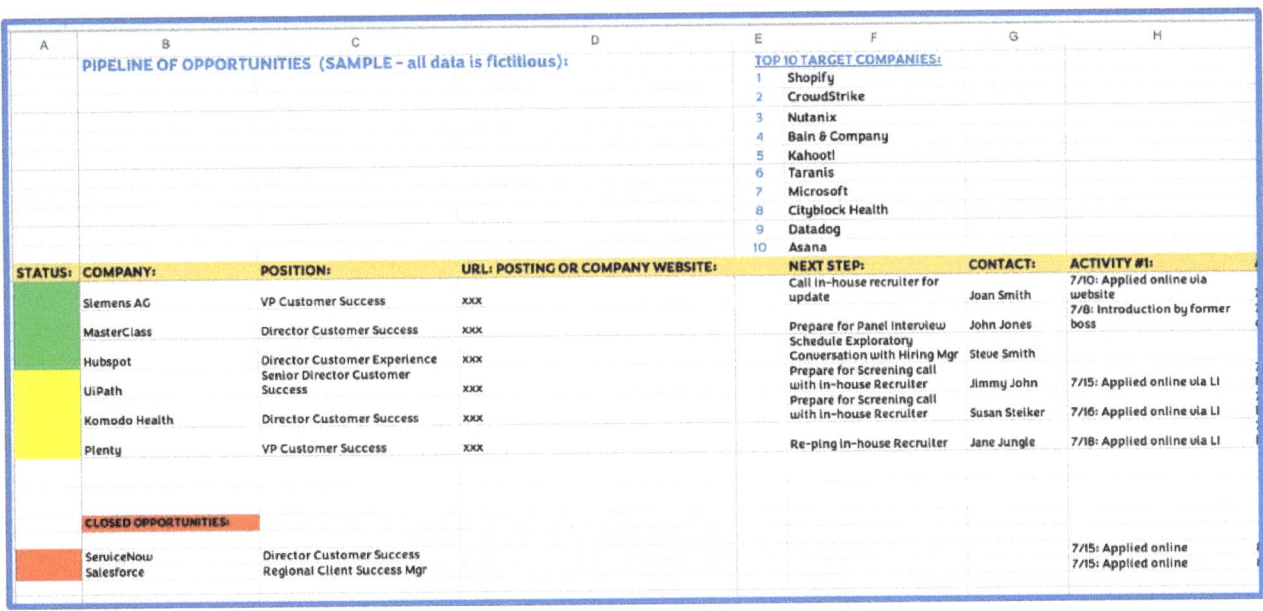

Stay agile and adaptable in your job search approach. Continuously seek feedback, learn from your experiences, and refine your strategy based on insights gained along the way. Stay proactive and persistent in pursuing your career goals.

By incorporating these components into your job search marketing plan, you can effectively market yourself to potential employers, differentiate yourself from other candidates, and maximize your chances of securing your next job opportunity.

In the next chapter, we will dig deeper into the importance of building and leveraging your network.

CHAPTER 14

NETWORKING

"Succeeding in business is all about making connections."

– Richard Branson

The word *networking* has developed a negative connotation over the years. Some people associate networking with being similar to a used car salesperson. So, let's reframe what effective networking is.

Professional networking refers to the process of establishing and maintaining relationships with other professionals in your field or related industries. It involves building connections with people who can provide valuable insights, advice, support, or opportunities for career advancement.

Networking is a critical component of any job search marketing plan. Positions not posted on job posting sites (hidden job opportunities) can be uncovered through your network. You should build and nurture relationships with other professionals via:

- Participating in or speaking at industry associations and conferences

- Attending networking events or social gatherings

- Engaging with alumni networks, online professional communities, and social media

- Attending seminars

- Participating in a mentoring program

By implementing best practices from this chapter, you will have the confidence to:

- Build or expand your network

- Leverage your network to ask for introductions

- Ask executives of interesting companies for an informational interview

Three Principles of Effective Networking

The first principle of effective networking is: *You should build a network before you need it.*

If your network is not where it should be, start *today* to improve the quality and size of your professional network. Your network can be your safety net when it's time to pivot to a new position, especially in a challenging labor market.

The good news is that networking is widely practiced in the tech industry, so you will find many people who enjoy engaging with others and would be willing to talk with you.

If you are actively working, I recommend setting a goal of meeting at least five new people every month. A good rule of thumb is to connect at least twice a year with each person in your existing network.

If you are actively seeking your next career opportunity, set a goal of meeting at least two people a day.

The second principle of networking is: *It's not about you. It's about the other person.*

When I was in graduate school at Chapman University, we had an evening when business leaders from local companies came to the university, and we networked with them. I asked an owner of a successful business what the key to effective networking is, and he told me, "Networking should be about what you can give, not what you can take." That had a lasting impact on me. The best networking approach, both for you and the people you want to talk with, is to just *be curious*. Ask yourself, "What interesting people can I meet today? What can we learn from each other? How can I support and encourage them?" I ask you: Who doesn't need a little more affirmation in their life?

If you genuinely engage with others and want the best for them, you shouldn't hesitate to ask them for help when you need it.

The third principle of networking is: *Be authentic.*

Authenticity is key to building trust and rapport with others. Be yourself. To help you feel more comfortable, you can consider preparing a list of questions to start conversations with. I provide sample questions later in this chapter that you can tailor for various networking opportunities.

How to Become an Effective Networker

Becoming an effective professional networker involves both planning and relationship-building skills. Effective networking is natural. Here are some steps you can take to improve your networking abilities:

- **Set clear goals**: Determine what you want to achieve through networking, whether it's gaining industry insights, uncovering leads for a new career opportunity, or expanding your customer base. Having specific goals will guide your networking efforts.

- **Identify your target audience**: Identify the individuals or groups you want to connect with based on your goals. This could include professionals in your industry, potential mentors, colleagues, customers, or experts in related fields. Find people who will strengthen your network.

- **Be approachable and engaging**: Approach networking with a positive attitude and genuine interest in others. Be open to initiating conversations, listening attentively, and asking insightful questions. Show empathy, respect, and enthusiasm when interacting with others.

- **Perfect your elevator pitch**: Prepare a concise and compelling introduction that highlights your skills, experiences, and goals. The good work you did in Chapter 10 will serve you well. The top paragraph of your resume serves as your elevator pitch. Practice delivering your elevator pitch in a clear and confident manner. Make it easy for others to understand what you do and how you can add value.

- **Follow up**: After meeting someone new, follow up promptly to express gratitude for the conversation and reinforce your interest in staying connected. Send a personalized message, connect on LinkedIn, or schedule a follow-up meeting to continue the conversation.

- **Provide value**: Offer help, support, or resources to your network contacts whenever possible. Share relevant information, make introductions, offer assistance, or provide insights that demonstrate your expertise and willingness to contribute.

- **Maintain relationships**: Networking is not just about making initial connections; it's also about nurturing and maintaining relationships over time. Stay in touch with your contacts through periodic check-ins, provide updates on your own activities, and participate in mutual interests or projects.

Networking requires persistence and patience. Rome wasn't built overnight, and growing your network will take time as well.

Tips for Starting a Conversation at a Tech Conference

Starting conversations at a tech conference can be a great way to network and build connections. The key is to start the conversation focused on the other person. It is a turnoff for most people when others just want to talk about themselves. Try to find something the other person is interested in discussing with you. Here are some conversation starters:

1. **Comment on the conference**: "What sessions have you found most interesting so far?"

2. **Discuss industry trends**: "What emerging technologies are you most excited about?"

3. **Discuss industry events**: "Have you attended any other tech conferences recently? Any recommendations?"

4. **Ask about their background**: "How did you get started in the tech industry?"

5. **Ask about their work**: "What projects are you currently working on?"

6. **Seek advice or insights**: "I'm considering [a new technology or approach]. What are your thoughts on it?"

7. **Find common ground**: "I noticed you're interested in [a specific topic or area]. I'm also passionate about that. What sparked your interest?"

8. **Share experiences**: "Have you encountered any interesting challenges or successes in your recent projects?"

Listen actively, show genuine interest in the other person's responses, and be prepared to share your own experiences and insights. Engaging conversations help build trust.

How to Network Effectively Online

Networking online offers numerous opportunities to connect with professionals from around the world and build valuable relationships. Here are some effective ways to network online:

- **Utilize professional networking platforms**: LinkedIn gives you access to a vast pool of potential professional connections. See the recommendations in Chapter 10 to ensure that your LinkedIn profile is at an optimal state.

  - Join relevant LinkedIn Groups, participate in discussions, and connect with professionals in your industry or field of interest.

  - When I was an executive recruiter, I would like or comment on interesting posts, people's career promotions or work anniversaries, etc. On average, I liked or commented on five to ten posts a day. I didn't think this was a lot. It certainly didn't take much of my time. However, the impact was greater than I thought. When I talked with tech professionals on the phone, quite a number of them commented that they saw me everywhere on LinkedIn; I was always popping up on their LinkedIn feed.

- **Engage in social media**: Platforms like X, Facebook, and Instagram can also be valuable networking tools. Follow thought leaders, industry experts, and companies in your field. Share content, comment on posts, and engage in conversations to establish your presence and connect with others.

- **Attend virtual events and webinars**: Many conferences, seminars, and industry events have moved online, providing opportunities to network with professionals from anywhere in the world. Attend virtual events, participate in Q&A sessions, and connect with speakers, organizers, and fellow attendees through chat features or social media.

- **Participate in online workshops and courses**: Enroll in online workshops, courses, or training programs related to your field. These platforms often provide opportunities to interact with instructors and fellow participants, ask questions, and exchange ideas. Make a concerted effort to connect with other students on the chat line who are interesting to you, then follow up privately to schedule a phone call.

- **Host or participate in virtual meetups**: Organize or participate in virtual networking events, meetups, or coffee chats with professionals in your network. Platforms like Zoom, Google Meet, and Microsoft Teams make it easy to host virtual gatherings and facilitate meaningful conversations.

- **Create and share valuable content**: Establish yourself as a thought leader by creating and sharing valuable content related to your industry or expertise. Write white papers, articles, blog posts, or LinkedIn posts sharing your insights, experiences, or tips. Engage with comments and feedback to spark conversations and connect with others. Hiring executives look for content on your LinkedIn profile so they can view samples of your work and thought leadership.

- **Offer help and support**: Look for opportunities to help and support others in your network. Offer advice, share resources, or make introductions to people who may benefit from connecting with each other. Being generous with your time and expertise can help you build strong and lasting relationships.

- **Follow up and stay connected**: After engaging with someone online, follow up with a personalized message to express gratitude and continue the conversation. Stay connected by periodically checking in, sharing updates, or congratulating them on achievements to maintain the relationship over time.

By leveraging these strategies and actively participating in online networking activities, you can expand your professional network, establish your presence in your industry, and unlock new opportunities for collaboration and growth.

Keep Your Network Active

Tracking and following up with networking contacts effectively is essential for maintaining relationships and maximizing the benefits of your network. Here are some of the most effective ways to do so:

- **Use a CRM (customer relationship management) system**: Utilize a CRM system to organize and manage your contacts, including names, contact information, notes from conversations, and follow-up tasks. Popular CRM tools include Salesforce, HubSpot, and Zoho CRM. I also came across a professional networking app called Contacts+ that is designed for managing professional contacts.

- **Maintain a spreadsheet**: If you prefer a simpler approach, you can use a spreadsheet to track your networking contacts. Create columns for contact details, notes, follow-up dates, and any other relevant information.

- **Set reminders**: Whether you're using a CRM system, spreadsheet, or calendar app, set reminders for follow-up tasks and important dates, such as birthdays, work anniversaries, or upcoming events. This ensures that you stay proactive in nurturing your relationships.

- **Segment your contacts**: Categorize your networking contacts based on factors such as industry, location, level of relationship, or specific interests. This allows you to tailor your follow-up messages and interactions to each group's preferences and needs.

- **Personalize your follow-ups**: When following up with contacts, avoid generic messages and instead personalize your communications based on your previous interactions. I can tell when I receive a generic email to a distribution list that asks to connect with me versus a more personalized email that was sent to only me. The latter are the ones I respond to. Reference specific conversations, shared interests, or mutual connections to demonstrate your genuine interest and attention to detail.

- **Schedule regular check-ins**: Establish a cadence for reaching out to your networking contacts, whether it's quarterly, semiannually, or annually. Schedule regular check-in calls, coffee meetings, or virtual catchups to stay updated on their activities and maintain the connection. Schedule a fifteen- or thirty-minute phone call on Fridays since people are generally more available on this workday.

- **Offer value**: In your follow-up communications, look for opportunities to provide value to your contacts. Share relevant articles, offer introductions to other professionals in your network, or assist with their projects or challenges. This reinforces your relationship and encourages reciprocity.

- **Evaluate and adjust**: Periodically review your networking efforts to assess what's working well and where there's room for improvement. Adjust your approach based on feedback, changes in your goals, or evolving priorities to ensure that your networking activities remain effective and aligned with your objectives.

Keeping your networking contacts and activities organized will put you more in control of expanding your network and allow you to maximize the benefits of your professional network.

Make the Most of Informational Interviews

An informational interview is a networking conversation in which an individual seeks to gather insights, advice, and information about a particular career field, industry, company, or role from someone who is already established in that area.

Before you finalize your career path and career action plans, conducting informational interviews is a great way to validate, or invalidate, assumptions you have about a job, company, or industry.

These informal conversations tend to last twenty to thirty minutes; though, if you've made a strong connection, they can last up to an hour. They can be conducted via phone, via video conference, or in person (e.g., for coffee).

Prepare Questions Ahead of Time

For informational interviews, *you* are the interviewer; the professional you are seeking advice from is the interviewee. So, it's important to be prepared with specific questions that are on your mind. First, think about the insights or information that would be helpful with planning your career. Second, prepare a set of questions.

Below are sample questions to spur your thoughts:[77]

- "Can you tell me about your career trajectory?"

- "What made you decide to pursue this career path?"

- "What does a typical day or week look like for you?"

- "What skills do I need to succeed in this career?"

- "Can you recommend anyone else I could speak to?"

The interviewee will share their experiences, expertise, and insights, and they'll likely provide valuable guidance and perspective for you.

Unlike a job interview, the primary goal of an informational interview is not to secure employment. Instead, it's to gather information, expand your network, and gain a better understanding of a particular field or role. However, if you handle yourself professionally, informational interviews can ultimately be a gateway to future opportunities.

Follow up with a personalized thank-you as soon as possible to express your gratitude for their time and insights; it can be via LinkedIn or email.

If the interaction was positive, keep in touch and continue to build the relationship.

Exercise: Evaluate Your Professional Network

Review the list of people you have listed on the My Network tab in your marketing plan. What are the strengths of your network? What are the gaps? List the key gaps below, along with actions you will take to broaden your network. Be specific with the actions and then block time on your calendar to make this happen. A robust professional network is worth its weight in gold.

---

[77] https://www.coursera.org/articles/informational-interview-questions

Key Gaps: **Actions to Take:**

-
-
-
-
-
-
-
-

The tech industry has always embraced the concept of lifelong learning to encourage tech employees to continue to learn and grow. Analogous to this is lifelong networking since we are all free agents in the tech industry. Your network will be there for you when you are ready to make your next career move as long as you regularly reach out to key people in your network and continuously grow your network. It's one of the most important job search execution actions you can invest in.

In the next chapter, we will discuss another group of people you should be cultivating long-term relationships with—executive recruiters.

CHAPTER 15

WORKING WITH RECRUITERS

"The bigger the dream, the more important the team."

– Robin Sharma

To effectively manage your career, you need a team around you. As we discussed in Chapter 14, your network is worth its weight in gold. Recruiters should be a part of your network as well.

There are many benefits to interacting with recruiters:

- Recruiters can introduce you to open positions that may not be advertised publicly.

- Recruiters can help you assess whether a company and role are the right fit for you.

- Recruiters can provide feedback on your resume before it is sent to the hiring executive.

- A good recruiter will help you navigate the interview process and provide insider knowledge about the company, the culture, and the hiring executive.

Having said all that, recruiters are not career coaches. Recruiters are paid to find qualified talent for open positions. If you know the type of position you are looking for next, you should work with recruiters. If you don't know what your next position should be, you should hire a career coach.

There are distinct differences between in-house recruiters and executive recruiters (often referred to as headhunters).

In-House Recruiters

In-house recruiters conduct searches for solely one company. Their title could be recruiter, or it could be talent acquisition specialist. It is a common practice for tech companies to hire recruiters on a contract basis to enable the recruiting team to level up during peak hiring seasons and scale back down during low-hiring seasons. So the in-house recruiter you are working with might be an employee of the company, or they could be an independent contractor.

There are two factors to consider when working with in-house recruiters in tech:

- Many in-house recruiters stay with an employer for only two to three years before considering a move to another organization. There is a lot of job hopping.

- In-house recruiters could be working on thirty to forty open requisitions concurrently, which is a large workload.

Some in-house tech recruiters are junior and may not understand what you do or what differentiates you from other candidates. So, the following is my advice when you are pursuing posted open positions:

- Apply for the position on the company's website. But don't stop there. When candidates apply for positions online, they commonly refer to it as the black hole. Your resume goes into the portal, but no response comes back.

- Try to identify who the in-house recruiter is and reach out to them directly via LinkedIn. Often, the in-house recruiter's name will be listed on the job posting on LinkedIn, Indeed, etc. You want to get their attention to get your resume to the top of their pile.

- You must connect the dots for them as to why you are a strong candidate. When speaking with them, use the terminology and keywords from the job description. Remember, if they are junior, they likely have very little business experience outside recruiting.

- Be friendly and accommodating. Follow up quickly on any requests they make of you.

- In-house recruiters decide which resumes to provide to hiring managers, and they can overlook excellent talent because they just don't understand the context of the role enough.

- Some in-house recruiters view themselves as gatekeepers; they want to control all the communication between you and the hiring executive, but you should not put your career in their hands.

- Conduct a search on LinkedIn to try to identify who the hiring executive is for the role. This can be straightforward with small to medium companies but more challenging with larger companies. Reach out to the hiring executive directly via LinkedIn and make a two- or three-sentence introduction. Express your enthusiasm for the role, mention several capabilities you have that meet requirements on the job description, and state that you have applied via their career portal. You want the hiring executive to contact the in-house recruiter and tell them to schedule an interview with you.

Going directly to the hiring executive may annoy the in-house recruiter, but it's better to beg for forgiveness than let a great opportunity pass you by.

Executive Recruiters

Executive recruiters tend to work for firms that fall into two camps:

- Boutique recruiting firms that specialize in specific niche areas

- Large recruiting firms, like Korn Ferry or Spencer Stuart, which focus on talent searches in the tech and tech-adjacent industries

These two types of recruiting firms have very different business models and, thus, operate differently.

Boutique Recruiting Firms

Boutique recruiting firms can be solopreneurs by design (no employees) or larger firms with as many as more than a hundred employees.

- Executive recruiters are typically very knowledgeable about the role and what makes a great candidate.

- Some executive recruiters held roles similar to what they are recruiting for, so they may speak your language.

- These boutique firms intentionally differentiate themselves from large recruiting firms by building relationships with candidates who are in their niche areas. When I was an executive recruiter, I scheduled fifteen-minute phone calls with candidates in my recruiting niche areas to get to know them and what they were looking for. When I received a new search from one of my clients, I went first to my database of candidates. Over the years, I've contacted many candidates for a variety of searches.

- The hiring executive and their in-house recruiting team often exhaust their resources before they hire an executive recruiter. So there is a high sense of urgency for the executive recruiter to identify and submit qualified candidates to their client. Being responsive to executive recruiters is key. Otherwise, you might miss the window to be submitted as a candidate.

Large Recruiting Firms

Many candidates I have talked with describe their experiences with large recruiting firms as transactional. Executive recruiters from large firms might talk with you only if they perceive that you are a qualified candidate for a position they are *currently* trying to fill.

I came across an article on Korn Ferry's site that makes this clear:

One day, the recruiter spoke with more than a dozen potential candidates about various positions she was recruiting for clients. While she worked, she got more than six hundred new messages from job seekers asking for her help. "I have a ton of people in my inbox who say, 'I'm in the job market. I want a Zoom meeting and grab coffee,'" she says. "I'm like, 'No.'"

According to one survey, about 75 percent of people applying for jobs say they never heard back from the large recruiting firm—and that was before the pandemic. Now overwhelmed with millions of unemployed people and often working with reduced resources, HR officials and headhunters alike may fit the cliché of being next to impossible to reach.[78]

It's easy to become frustrated by this phenomenon, but it's more productive to understand how these large recruiting firms work and try to get them to notice you using the methods they are accustomed to.

Four Ways to Get on a Recruiter's List[79]

- **Be Findable**: Recruiters search LinkedIn and trade association sites affiliated with the industry or sector they are trying to fill a position in.

  "Nothing stands out more than candidates who have written articles or given presentations or other displays of insights about the industry or role. The more people demonstrate thought leadership, the easier they are to find, and those are the people clients often want to speak to," says Dan Kaplan, a Korn Ferry senior client partner in the firm's CHRO practice.

- **Get into Their Database**: Many large recruiting firms have a portal where you can enter your contact information and resume. Some of the sites are a bit cumbersome, but executive recruiters do search their company's databases for candidates when they get a new search. I have had recruiters contact me many years after I was first placed in their database.

- **Have an Elevator Pitch**: Whether it's on the phone or over email, candidates should have a concise story to tell executive recruiters. They don't need to know a full career history—for executives, they can usually get that from a corporate biography page. Experts say recruiters want to know two or three valuable skill sets a candidate has, what role a candidate has now, and some idea of what type of emotional intelligence—so-called 'soft skills'—the candidate demonstrates. "Sell yourself fast," says Deepali Vyas, cohead of fintech for Korn Ferry's Global Financial Markets practice.

  "That type of information should come across quickly on a resume as well. Sometimes, resumes are too broad", says Mary Elizabeth Sadd, Korn Ferry senior client partner. "At the executive level, you have to know who you are and what you are," she says.

  The elevator pitch on the top part of your resume that you built in Chapter 10 is so important, as is being able to articulate this elevator pitch. So, do yourself a favor and invest in that top paragraph on your resume until you feel like you've nailed it and other people tell you that you've nailed it.

---

[78] https://www.kornferry.com/insights/this-week-in-leadership/how-to-find-a-recruiter
[79] Adapted from https://www.kornferry.com/insights/this-week-in-leadership/how-to-find-a-recruiter

- **Help the Headhunter**: "The most successful people will develop good relationships with a few good recruiters who can help them throughout their entire careers," Vyas says. "That can mean telling recruiters about other people who might fit open roles. Recruiters are always looking to broaden their network and industry knowledge. Anyone who can do that now will be one of the first people a recruiter wants to talk to about a related open role in the future," Kaplan says.

The three networking principles covered in Chapter 12 apply to working with executive recruiters as well.

Last tip I will offer:

<u>Don't Play Cat and Mouse Games:</u> This was my pet peeve when I was an executive recruiter. Recruiters want to know if you are interested in exploring an opportunity. Saying things like "I'm just casually looking" or "I'm not really looking right now, but what you got?" sends off red flags for the recruiter. They will assume you are not serious about exploring new opportunities, which is a waste of your time and theirs.

It's fine if you aren't ready to make a move right now. Let the recruiter know that the timing isn't right but that you'd like to stay in touch for future opportunities. But if you *are* open to hearing about new opportunities, just say so! Recruiters don't assume you are trying to run from your current role. They think you are smart for listening to new career opportunities.

Exercise: Evaluate Your Relationships with Executive Recruiters

Review the list of people you have listed on the Executive Recruiter tab in your marketing plan. Do you have at least a dozen recruiters you touch base with several times a year? If not, identify recruiters you will build relationships with and add them to your marketing plan spreadsheet. Ask executive recruiters what they are seeing in the market and whether they have opportunities that might fit your next career move. Then track each conversation you have with them to ensure that you are touching bases at least twice a year, even if you aren't specifically looking to make your next career move yet. Build relationships with them and keep a pulse on what hiring executives are looking for.

A final comment on executive recruiters: Don't be discouraged if executive recruiters don't respond to you. They are heads down and focused on finding qualified candidates for their clients' open positions. They likely kept your resume and entered it into their applicant tracking system so they can contact you in the future if they have a position you would be a qualified candidate for. Many candidates who are searching for their next position have found more success working with smaller boutique recruiters who do invest in building relationships with candidates. So, talk to as many executive recruiters as you can and contact a diverse size of firms, both smaller and larger.

In the next chapter, we will cover another important component of your job search execution: effective interviewing.

CHAPTER 16

EFFECTIVE INTERVIEWING

"One important key to success is self-confidence.
An important key to self-confidence is preparation."

– Arthur Ashe

Most of us don't interview very often. It's a set of skills that can get rusty or be underdeveloped. So, in this chapter, we will look at the interview process from the hiring executive's perspective, discuss key steps for preparing for an interview, and review the land mines to avoid during an interview.

The Process of Interviewing

Interviewing for a new job is a process. The more prepared you are, the more likely you will have a strong outcome—ideally, a strong offer.

Each step in the process serves to progressively narrow down the pool of candidates and ensure a good match between the candidate and the company. And it is an opportunity for you, the candidate, to get to know the company and key members of the team to assess whether the company and position are a good fit for you.

It is a large undertaking for a company to conduct a search for a new employee. Below is the typical interview process that hiring executives in tech companies deploy:

- **Job Posting**: The hiring company invests money to post the open position on job boards where candidates are looking for new positions. This is typically done by the in-house recruiter or HR representative.

- **Recruiter**: If the position is particularly difficult to fill, is a confidential search, or is a key leadership role, the hiring company may engage an external recruiting company to conduct the search. If not, the in-house recruiter will conduct the search.

- **Job Application**: You submit your resume, cover letter, and any other required documents to the hiring company or recruiter.

- **Review of Applications**: Applications are reviewed, and a short list of candidates who meet the job requirements is prepared by the recruiter.

- **Initial Screening**: This is typically a phone call conducted by a recruiter or HR representative. The objective is to confirm the candidate meets the basic requirements.

- **First Interview**: Next, an initial interview lasting thirty to sixty minutes is conducted by phone or video with qualified candidates. The focus of the interview is on your background and experience and why you are interested in the role.

- **Assessment**: You might be asked to complete a task (e.g., a mini project) or take a test or assessment relevant to the position to demonstrate your abilities.

- **Second Interview**: Next, a more in-depth interview with the hiring executive or team members is conducted in person or via video. This interview often includes behavioral and technical questions.

- **Panel Interview**: Then, you'll engage with a group of interviewers from different functional departments or levels in the company. Panel interviews are very common and efficient for the interview team. Cultural fit, technical abilities, and assessment of your ability to collaborate with cross-functional teams are typically the focus of the interview. You may also be asked to prepare a short presentation for the panel of interviewers.

- **Final Interview**: A final interview round with higher-level executives or the hiring executive is conducted to address any open areas and assess your long-term potential with the company.

- **Background Check and References**: The hiring company may conduct background checks and contact your references to verify your employment history and qualifications.

- **Job Offer**: If you are the selected candidate, you will receive a job offer outlining the terms of employment, including compensation, benefits, and start date. You may opt to negotiate the offer before accepting it.

- **Onboarding**: Once you accept the offer, the onboarding process begins. It includes necessary paperwork, work equipment setup, and employee orientation.

Preparing for an Interview

Based on the above process, the hiring company invests significant time and resources to hire an employee. It is also an investment of a candidate's time to participate in an interview process. And your objective is to assess whether the hiring company and its team members are a good fit for your next career move.

Candidates engage in seven key activities to prepare for an interview process and increase the possibility of receiving a job offer:

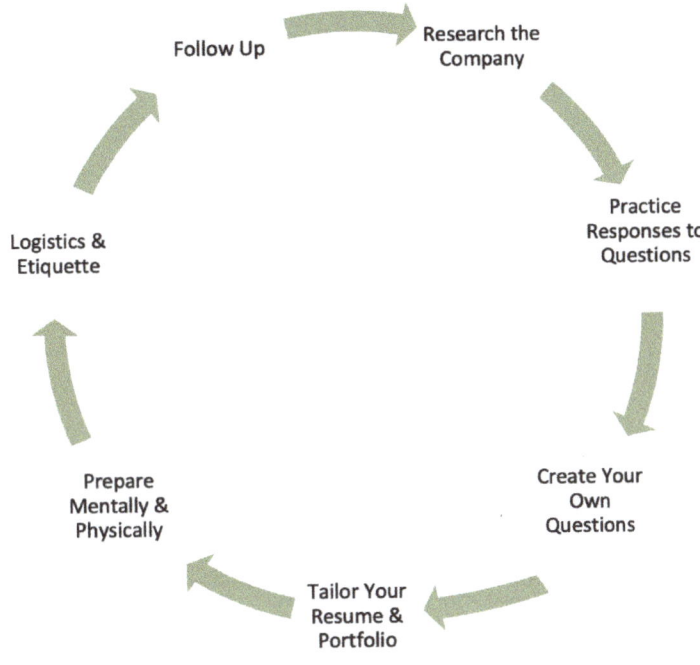

Research the Company

Prepare for an interview like you would prepare for an important business meeting. Research the following:

- **Understand the Company's Mission and Values**: Visit the company's website to learn about the mission, values, and culture. Look for recent news or public company filings in which they discuss their key objectives for the year.

- **Know the Products or Services**: Be familiar with what the company offers and any major achievements, projects, or initiatives.

- **Understand the Industry**: Gain insights into the industry the company operates in, including competitors and market trends.

- **The Interview Team**: Ask the recruiter or HR representative whom you will be interviewing with so you can review their LinkedIn profile to understand their work experience. This could help you anticipate questions they might ask you.

Hiring executives have business problems, and you are the solution to that problem. The more you uncover about the company's business objectives, the more you can position your experience and strengths to help them see that you can become part of the solution.

Understand the Job Description:

- **Identify Key Requirements**: Highlight the skills, experiences, and qualifications that the job requires. These are typically listed in priority order on the job description, with requirements at the top being more critical and those at the bottom being more likely to be nice to have.

- **Match Your Skills**: Be prepared to discuss how your skills and experiences align with the job requirements.

Focus on pursuing positions that play to your strengths yet still give you an opportunity to grow and build new skills.

Practice Responses to Common Interview Questions

Interview questions fall into three categories:

1. Behavioral
2. Technical
3. Company-specific

Behavioral Interview Questions*:*

Prepare for behavioral interview questions by completing stories using the STAR method.

STAR stands for *Situation*, *Task*, *Action*, and *Result*. It's a method for structuring your answers to make them as compelling and concise as possible.

Provide answers that are honest and thorough, without rambling. Give only the most relevant details to keep your answers concise. The interviewer will ask you to elaborate if they want more information.

Sample Behavioral Interview Question:

"Tell me about a time when you were under a lot of pressure at work. How did you handle the situation?"

Example Answer Using the STAR Method:

Situation – What were the circumstances? What was the challenge?

"In my previous role, an important member of the team quit suddenly in the middle of a major project. We knew we wouldn't be able to hire and onboard a new team member before the project's deadline, but this was a major project for a large client. We didn't want to lose the account."

Task – What goal were you working toward?

"I was tasked with taking over their responsibilities, in addition to my own, to ensure that the project was successful."

Action – What did you do specifically to address the situation?

"I worked with my manager to deprioritize some other projects I was working on so I could dedicate more time and effort to this account. I made myself completely available to the client, including taking calls with them some evenings to ensure that they were wholly satisfied."

Result – What was the outcome? What did you learn?

"The project was delivered on time and to a high standard. The client was so happy that they went on to sign a larger contract with us."

Exercise: STAR Method Stories

Document six stories using the STAR method so you can be prepared for common behavioral interview questions.

Story #1:

Situation – What were the circumstances? What was the challenge?
Task – What goal were you working toward?
Action – What did you do specifically to address the situation?
Result – What was the outcome? What did you learn?

Story #2:

Situation – What were the circumstances? What was the challenge?
Task – What goal were you working toward?
Action – What did you do specifically to address the situation?
Result – What was the outcome? What did you learn?

Story #3:

Situation – What were the circumstances? What was the challenge?
Task – What goal were you working toward?
Action – What did you do specifically to address the situation?
Result – What was the outcome? What did you learn?

Story #4:

Situation – What were the circumstances? What was the challenge?
Task – What goal were you working toward?
Action – What did you do specifically to address the situation?
Result – What was the outcome? What did you learn?

Story #5:

Situation – What were the circumstances? What was the challenge?
Task – What goal were you working toward?
Action – What did you do specifically to address the situation?
Result – What was the outcome? What did you learn?

Story #6:

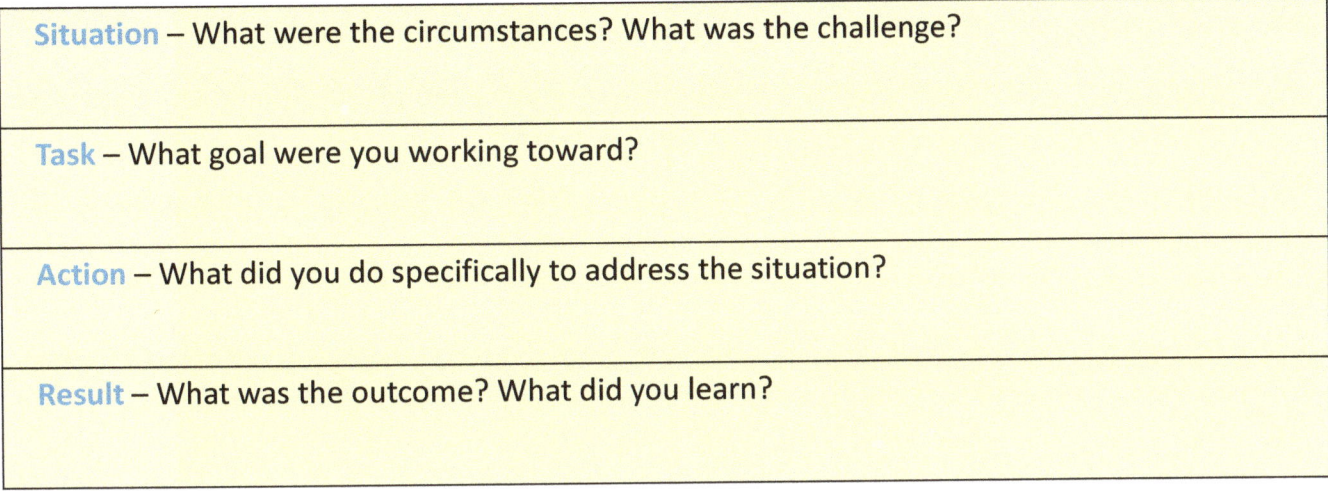

Situation – What were the circumstances? What was the challenge?
Task – What goal were you working toward?
Action – What did you do specifically to address the situation?
Result – What was the outcome? What did you learn?

Practice telling your stories out loud. Keep the stories short and punchy. Add quantitative results as often as possible.

Common Behavioral Interview Questions and Expected Responses

Below are common behavioral questions compiled by LinkedIn. "We surveyed nearly 1,300 hiring managers about the soft skills they look for and the behavioral questions they ask." [80] Below is a list of hiring managers' top interview questions and what hiring managers listen for in the candidate's responses.

The top six skills, in order of importance, are:

1. Adaptability

2. Culture fit

3. Collaboration

4. Leadership

5. Growth potential

6. Prioritization

Below is an excerpt from the LinkedIn survey. For each of the six skills, the first question in each category was the most popular question asked by hiring managers.

---

[80] https://business.linkedin.com/content/dam/me/business/en-us/talent-solutions/resources/pdfs/guide-to-screening-candidates-30-essential-behavioral-interview-questions-to-ask-ebook-v2.pdf

Adaptability: "Adaptability is essential for thriving in a rapidly changing work environment. Given that 54 percent of employees may require significant reskilling or upskilling over the next few years to keep pace with new technology and evolving business needs, adaptability is essential.

Question 1: Tell me about a time when you were asked to do something you had never done before. How did you react? What did you learn?

What the Interviewer Listens For: Excitement about tackling new challenges and willingness to leave their comfort zone, knowing they'll learn something valuable from the experience.

Question 2: Describe a situation in which you embraced a new system, process, technology, or idea at work that was a major departure from the old way of doing things.

What the Interviewer Listens For: Eagerness to explore new ways of working and improve based on what they learn; if they discovered a better way, did they embrace the change?

Culture Fit: Employees who fit in with your culture have the potential to do great things at your company. They should be fundamentally aligned with your company's mission and core values.

Question 1: What are the three things that are most important to you in a job?

What the Interviewer Listens For: Alignment between what's most important to them and what the role and company have to offer.

Question 2: Tell me about a time in the last week when you've been satisfied, energized, and productive at work. What were you doing?

What the Interviewer Listens For: An indication that the work environment and day-to-day responsibilities are right for them.

Collaboration: When a role requires teamwork, strong collaboration skills make a big difference. Done right, collaboration improves productivity, morale, and order. But when people aren't good at collaborating, they can create roadblocks for colleagues.

Question 1: Give an example of a time when you had to work with someone who was difficult to get along with. How did you handle interactions with this person?

What the Interviewer Listens For: A willingness to try to see things from the other person's perspective by identifying the cause of the tension and finding ways to improve the relationship.

Question 2: Tell me about a time when you were communicating with someone and they did not understand you. What did you do?

What the Interviewer Listens For: Patience. Great collaborators take the time to make sure they're being understood and can adjust their style to align with others.

Leadership: Even when you're not interviewing for a leadership role, hire people who can inspire. Organizations with strong leadership are 13x more likely to outperform their competition.

> **Question 1:** Tell me about the last time something significant didn't go according to plan at work. What was your role? What was the outcome?
>
> **What the Interviewer Listens For:** Thoughtful reflection and a strong sense of ownership. True leaders don't try to shift the blame to others but consider what they could have done differently.
>
> **Question 2:** Describe a situation in which you needed to persuade someone to see things your way. What steps did you take? What were the results?
>
> **What the Interviewer Listens For:** Strong leaders establish credibility and use compelling evidence to reinforce their viewpoint rather than acting like they know best.

Growth Potential: Hire someone with growth potential so they can develop the role and make it their own.

> **Question 1:** Recall a time when your manager was unavailable when a problem arose. How did you handle the situation? Who did you consult with?
>
> **What the Interviewer Listens For:** The ability to rise to the occasion without stepping on toes. Great candidates respect all stakeholders and explore options before making a decision.
>
> **Question 2:** Describe a time when you volunteered to expand your knowledge at work, as opposed to being directed to do so.
>
> **What the Interviewer Listens For:** Eagerness to learn and a willingness to ask for the resources. Invest in continuous learning and actively seek out new opportunities.

Prioritization: Candidates who have mastered prioritization can juggle key tasks. When employees know how to prioritize, they're less likely to drop the ball, or to burn themselves out.

> **Question 1:** Tell me about a time when you had to juggle several projects at the same time. How did you organize your time? What was the result?
>
> **What the Interviewer Listens For:** A clear and proactive process for organizing their time, like blocking off their calendar, creating a to-do list, and confirming deadlines.
>
> **Question 2:** Tell me about a project that you planned. How did you organize and schedule the tasks?
>
> **What the Interviewer Listens For:** A methodical approach to planning and strong self-discipline when meeting deadlines and driving a project through to completion." [81]

---

[81] https://business.linkedin.com/content/dam/me/business/en-us/talent-solutions/resources/pdfs/guide-to-screening-candidates-30-essential-behavioral-interview-questions-to-ask-ebook-v2.pdf

Technical Interview Questions:

If applicable, prepare for technical questions related to your field. Conduct research ahead of time to understand the technologies the tech company is focused on. You can review press releases on their website and some of their executives' LinkedIn profiles to try to identify clues as to the company's key business initiatives.

Company-Specific Interview Questions:

Think about why you want to work at that specific company and how you can contribute to its goals. Below are sample questions you might be asked:

- What motivates you to come to work every day?

- What would motivate you to make a move from your current role?

- What does impact at a business mean to you?

- Where do you see yourself five years from now?

Create Your Own Questions

From the LinkedIn survey referenced above, interviewers are encouraged to pay attention to the questions that candidates ask since high-potential candidates are often highly curious and invested in learning about the role and the company.

Your questions could fall into the following categories:

Role-Specific: Ask about day-to-day responsibilities, team structure, and performance metrics.

- What's the most challenging aspect of this role?

- What does success in your position look like?

- If you could describe your team in three words, what would they be and why?

- What type of person works well with this team?

- Was there someone in this role, and were they successful? If the answer is no, why not?

Company Culture: Inquire about the company culture, work environment, and values.

- How did the company determine its mission?

- How does this role help the company achieve its key objectives for the year?

Career Development: Ask about opportunities for growth, training, and career progression.

- Are there opportunities for continued education and growth?

- Does the company provide paid training or education?

- What is the typical career path for this role?

Tailor Your Resume and Portfolio

Tailor your resume to help connect the dots for the recruiter, HR representative, and interview team as to why you are the top candidate.

Title: Put the title of the position you are applying for at the top of the resume. This reinforces your enthusiasm for the position that the hiring executive is hiring for.

Core Competency Keywords: In Chapter 10, you created a master list of keywords that articulate your competencies to include in your resume. Whittle this list down so that the relevant core competencies are listed, especially the competencies that are documented in the job description.

Work Experience Descriptions: Pare down the bullet points under each position you have held to ensure that the relevant experience and accomplishments are listed. Don't make the reader read any more than what is relevant.

Prepare Your Portfolio: If applicable, prepare a portfolio of your work to demonstrate your skills and achievements.

Email your tailored resume to the recruiter or HR representative, ideally forty-eight hours before the interview, so the interview team can review it. If you are presenting a portfolio of your work, you can email this along with your resume.

Prepare Mentally and Physically

Rest Well: Get a good night's sleep before the interview.

Stay Calm and Confident: Ensure that you have a positive mindset. Meditation or relaxation techniques can help calm nerves and increase confidence.

Attire: Choose professional attire that fits the company's dress code. When in doubt, it is better to be slightly overdressed. Many candidates, including executives, are dressing too informally during interviews. This can be viewed as a sign of disrespect or disinterest on your part. I suggest that casual attire is not appropriate. Wear business casual at a minimum and ask the recruiter or HR representative if business attire is suggested.

Logistics and Etiquette

Ensure that you have all the logistics covered so the small details don't get in the way.

Know the Interview Format: Confirm whether the interview is in person, over the phone, or via video call. *Always* be prepared for a video call. Candidates who say, "Oh, I didn't realize this would be a video interview," come off as unprepared and unprofessional.

Be on Time: If the interview is in person, plan your route and leave early to account for any delays. It is not helpful to be rushing to get to the interview on time.

Video Interviews: For video interviews, ensure that you have a quiet, clean, and well-lit space with a reliable internet connection. You should use a laptop, not a cell phone or iPad. Set up your video on your PC and ensure that you are at eye level.

Etiquette: Be polite and professional. Greet everyone warmly, make eye contact, and listen actively.

Follow-Up

Send a Thank-You Note: After the interview, send a thank-you email to express your appreciation for the opportunity to interview with the team and reiterate your interest in the role.

Checkpoints: Follow up with the interviewer per the agreed-upon time. If you are one of the first candidates who were interviewed, it could be several weeks (or months) before the interview process progresses. It's good to continue to show your interest by following up with either the recruiter, HR representative, or hiring executive. Ideally, follow up with the hiring executive directly unless you have been told to do otherwise.

Following up once a week is a good cadence to demonstrate your continued interest.

The process repeats itself for each subsequent interview.

- Prepare for second and subsequent interviews.

- Address panel interviews.

Land Mines to Avoid During an Interview

Avoiding certain pitfalls or land mines in the interview process can make a significant difference in your success. Here are some common land mines to be aware of and tips on how to avoid them:

Talking Too Much: When I was an executive recruiter, the number-one objection I heard from my clients when interviewing candidates was "they talked too much." All levels of candidates, including executives, fall into this category. You must put yourself into the hiring team's shoes and tailor your communication to address their questions.

Respect that they have a limited amount of time to get to know you and are coming to this interview with their own set of questions they want to get through.

- *Tips:* Stay on topic. With a buddy, practice concise and relevant responses to common questions. And practice telling your STAR method stories. Ask your interview buddy for their honest feedback about how to keep the responses to a ten-thousand-foot level. This means you should describe what you did and the results you accomplished.

Candidates get into trouble when they start describing *how* they did something. This is where the responses are too detailed and in the weeds.

If you go deeper into the interview process—for example, you have a panel interview—you might get questions about how you accomplished something. But offer detailed responses only if they ask for that level of detail.

Unprofessional Behavior: The number-two objection from my clients is annoyance with candidates who interrupt the interviewers. Please let the interviewer finish speaking before you speak.

Also, avoid being late, using informal language, using curse words, or checking your phone during the interview.

- *Tip:* Arrive five or more minutes early for phone, video, or in-person interviews.

Lack of Preparation: Avoid going into an interview without sufficient knowledge about the company, role, or industry. It is a sign of disrespect to waste people's time by not being prepared. I put a great candidate in front of a client, and he was immediately disqualified for not being prepared for an interview. He gave excuses as to why he didn't complete the task that was assigned to him, but there is no excuse if you have at least several days to complete the task.

- *Tip:* Plan ahead and don't wait for the day of the interview to complete a task. If you have a family or work emergency, you are better off trying to reschedule the interview than going into the interview unprepared.

Negative Talk: Avoid speaking poorly about previous employers, colleagues, or experiences.

- *Tip:* Focus on the positive aspects of your previous roles and what you learned from challenging situations. For each position that you have left, prepare a response as to why you left that position or company.

Dishonesty: Refrain from exaggerating your qualifications, experiences, or achievements.

- *Tip:* Be honest about your skills and experiences. Emphasize your strengths without embellishment. If you were the leader of a project or initiative, state that. It shows your maturity when you also state the contributions of others who worked in collaboration with you.

Poor Body Language: Avoid negative body language, such as crossing arms, failing to make eye contact, fidgeting, or slouching.

- *Tip:* Maintain good posture, make eye contact, and use open gestures to convey confidence and engagement.

Inadequate Questions: Don't fail to ask any questions when given the opportunity. And don't ask inappropriate or self-centered questions (e.g., about compensation or benefits before you get to that stage).

- *Tips*: Prepare thoughtful questions about the role, team, company culture, and career growth opportunities. Before you enter an interview process, ask the recruiter or HR representative what the salary range is for the position and whether incentive or equity compensation is included in the role. That is the time to ask this initial question, not during an interview with the hiring executive, since that could break the flow of building a relationship with them.

Failure to Connect Your Skills to the Role: Avoid talking about your skills and experiences without relating them to how they benefit the company or the specific role.

- *Tip:* Tailor your answers to highlight how your background, skills, and experiences make you a strong fit for the position. Remember that the interview team has a list of criteria they are looking for. Focus on those and ensure they get the answers to their questions.

Lack of Enthusiasm: Avoid appearing disinterested, unenthusiastic, or unsure about the role.

- *Tip:* Be curious and show genuine interest in the position and the company. Express your enthusiasm and explain why you are excited about the opportunity. It's okay to have reservations in your own mind, but use the interview process to gather more insight into the company and the role so you can assess if it's the right fit for you. Sometimes, you need to get deeper into the interview process before you can make a good assessment.

Forgetting to Follow Up: Failing to send a thank-you note after the interview will likely be noticed.

- *Tip:* Send a brief, courteous thank-you email the same day of the interview to express your appreciation and reiterate your interest. Most of my clients took careful note of candidate follow-ups, and the interview team compared notes as to whether they received one. It shows maturity and thoughtfulness, and it reiterates your enthusiasm for the role and the company. Ask the recruiter or HR representative for the interview team's email addresses. If they won't provide them, ask the recruiter or HR representative to forward your email to the interviewer(s).

When I was an executive recruiter, one of the more frustrating situations I heard from candidates who didn't move forward in the interview process was not getting feedback from the interview team on what didn't go well during an interview. Unfortunately, most companies will not provide feedback on a candidate's effectiveness during an interview due to legal risks.

My suggestion is to use the list above "Land Mines to Avoid During an Interview" and assess yourself the best you can after you participate in an interview. And keep refining and practicing your STAR stories. As with any skill, improving your ability to interview can improve the more you exercise this muscle. And use your interview buddy to debrief after interviews to get another person's perspective.

Exercise: Assess Your Gaps and Improve Your Interview Skills

Building and maintaining interview skills is critical for progressing toward your career goals. You could engage in an interview process as often as every year. Or maybe years and years go by before you exercise your interviewing muscle.

I encourage you to assess the gaps in your interview skills and then invest some time before you begin an interview process to brush up on and enhance your interview skills.

Top Three Interview Gaps: **Training Resources Identified:**

•	•
•	•
•	•

Training Resources to Enhance Your Interview Skills:

- **LinkedIn**: Mastering Common Interview Questions

- **Mock Interview Platforms**:
    - *Pramp:* Peer-to-peer mock interviews, real interview questions, peer feedback, technical and behavioral interviews
    - *Gainlo:* Mock interviews with experienced interviewers from top tech companies, detailed feedback, coaching, and interview tips

- **Glassdoor**: Company reviews, interview questions, salary information, insights from current and former employees, interview tips specific to companies

- **Book**: *Tell Me About Yourself: Storytelling to Get Jobs and Propel Your Career* by Holley M. Murchison, which focuses on crafting compelling personal stories for interviews

Typically, hiring executives will take two candidates to the final rounds of interviews. If you have been selected for final interviews, you should be prepared to provide professional references. It is ideal to include one or more of your prior bosses as references or other senior leaders you had a productive working relationship with who can speak to your performance.

Hopefully, this provides a broader perspective of the typical tech interview process, steps you can take to prepare for an interview, and land mines to avoid during interviews.

Steve Jobs, former CEO of Apple, was an incredible public speaker; he made it look easy. Years ago, I saw a video he made about his preparation process before he would deliver a speech. He invested hours and hours to give a thirty-minute speech. He said that a compelling speech is all about preparation.

The same can be said for effective interviewing; you should appear comfortable and confident in the eyes of the interviewer. Preparation with an interview buddy is key to achieving this.

In Phase 5, "Job Search Execution," we have covered the marketing plan, the importance of networking, how to work effectively with executive recruiters, and how to prepare for an effective interview.

The final topics are negotiating offers and ensuring a graceful exit, which we will cover in the next, final chapter.

CHAPTER 17

NEGOTIATING OFFERS AND ENSURING A GRACEFUL EXIT

"Let us never negotiate out of fear.
But let us never fear to negotiate."

– John F. Kennedy, thirty-fifth president of the United States

Historically, compensation has been shrouded in mystery in the tech industry. Tech companies made it taboo for employees to discuss their base pay, bonuses, etc. This made it challenging for a tech professional to benchmark their own compensation to see how well it was keeping up with the industry.

Well, that is all changing, and for the better. Pay equity and salary transparency laws are making base pay compensation more transparent on open job postings, which enables you to see what the going rate is for the role you are playing or the role you would like in your next career move. There are also many salary surveys conducted on specific tech job families to allow you to benchmark your compensation against others who are in the same role you are in.

In this chapter, we will cover pay equity and salary transparency laws, noncompete agreements, what a good offer should include, and how to have a graceful exit from your current employer.

As an executive recruiter, I have seen a wide variety of job offers. Some are very detailed—up to fifteen pages long. Others are lacking in detail at just a page or two. This is a contract between you and your future employer, so if you have important questions that aren't answered in the job offer, now is the time to get them clarified—ideally in writing.

Let's start with compensation.

Pay Equity and Salary Transparency Laws

At any time before, during, or after interviews, a potential employer or recruiter is not supposed to ask you what your current compensation is. This is true in many states across the United States and is becoming a practice nationwide. And the hiring company is required to tell you what the salary range is for a particular position. See 2024 State-by-State Pay Transparency Laws for additional insight.[82]

The initial problem that salary transparency laws are trying to resolve are disparities in how women are paid relative to how men are paid for the same job. According to Forbes, "In 2024, women working full time, year-round earned only 84 cents for every dollar earned by men. In more than 90 percent of occupations, women earn less than men. For lawmakers, these figures highlight the urgent need for measures that address gender pay inequality and promote wage transparency."[83]

It chaps my hide that we still have pay inequality for women, which has persisted for decades in the tech industry. Here's an example of why.

If a female candidate is asked what her current base salary is and the potential employer offers her a 10 percent higher base salary, she still might be paid well below what men are being paid for the same job. It is difficult, if not impossible, to close the gender pay disparity gap when candidates are asked to reveal their current compensation.

Many potential employers will ask, "What is your preferred or required compensation?" This is a fair question, but you don't have to answer it. You can politely respond with your own question: "What is the pay range for this position?" As a candidate, you want the potential employer to put their cards on the table first by telling you the pay range for the position. Then you can tell them whether that range works for you or not. It is ideal to have this dialogue before committing to the first interview. However, if that didn't happen, now is the time to have the conversation.

In my executive recruiting practice, I found that pay transparency laws not only help close pay disparities for women but also provide benefits to many other candidates. For example, I know many candidates who have had very successful careers in tech, made a lot of money, and now want to pivot to either a new role or a smaller company, and they don't want to be branded as overqualified for the position because of their relatively high salary. Being able to withhold comments about your current compensation can be beneficial for all candidates. And requiring employers to communicate the salary range for a position provides critical information that candidates need to negotiate their salaries in an optimal way.

Noncompete Agreements

Companies that required candidates to sign noncompete agreements put their employees in a situation in which it could be very difficult for them to earn a living for themselves and their families. I have always felt that noncompete agreements are an unfair business practice.

---

[82] https://www.forbes.com/sites/alonzomartinez/2024/06/14/2024-state-by-state-pay-transparency-laws-key-insights-for-employers/

[83] https://www.forbes.com/sites/alonzomartinez/2024/06/14/2024-state-by-state-pay-transparency-laws-key-insights-for-employers/

It is heartening to see federal legislation effectively banning workplace noncompete agreements. I'm typically not big on having a lot of legislation, but I am a big fan of the recent noncompete legislation and the pay transparency law mentioned above.

On April 23, 2024, The Federal Trade Commission (FTC) "issued a final rule to promote competition by banning noncompetes nationwide, protecting the fundamental freedom of workers to change jobs, increasing innovation, and fostering new business formation. Noncompete clauses keep wages low, suppress new ideas, and rob the American economy of dynamism, including from the more than 8,500 new startups that would be created a year once noncompetes are banned. The FTC's final rule to ban noncompetes will ensure Americans have the freedom to pursue a new job, start a new business, or bring a new idea to market."[84] Amen!

For any of you who signed a noncompete agreement with your current or prior employer, this might apply to you as well. "Under the FTC's new rule, existing noncompetes for the vast majority of workers will no longer be enforceable after the rule's effective date." There are exceptions for senior executives with existing noncompetes (less than 0.75 percent of workers), but there are to be no new noncompetes at any level of position.[85]

I am not an attorney, so if you have concerns about an offer you are receiving from a potential employer, I encourage you to consult an attorney before signing it. Fees can be very reasonable for this type of service.

Next, we will review what should be included in an offer. When it comes to compensation, you want it to be very clearly written in the offer letter.

The Compensation Should Be Clear in the Offer

Below is a list of components to look for in an offer letter:

- What is the base salary? How often will you be paid?

- If there is a sign-on bonus, how long do you need to work for the company to ensure that you don't have to pay this bonus back to the employer?

- What is the bonus opportunity? Bonuses can be at the company level, often referred to as company performance bonuses. Or bonuses can be at the individual level. It should be clear what the percentage of the bonus is and how it is calculated.
  - For example, there is a 30 percent bonus opportunity. Does that mean your base salary is $100,000 and the bonus *on top* of the salary is a $30,000 opportunity? Or does it mean your base salary is $70,000 and you have to earn the $30,000 to get to the $100,000? They should make it clear what your total compensation opportunity is, what percentage is base salary, and what percentage is bonus.

- Is there an equity component? For publicly held companies, this should be straightforward. You can do your own research to see what the value of one share of stock is, then understand how many stock options the company is willing to give you. If it is a privately held company, this can be a more opaque process. Founders of privately held companies don't typically like to tell you what a company is worth. So, try to get as much detail as you can. If equity compensation is a significant portion of your compensation, I recommend you ask for a discussion with the chief financial officer so you understand what you're getting into.

Once you sign your offer letter and pass your background check, it's time to prepare to resign from your current employer.

You should resign from your current employer only when you have a final, signed offer letter as well as a cleared background check.

Submitting Your Resignation and Having a Graceful Exit

There are two critical times when you have control in your career with respect to your employer:

1. When you are negotiating a new offer of employment with a potential employer

2. When you resign from a company

This is your career. You are deciding which company to work for and which company it is time to move on from. You will need to be clear and confident with your communication when it comes time to leave your current employer voluntarily.

You can resign in a respectful way to maintain as many relationships as possible.

Below are best practices.

Tell Your Manager You Need to Talk

- Send a text or a meeting invitation for today (the day you plan to resign).

- Use wording like: "I need to talk with you confidentially at your earliest convenience, please."

  - You are alerting your manager and preparing them for an important conversation.

- It's okay to feel butterflies at this step in the process. I did every time I resigned from a company. But don't let the nervousness keep you from moving forward. Remind yourself why you want to leave and why you accepted your new employer's offer.

Resignation Conversation – Verbal with Your Direct Manager

- "[Name], I want to let you know I've decided to leave [Employer's Name]." [Be clear.]
  - [Pause and let the surprise soak in. People handle surprises differently. You cannot control their response, and you are not responsible for their response.]
- "I want to let you know before I put it in writing."
  - [This shows respect for your relationship. Pause. Let them ask questions.]
- Possible questions from your manager:
  - "Where are you going?"
  - "What will your role be?"
  - "Why are you leaving?"
  - "Is there anything I can do to make you stay?"
  - "When are you leaving?"
    - "My last day with [Employer's Name] is [Date]." [Be clear and confident.]
    - "If you like, I can hold off until tomorrow to submit my letter of resignation to HR so you can think about a transition plan."
      - [This gives your manager a day to start thinking about the transition and how they will plan for your departure.]
    - "I will also keep this confidential until you send out a message about my impending departure."
    - From the employer's perspective, there is never a good time for a high performing employee to leave. You just have to rip off the Band-Aid and have this conversation.
- Your Manager's Reaction:
  - There is likely going to be a sting for your manager because now they have to figure out how to cover your responsibilities. *This is business. It's not personal.*
  - You will likely feel bad, but it is your manager's responsibility to staff their team and cover the business. It is your responsibility to make decisions about your career and what is best for you and your loved ones.
  - Don't be surprised if you get a bit of a cold shoulder from your manager. When your manager announces your departure to the broader organization, you will get warm fuzzies from your colleagues who enjoyed working with you.
- Best-case scenario: Your manager will be happy for you and professional about taking responsibility for staffing their own team.
  - Your response: "I've enjoyed working for you, [Manager's Name], and I wish the best for you and [Employer's Name]."

- Close the call as quickly as you can and as soon as it makes sense. Let your manager move on and start thinking about the transition plan.

- Worst-case scenario: Your manager gets verbally frustrated and lacks professionalism:

  - Let them vent—but you are not changing your mind. Remember that you have control over your career decisions and have accepted another company's offer.

  - Your response: "I see you are a bit upset. Should we take a pause and connect tomorrow? I'll keep this confidential until we have a communication plan."

  - If the conversation degrades, you should contact HR.

Send Resignation Email to HR and Copy Your Direct Manager

Send your resignation letter no later than twenty-four hours after your verbal conversation with your manager. If you haven't heard back from your manager about a transition plan within twenty-four hours of your verbal conversation, tell them you will be submitting your letter of resignation *today* to HR.

Sending the resignation letter to HR and copying your manager makes it less personal for the manager. You are resigning to the company HR official instead of to your manager. And the HR representative has offboarding processes to work through with you. If you wait for the hiring manager to tell HR, the HR representative could lose time to navigate you through the offboarding process.

Keep this letter short and to the point.

SAMPLE RESIGNATION LETTER:

Hello [HR Manager's Name],

I am submitting my formal resignation from [Employer's Company Name]. My last official day of employment will be [Date].

As discussed with [Manager's Name], I look forward to working to my term date of [Date] to support the transition activities.

Please let me know if there are any documents to fill out or any processes I need to follow before my last day.

I wish only the best for [Employer's Company Name] and my colleagues.

Thank you,

[Your Name]

Receive Acknowledgment from HR

- Ensure you receive an email response from HR acknowledging your letter of resignation.

- If HR has concerns about your new employer being a competitor, they will bring it up.

  - They might walk you out. If this is the case, you have done *nothing* wrong. Hold your head high. Remember that they are trying to protect their intellectual property. Try not to take it personally.

  - They might remind you that you will need to comply with the employment agreements you signed once you depart from the company.

    - Your response: "Please provide me with a copy of these documents so I'm sure to comply."

Handling Potential Counteroffers

Receiving a counteroffer can be instantly good for the ego, but it's important to take a number of things into consideration.

You have received a counteroffer only because you resigned. It is a purely reactive tactic from your employer. If your employer fully valued you, why didn't they improve your situation proactively?

- You may have a number of reasons for leaving—low compensation, no promotion in sight, don't like your boss, less than positive culture, don't feel valued, company is not positioned for growth, company is falling behind the market, etc.

- Despite what your employer is saying to you, if you were to accept a counteroffer, they would probably consider you a flight risk and may make contingency plans without your knowledge.

- The counteroffer could simply be an interim tactic from your employer to bridge a gap while they look to replace you.

Much research and many surveys have been completed over the years to measure what happens to employees who accept counteroffers. "80% of candidates who accept a counteroffer from their current employer end up leaving within six months. Nine of ten candidates who accept a counteroffer leave their current employer within the twelve-month mark."[86]

A lot of thought went into your decision to accept your new employer's offer. Be very careful about considering a counteroffer. How many of the dissatisfiers that you have with your current employer can be fixed? Only you can decide what is in your best interest.

---

[86] https://www.recruitment-software.co.uk/7-counter-offer-statistics-every-recruiter-needs-know/

Your Manager Will Send an Email Announcing Your Impending Departure

- Once your manager has figured out a transition plan, they will send an announcement regarding your impending departure.

- It's important to not let it leak out that you are leaving. Let your manager send the announcement to the team so they can also communicate the transition plan.

- You will get warm fuzzies from your colleagues once they see your manager's message.

The Transition

Once people hear you are leaving, you will likely receive many last requests that turn into action items for you.

Of course, we want to do what we can. But your employer also needs to start identifying who will be responsible for your work after your departure. Your time during the transition is best leveraged by transferring knowledge to other employees and helping them take on the action items versus doing all the work yourself.

There is only so much work one person can do in two weeks, so you'll need to help them prioritize what *you* will do versus what will be handed over to others.

Remember to also invest in your personal time during the transition and reserve some energy for your new career adventure. If you can negotiate a start date that gives you a week of vacation before you start your new role, that's even better. You deserve a break!

Thank-You Letter to Colleagues

- On the evening before your last day of employment, send an email to colleagues you have worked with.

- Keep in mind:
  - It's perfectly normal and honest to be excited and tell colleagues about your new opportunity. Remember, you are going to an incredible new opportunity and adventure while your colleagues are not. Be humble.
  - This is not the time to bring up anything that was frustrating for you in your current employer's environment. If you couldn't change it when you were there, just let it be.

SAMPLE THANK-YOU LETTER:

SUBJECT: Thank you

Hi Everyone,

I joined [Employer's Name] [X] years ago to [describe your charter].

[Say something nice about your employer and your colleagues—something about the culture or what you've accomplished together. If you can add a bit of humor or mention a funny situation, that helps add a bit of levity.]

I want to say a big thank-you to all of you for enriching my experiences here at [Employer's Name].

I wish you much success this year and onward. In my humble opinion, [Employer's Name] is a special company with amazing people. I've enjoyed working with each and every one of you.

I wish you all the best,

[Your Name]
[Email]
[Phone]

You will likely feel a huge sigh of relief after resigning and working through the offboarding process with HR. Enjoy the kind words that colleagues offer you. When leaving a company, it's a unique time to hear words of appreciation from people. Some people will even surprise you! It's a shame we don't communicate appreciation more often, but such is human nature.

While you are working the last several weeks of transition with your current employer, your new employer will have you start the onboarding process with them.

Onboarding

Onboarding processes vary widely across industries and companies. Below are some of the components you may experience with a tech or tech-adjacent company:

Pre-Boarding: Before your first day, there are a number of activities to ensure you are productive on day one with your new company. The trend with tech and tech-adjacent companies is to have most of these activities completed before your first day so you can hit the ground running.

- **Offer Acceptance**: Confirm receipt of the signed offer letter. You should resign from your current employer only once you have a final, signed offer letter as well as a cleared background check.

- **Welcome Package**: An HR representative will send you a welcome email with important information, such as your start date, first-day schedule, dress code, and company policies.

- **Paperwork**: Complete the necessary pre-employment paperwork, such as tax forms, nondisclosure agreements, and benefits enrollment forms.

- **Equipment Setup**: The company will provide a computer, software, and other necessary equipment. If you are working remotely, they will typically ship you a preconfigured set of equipment.

First-Day Orientation: A growing number of companies have new employees join them in an office for the first week of employment to get the employee integrated into their new work environment. If the orientation will be conducted remotely, some companies have become creative in making the orientation process both productive and fun via video conference.

- **Introduction to the Team**: You will be introduced to the team and key people you will collaborate with.

- **Office Tour**: A tour of the office, or a virtual tour for remote employees, will be conducted.

- **Company Overview**: A presentation of the company's history, mission, values, and culture will be provided.

- **IT Setup**: The IT team will assist with setting up email accounts and accessing necessary software or tools.

Training and Development: Depending on your experience and the level of the position you accepted, you may be expected to hit the ground running and get to work. Or there might be training and development to help point you in the right direction.

- **Role-Specific Training**: You might receive training specific to your new role, including technical training, tools, or processes.

- **Company Policies and Procedures**: Education on company policies, code of conduct, security protocols, and compliance requirements should be provided.

- **Product and Services Training**: Training on the company's products, services, and any relevant industry knowledge should also be provided.

Integration into the Team: At a minimum and sooner rather than later, your hiring executive should create a list of the key people you should spend time with. You will then reach out and set up one-on-one time with each person to introduce yourself and understand each person's key initiatives, objectives, and performance metrics. Be sure to also take advantage of social activities to start building relationships with colleagues.

Goal-Setting and Performance Expectations: Don't shy away from this conversation. The earlier you have this conversation with your new boss, the less likely there will be confusion about what is expected of you.

- **Initial Goals**: Ensure you and your manager set clear, achievable, measurable goals and objectives for your first few months in your new role.

- **Performance Metrics**: Ensure you understand how your performance will be measured and what success looks like in this new role.

With every new position I took on in my career, I found it so exciting to figure out where I could make contributions. I embraced each career change as an adventure.

I wish you all the best with your next career adventure!

And finally, I offer some closing thoughts.

CLOSING THOUGHTS

*"Be who God meant you to be
and you will set the world on fire."*

— St. Catherine of Siena

My husband and I moved our family from Southern California to Northern California for a promotional opportunity with Hewlett-Packard. We had a young family at the time, so the relocation was a big deal for us.

I was fretting over making the most of this career opportunity since my family was making sacrifices to be away from our extended family in Southern California.

About a year after I took this new role, my boss was moved into a new role in a different part of the company, so her position became open. I wanted to be promoted into her position. My boss's boss posted the position, so I started preparing to interview.

And then I had an especially poignant moment . . . what some call a *close moment*.

I was lying in bed, just waking up one morning, and I heard a clear message: "It's going to be all right." A great peace came over me, and I was eager to experience the day to see what would unfold.

Well, my boss's boss came into my office that morning and said, "The job is yours if you want it." No interviews. He just offered it to me. I was elated!

It was at this moment that I realized God cared about my career. Prior to this close moment, I assumed God was busy with other things that were way more important than what I was fretting about, but this isn't so. He cares about the myriad of details in our lives.

I believe God cares deeply about your career too.

Our lives and careers will have high points and low points. Over the years, my career certainly had some painful low points. So my advice is:

Do your very best . . . and give the rest to God.

We never walk alone.

APPENDIX

List of Chief Customer Officer Competencies from ChatGPT

ChatGPT prompt: Please provide a list of competencies for chief customer officers in the technology industry.

ChatGPT response:

Here's a comprehensive list of competencies for Chief Customer Officers (CCOs) in the technology industry, categorized into relevant skill areas:

1. Customer-Centric Strategy

- **Customer Advocacy**: Acting as the voice of the customer within the organization to align strategies with customer needs.

- **Customer Journey Mapping**: Understanding and improving the customer lifecycle and experience across all touchpoints.

- **Data-Driven Decision-Making**: Leveraging customer data and insights to drive strategies and initiatives.

- **Outcome-Oriented Mindset**: Ensuring customers achieve measurable results and value from the company's products or services.

2. Leadership and Collaboration

- **Cross-Functional Leadership**: Aligning sales, marketing, product, and support teams around customer success objectives.

- **Change Management**: Leading organizational transformations to instill a customer-first culture.

- **Team Development**: Building, mentoring, and retaining high-performing customer success teams.

- **Influencing Skills**: Persuading executive leadership and stakeholders to prioritize customer-focused initiatives.

3. Customer Relationship Management

- **Executive Relationship Building**: Engaging with key customer executives to deepen strategic relationships.

- **Conflict Resolution**: Navigating and resolving high-stakes customer challenges effectively.

- **Customer Retention Strategies**: Developing plans to reduce churn and drive long-term customer loyalty.

- **Expansion and Upselling**: Identifying opportunities for additional value creation through existing relationships.

4. Technical and Industry Expertise

- **Technology Ecosystem Knowledge**: Understanding cloud, SaaS, enterprise software, and other tech landscapes.

- **Product Knowledge**: Deep familiarity with the organization's technology offerings and their application to customer needs.

- **Digital Transformation Expertise**: Guiding customers through complex technology implementations and transitions.

- **Emerging Trends Awareness**: Staying ahead of trends like AI, machine learning, and customer analytics to create innovative customer solutions.

5. Operational Excellence

- **Metrics and KPI Management**: Establishing and tracking metrics such as Net Promoter Score (NPS), Customer Lifetime Value (CLV), and churn rates.

- **Process Optimization**: Implementing scalable processes for customer onboarding, support, and account management.

- **Revenue Alignment**: Collaborating with sales and finance teams to link customer success to revenue growth and profitability.

- **Technology Enablement**: Leveraging tools like CRM, customer success platforms, and analytics software to streamline customer operations.

6. Communication and Storytelling

- **Customer Storytelling**: Sharing success stories internally and externally to drive credibility and brand loyalty.

- **Executive-Level Communication**: Presenting insights and initiatives clearly and persuasively to boards and C-level stakeholders.

- **Empathy and Listening Skills**: Understanding customer pain points and needs to create tailored solutions.

- **Crisis Communication**: Managing communication during product issues or escalations.

7. Innovation and Continuous Improvement

- **Customer Feedback Loop**: Establishing systems to gather, analyze, and act on customer feedback.

- **Value Realization**: Continuously demonstrating the ROI of the company's products to customers.

- **Creative Problem-Solving**: Developing innovative solutions to complex customer challenges.

- **Scalability and Growth**: Driving customer success strategies that support company growth and market expansion.

These competencies enable CCOs in the technology industry to enhance customer satisfaction, foster loyalty, and drive revenue growth while ensuring that customers derive maximum value from their solutions.

Sample Resume

TOM SMITH

St. Paul, MN

tsmith@gmail.com | 305.321.1234 | www.linkedin.com/in/tsmith

Senior Executive Customer Support / Cloud Operations

Global Operating Models | Business Transformation | Enterprise Software | Customer Experience | Customer Success
Cloud Services | SaaS | Strategic Planning | Application Support | Leadership | Managed Services | Digital Strategies

Consistent track record leading global Support and IT organizations in SaaS, Cloud Services, Managed Services, and on-premise Enterprise Software business models for large public and private growth technology companies. History of improving the customer experience while significantly reducing costs. Holistic, critical thinker who contributes to broader company initiatives that accelerate software sales, improve product quality, and increase renewal rates.

KEY BUSINESS RESULTS

- **Improved Customer Experience**: Increased CSAT by 18 points. Improved the support experience by building a "Customer First" culture, offering real-time self-service capabilities, and meeting changing customer demand.
- **Customer Success:** Improved Net Promoter Score by 30 points and contributed to 8-point improvement in retention rates. Drove multiple cross-functional initiatives aimed at building loyalty, retention, and product adoption.
- **Innovation:** Continuously identified trends in the market place based on changing customer needs. Leveraging an agile methodology, nimbly develops and deploys tools that align with customer journeys.
- **Cost Optimization**: Decreased support costs by 12%. Established and executed Horizon 1 and 2 plays including leadership alignment, low cost geography utilization, and work reduction (self-service, assisted support, and automation).
- **Digital Strategies**: Decreased cost per interaction by 22%. Deployed digital transformation projects including process re-engineering, internal technologies, and customer facing digital platforms to enable self-service and automation.
- **Millennial & GenZ Workforce Retention**: Reduced employee attrition to 8% in labor markets with an average of 30%. Established intrinsic value culture for the modern workforces while prioritizing employee engagement.

KEY SKILLS

Transforms global operating models to rebalance onshore, offshore, and near shore support operations to expand coverage and create scale. Drives digital strategies leveraging omnichannel, self-service capabilities, and intelligent routing to drive down cost per interaction. Builds a growth-mindset culture which motivates and inspires diverse global teams toward continuous improvement and innovative change for optimal customer and business impact.

PROFESSIONAL EXPERIENCE

Kronos
June 2011 - Present
St. Paul, MN

Senior Vice President, Global Technical Support (Feb 2018-Present)

Accountable for global strategy and execution of technical support delivery models including SaaS, Cloud Services, Managed Services and on-premise Enterprise Software. 1,800 global support personnel in 20+ countries provide world class support to over 300,000 customers and trading partners. 2 million+ tickets transacted annually in support of $4B in ARR. 95% CSAT scores.

- **Global Operating Model Optimization:** Built and led the strategy to consolidate siloed support teams into a globally unified support model.
- **Proactive Service Transformation:** First-phase pilot executed on journey mapping, process engineering, videos, and knowledge base to build the foundation for proactive technical services, with the objective of reducing demand for labor by 25%.
- **Product Quality Improvements:** Improved tickets assigned to defects by 8 points. Formed partnership with Engineering and implemented serviceability, manageability, and quality processes to drive product quality.
- **Improved Customer Experience:** Increased CSAT by 18 points. Improved the support experience by building a "Customer First" culture, offering real-time self-service capabilities, accommodating customer demands, and implementing best practices.

Vice President, Business Network Support (Dec 2014 – Jan 2018)

- **Growth-Mindset Culture:** Built a growth-mindset culture to motivate and inspire diverse global teams toward continuous improvement and innovative change for optimal customer and business impact.
- **Digital Strategies:** Executed automation strategies that reduced transaction and system alerts by 35% while executing self-service options that reduced tickets by 15%.

Strengthens the Customer Experience while Improving Margins

Sample Resume

- **Employee Retention:** Established an employee engagement survey with an approach to identifying specific pain points with employees. Initiatives targeted key areas resulting in higher employee engagement and lower attrition rates.

Vice President, Global Messaging Support (July 2013 – Nov 2014)
- **Mergers & Acquisitions:** Directed support services integration of acquisitions into newly formed Business Network organization. Oversaw strategic global initiatives to drive transformation and scaled growth.
- **Support Process Optimization:** Drove internal and cross-functional initiatives to reduce support costs. Resulted in 52% reduction in repetitive work, allowing for focus on more critical issues.
- **Scale for Growth:** Led operational transformation initiatives to scale business for major growth, elevate the customer experience, and reduce cost structures via cross-training, up-skilling, self-service, and automation.

Vice President, Global Support Services, Strategy & Operations (June 2011 – June 2013)
- **Net Promoter Score:** Fueled 30-point improvement in NPS in two years while generating 22% productivity increase across global support services operations.
- **Productivity & Operational Improvement:** Established business intelligence and reporting framework, trending and analytics capabilities, ticket management, and global resource management model (>95% accuracy).
- **Eliminate Work & Improve Product Quality:** Implemented product trend and customer trend analysis processes to define specific product enhancement, implementation improvements, training opportunities, and knowledge articles for reducing and eliminating work.

Dell Technologies   Palo Alto, CA
Sept 2005 – May 2011

Senior Director, Global Support Services, Productivity Improvement Office (April 2010 – May 2011)
Led business operations for global support services with 7,500 employees. Drove improvements to a growing global remote and field services technical support organization. Drove a services integration project saving over $2M per week on technical service agreement costs.

Chief of Staff, Global Support Services, Business Planning & Strategy (Mar 2008 - Mar 2010)
Senior Director, Global Support Services, Business & Technical Operations (Nov 2006 – Feb 2008)
Director, Global Support Services, Business Operations (Sept 2005 – Oct 2006)

- **M&A Integration:** Established and led a program office to transition people, process, and technology from acquired company to Dell, resulting in $2M per week in cost savings. Project was completed 5 weeks ahead of deadline.
- **Cross-Functional Leadership:** Led cross-functional team to establish 40 initiatives using "fact-based modeling". Increased support capacity by 12%, resulting in achievement of gross margin targets and improved customer and employee experience.
- **Digital Strategies:** Decreased cost per interaction by 22%. Deployed digital transformation projects including process re-engineering, ticketing system, and customer-facing digital platforms to enable self-service, assisted support, and automation.

TRAVEL SABBATICAL
Explorer of the South Pacific (Sept 2004 – Aug 2005)
Explored the islands of the South Pacific to learn about Polynesian culture and understand what makes them so happy.

SAP   Redwood Shores, CA
Jan 1998 – Aug 2004
Promoted rapidly through progressive roles in strategy, IT application development and support, business platform operations, and tool development.

Director Support Services, Business Operations & Systems Technologies (2004-2004)
Director IT Services, Applications Support (1999 – 2004)
Senior Manager Support Services, Business Planning & Strategy (1998 – 1999)
Manager Support Services, Development Tools (1998 – 1998)

EDUCATION

Bachelor of Science in Business Administration, San Diego State University
MIT's Professional Certification in Machine Learning and Artificial Intelligence

HONORS AND PROFESSIONAL ASSOCIATIONS

- J.D. Power & Associates Award for Technology Service and Support Operations for four consecutive years.
- Recipient of 3 TSIA STAR Awards for: "Excellence in Mission Critical Support", "Excellence in Continual Improvement", and "Best Knowledge Management Practices".

Strengthens the Customer Experience while Improving Margins

ABOUT THE AUTHOR

JULIA STEGMAN, CCMC, MBA is a certified career management coach, trained by The Academies for Coaching, Inc. With over thirty years of experience in the technology industry, she has worked as an executive recruiter and spent two decades as an executive at Hewlett-Packard. She also served as Vice President of a research and advisory services practice at the Technology Services Industry Association, where she partnered with leading tech companies.

Drawing from her deep industry expertise and proven coaching methodologies, Julia has helped countless professionals successfully navigate career transitions. She is passionate about guiding individuals to uncover their unique talents and apply them toward meaningful, fulfilling work that aligns with their broader life priorities.

Julia lives on the Central Coast of California with her husband. She enjoys spending time with her sons and grandchildren as well as tending to her garden.

Contact: Julia@DiscoverMeaningfulWork.com

Thank you for reading my book!
I hope it was helpful to you.
May I ask a favor?

Will you please take two minutes now to leave a review on Amazon letting me know what you thought of the book?

You can find the book's Amazon listing posted on my website: https://DiscoverMeaningfulWork.com/

I would greatly appreciate it!

Thank you,

Julia Stegman